GROUP
PSYCHODYNAMIC-
INTERPERSONAL
PSYCHOTHERAPY

GROUP PSYCHODYNAMIC-INTERPERSONAL PSYCHOTHERAPY

Giorgio A. Tasca, Samuel F. Mikail, and Paul L. Hewitt

 AMERICAN PSYCHOLOGICAL ASSOCIATION

Published by
American Psychological Association
750 First Street, NE
Washington, DC 20002
https://www.apa.org

Order Department
https://www.apa.org/pubs/books
order@apa.org

In the U.K., Europe, Africa, and the Middle East, copies may be ordered from Eurospan
https://www.eurospanbookstore.com/apa
info@eurospangroup.com

Typeset in Charter by Circle Graphics, Inc., Reisterstown, MD

Printer: Sheridan Books, Chelsea, MI
Cover Designer: Beth Schlenoff, Bethesda, MD
Cover Art: Barbara L. Calvert, *Resolving the Triangles*, acrylic, 2019

Library of Congress Cataloging-in-Publication Data
Names: Tasca, Giorgio A., author. | Mikail, Samuel F., author. |
  Hewitt, Paul L. (Paul Louis), author. | American Psychological Association,
  issuing body.
Title: Group psychodynamic-interpersonal psychotherapy / Giorgio A. Tasca,
  Samuel F. Mikail, Paul L. Hewitt.
Description: Washington, DC : American Psychological Association, [2021] |
  Includes bibliographical references and index.
Identifiers: LCCN 2020014949 (print) | LCCN 2020014950 (ebook) |
  ISBN 9781433833618 (paperback) | ISBN 9781433833953 (ebook)
Subjects: LCSH: Group psychotherapy. | Interpersonal psychotherapy. |
  Psychodynamic psychotherapy.
Classification: LCC RC488 .T37 2021 (print) | LCC RC488 (ebook) |
  DDC 616.89/152—dc23
LC record available at https://lccn.loc.gov/2020014949
LC ebook record available at https://lccn.loc.gov/2020014950

https://doi.org/10.1037/0000213-000

Printed in the United States of America

10 9 8 7 6 5 4 3 2 1

Contents

Foreword

Having the opportunity to read this excellent book, authored by Drs. Tasca, Mikail, and Hewitt, and to write this foreword in the midst of the self-isolation necessitated by the COVID-19 pandemic highlighted evermore for me the importance of our groupness. Our groups in society define us all. For group psychotherapists, their groups play a key role in the healing process for our clients, who come to us seeking help in dealing with difficulties in their relationships, depression, anxiety, trauma, addictions, and eating disorders. The value of social integration to our physical and emotional health is clear through abundant research and accrued wisdom. That resonates loudly for me at this time in particular.

That is why this book is such an important resource for our field. We know that group psychotherapy works. It can be referred to as a "triple-E treatment": It is effective; it is equivalent to individual treatment, by and large; and it is efficient with regard to therapist use and costs.

We know, as well, that group therapy is implemented widely in most agencies, institutions, hospitals, residential and addiction programs, and outpatient settings. But we also know that group therapy is hard to do well and often is not delivered in a way that is commensurate with its potential and effectiveness. In mental health care at large, and the delivery of group psychotherapy specifically, there is a quality gap and a significant implementation gap. This book seeks to address that and does so to good effect.

The text is a combination of handbook and textbook with clearly articulated links between theory and practice, with exercises and questions posed to the reader. It provides a deep dive into how to maximize one's effectiveness as a group psychotherapist.

It is widely recognized in our field that effectiveness in group psychotherapy is a reflection of the relationships that therapists develop with their clients, the quality of group cohesion in the group, and the quality of the therapeutic alliance in treatment. Empathy is another key factor that unites all effective group leaders. How to build and sustain these "common factors" is not easy. This book illustrates how the group leader can marshal these important factors in this model of group psychotherapy. It is truly an integrative model, bringing together psychodynamic, developmental, behavioral, and interpersonal elements. The great value of this approach is that it links depth of understanding and skill building. Too often, psychotherapy emphasizes one domain or the other at the expense of the other. This book is a response to the hazards of ideological singularity.

It reminds us that we must keep front and center that we treat individuals (and not groups) and that each individual needs their own tailored treatment. Tied inextricably to this is how the group leader uses herself as a therapeutic agent to maximize the learning and therapeutic opportunities within the group in the creation of a healing context. Doing this well is not easy and requires the kind of meaningful synthesis between theory and practice that this book articulates so well.

When group therapy is delivered by inadequately trained, inadequately supervised, and inadequately supported group therapists, the common result is an increase in stigmatization regarding mental illness and group therapy, devaluation of group as a useful modality, and the demoralization of both client and provider.

Having the capacity to demystify the work of psychotherapy provides both the group therapist and our individual clients a road map to understand the powerful links between early life experience, beliefs, and feelings one holds about oneself, the interpersonal behaviors that flow from that, and the impact of those interpersonal behaviors on the relational environment. We create interpersonal loops and cycles that have the potential to be either positive and virtuous or, all too often, negative and viciously destructive. Group therapy is the best forum for this illumination. It is at the heart of working in the here and now and within the group as a social microcosm.

This link between beliefs and behaviors, between early experience and contemporary experience, is at the heart of many contemporary models of group and individual psychotherapy. Consider Wachtel's cyclical psycho-dynamics, Strupp and Binder's misconstrual–misconstruction sequence, the Mount Zion psychoanalytic plan formulation model, or Luborsky's core conflictual relationship theme. Bringing the client into the therapeutic process as a fully informed and activated collaborator strengthens the central role of the alliance and promotes group cohesion. The best thera-peutic alliances emerge in the context of clarity and congruence between therapist and client about the goals of treatment, the tasks of treatment, and the quality of the relationship they will develop and hopefully maintain.

It takes therapist transparency and therapeutic demystification to achieve that. When this is in place and becomes illuminated within the group, an opportunity is afforded for the development of self-awareness and understanding of one's role in one's interpersonal world. Coupling this with the skills and the capacity to practice those skills in a supportive, albeit rigorous, therapeutic environment paves the way for improved client self-efficacy. This work requires tact, empathy, and precision. But helping our clients understand what they do in their relational world that brings them closer to what they prefer and further away from what they dread is one of the most important and exciting elements of the work we do.

This is the exact opposite of a kind of dated approach of "let's dive into the group and see what happens," or "everything we need to know will express itself in the group sooner or later." My preference, and the clear preference of these authors, is to come into the group with a mental map for each client that is coconstructed with the client. I liken it to holding in mind a psychological hologram for each member of the group so that it becomes possible to understand how each person is advancing or obstructing a personal cognitive, emotional, psychodynamic, and interpersonal view of self.

My trainees, largely residents in psychiatry, are often surprised at how much time is spent before the group begins in the assessment and formula-tion phase. Yet we soon see repeatedly that time refines the shared under-standing of each group member's chief concerns and allows anticipation of what to expect in the group before it happens in the group. I have had the experience many times of giving feedback to a client in the pre-group phase in the form of creating together a formulation and fine-tuning it together on the basis of clients' reactions and responses. This generally launches an effective trajectory of group therapy.

I recall vividly a woman I saw for an assessment for group therapy who, in the space of the first 60 seconds of our assessment, made me feel incompetent, shamed, and humiliated by her hostile dismissiveness of me.

My initial reaction was to wonder how I could disengage safely from this session. By taking some time to reflect, regroup, and metabolize my countertransference—the central data we must embrace and use fully—I was then able to focus on her chief concern, which was, in her words, her "uncanny ability to antagonize people." Having reflected on how quickly this arose within our session, I was able, with her willingness, to reflect back to her what had happened between us. She broke into sobbing, and I was concerned that I had destabilized her. Instead, what she said, as we processed this together, was that she felt understood and that this gave her some hope that therapy could be helpful to her.

Skill in metacommunication and being able to find palatable ways of saying unpalatable things are important capacities for group therapists to develop. This book provides constructive and helpful guidance in doing these effectively and empathically. It may be one of the most important skills we have to develop and refine.

I often remind myself, and my supervisees, of the need to always process, process, and process. Always aim to answer the question "Why is this happening in this way at this moment in time?" Explore, question, examine as a way not "to leave money on the table" in the form of therapeutic opportunities that have not been fully realized.

The book itself is a here-and-now illustration of the principles it espouses. Its fundamental premise is congruent with both its structure and style of writing. It advocates elegantly for the concept of identifying the core client issues, clarifying, collaborating, and reinforcing so that you actively foster client learning and behavioral change.

The reader of this excellent book should not expect a passive read but rather a deep and meaningful journey into greater psychotherapist effectiveness.

—*Molyn Leszcz, MD, FRCPC, CGP, DFAGPA*
Professor of Psychiatry, University of Toronto
President, The American Group Psychotherapy Association

GROUP PSYCHODYNAMIC-INTERPERSONAL PSYCHOTHERAPY

INTRODUCTION

From the beginning of our training 35 years ago, we found group therapy to be fascinating, challenging, sometimes frustrating, and always compelling. On the basis of our experiences, work, and research over the years, we developed group psychodynamic-interpersonal psychotherapy (GPIP), a comprehensive model of individual case formulation and group interventions informed by contemporary psychodynamic and interpersonal theories. We value evidence-based approaches, and so we empirically tested GPIP in randomized controlled trials, effectiveness studies, and group process studies (e.g., Hewitt et al., 2015; Hewitt, Qiu, et al., 2019; Tasca et al., 2013, 2019; Tasca, Ritchie, et al., 2006). GPIP is an evidence-based treatment.

Group therapy may be daunting for some trainees and therapists because of the amount of information coming at them in a group. Yet many trainees and therapists are capable of allowing the interactional forces of a group to pull them in, while at the same time, they remain capable of stepping back and reflecting when necessary to observe and comment on the process. We found over many years of practice, teaching, research, consultation, and

https://doi.org/10.1037/0000213-001

Group Psychodynamic-Interpersonal Psychotherapy, by G. A. Tasca, S. F. Mikail, and P. L. Hewitt

supervision that having a clear understanding of the interpersonal and intra-personal factors that underlie each patient's problems and a good grounding in group process theory was invaluable to helping our patients. Such an understanding, which informs GPIP, has given us and our trainees the ability to effectively participate in and work with the interactions and feelings inherent in therapy groups so that patients can benefit.

Dr. Smith,[1] a White woman in her early 30s, is a newly licensed psychologist who is hardworking and conscientious and wants to provide evidence-based therapy. She took a couple of group therapy courses in graduate school, during which she learned about the ample research demonstrating that group therapy is effective for a variety of mental disorders (Burlingame & Jensen, 2017), is just as effective as individual therapy, and is more cost-effective (Burlingame et al., 2016). She ran her first therapy group during her clinical internship with her supervisor as cotherapist, and she found the work exciting and stimulating. The experience allowed her to learn more about the value of here-and-now process work, interpersonal feedback among patients, group cohesion, and other group therapeutic factors (Yalom & Leszcz, 2020). She looked forward to group therapy being part of her professional career.

A mental health clinic employed Dr. Smith after she graduated and received her license. Shortly after she started, the clinic gave her responsibility for a time-limited, evidence-based, and symptom-focused therapy group for anxiety disorders. The group therapy included highly structured and sequenced activities with many psychoeducational components. Dr. Smith understood the evidence base for this treatment, but she became increasingly dissatisfied with the therapy group. Group members wanted to share their experiences and support each other, but the group's structure left little room for that. Dr. Smith wanted to get to know better the patients, their subjective experiences, and their lives to address the issues underlying their symptoms, but she felt pressure to get through the therapy's agenda in a brief time frame. Even though the group was for patients with similar anxiety disorders, Dr. Smith struggled to provide a coherent treatment given the great diversity of patients in terms of their personality functioning, interpersonal style, coping style, culture, and motivation. As a result, she spent a good portion of each group session talking at the group, and group members spent most of their time listening, taking notes, and reviewing their homework from the previous session.

Recently, Dr. Smith ran into a former group member, Rob, an Asian American male in his late 30s, in the clinic's otherwise empty waiting room. She recalled that Rob was a pleasant group member, but he often remained quiet in her group. In passing, Dr. Smith asked Rob how he was doing, and he proceeded to tell her.

---

[1]Here and throughout the book, all case examples are composites of real patients, and names of therapists and patients are pseudonyms.

ROB: I was certainly less anxious by the end of your therapy group, and I was grateful for that. I could go to the store and drive to work without worrying as much about having a panic attack. The tips and exercises you suggested were really helpful, and so I was having a better understanding of what triggered a panic attack.

DR. SMITH: But you're back here at the clinic?

ROB: Yah, well, other things in my life are still a mess. I don't think I ever told you, but my dad died around the time I was in your group [Dr. Smith remembered that Rob missed a couple of sessions], and after the end of the group, I started to feel more and more down.

DR. SMITH: Oh, I'm sorry to hear that.

ROB: Yah, well, you see, even though the anxiety was better, other things didn't really change much. I still feel taken advantage of at work by my boss, and my wife seems to have written me off. I can't seem to stand up for myself, which makes me feel like such a loser. And my relationship with my dad was pretty complicated, you know, he was so critical. Anyway, that's probably more than you want to hear.

DR. SMITH: And how's the anxiety?

ROB: That's the thing—it's starting to get worse again. I can't keep a lid on it with all of these other issues in my life. So, my family doctor referred me to see the psychiatrist this time. Maybe some medication might help.

The encounter with Rob troubled Dr. Smith. Unfortunately, this is not an uncommon story in mental health treatment. The way Dr. Smith ran the group did not allow her to get to know Rob and the important events in his life. Were his lack of assertiveness and quiet demeanor contributing to his problems with anxiety? Did others, such as his boss or wife, use him or neglect him because he was so passive? Did he expect others to take advantage of him and disrespect him? And what impact did this expectation have on his self-esteem? Why did he never mention his father's death? Did the other group members know? And how did it happen that she, Dr. Smith, missed all this?

We believe that questions like these make their way into the consciousness of mental health professionals trained exclusively in some protocol-based symptom-oriented interventions. For example, one could conceptualize an anxiety disorder, such as that experienced by Rob, as a conditioned response of a perceived threat (being in a crowded store) paired with bodily sensations (increased heart rate, sweatiness). Rob may have misinterpreted these bodily sensations as catastrophic and then began avoiding the perceived threatening situation. Eventually, the process and avoidance might generalize to other situations (driving, leaving his house). Interventions might include graduated exposure to the feared stimuli and challenging cognitions related to the physical sensations. But many clinicians may wonder about Rob's developmental history that made him vulnerable to anxiety in the first place, how he managed feelings like anger, and the current interpersonal and psychological factors that maintain the symptoms. And just as important may be Rob's current work and romantic relationships and the corrosive effect of his relational style on his self-esteem and self-concept. Dr. Smith might also wonder whether the group itself could have played a more prominent role in Rob's treatment. Rob's interpersonal problems were on full display in the group: He was quiet, passive, almost forgettable. However, Dr. Smith needed a way of understanding these problems, their role in maintaining Rob's symptoms, and how to use the group interactions to help Rob change his maladaptive interpersonal patterns, his means of coping, and his view of his self.

In this book, we outline a theory and practice of group psychotherapy that conceptualizes and treats those underlying transdiagnostic factors that can potentially cause or maintain many mental disorders and problems in living. We developed GPIP as a person-centered approach to treating the interpersonal and psychological factors that lead to and maintain many problems that our patients face in life. That is, we understand each patient's issues with an idiographic or personalized case formulation that is based on a developmental, interpersonal, and psychodynamic understanding of how problems evolve and what maintains them currently. For example, one can conceptualize Rob's lack of assertiveness, low self-worth, and anxiety as having developmental roots based on an insecure attachment and attendant relational behaviors. His current lack of assertiveness might be a form of avoidance to stave off potential rejection, and so group therapy may be a means of graduated exposure to interactions with others, to valuing his self, and to getting his attachment needs met in his relationships. We wrote this book for newer and more seasoned group therapists alike who are looking for a comprehensive, evidence-based way of conceptualizing patient problems and providing treatment that truly integrates individualized case formulations with group therapeutic factors to help patients live more fulfilling lives. Thus, our focus is not solely on reducing symptoms but enhancing the quality of people's lives by facilitating a shift in the individual's core relational pattern with both self and others.

A TRANSDIAGNOSTIC APPROACH

In GPIP, we take a transdiagnostic approach to understanding patients' problems. By *transdiagnostic*, we mean that the treatment focuses on those variables that underlie various diagnoses and syndromes and does not focus primarily on the symptoms themselves (Blatt et al., 2006; Hewitt et al., 2008, 2015). Current diagnostic schemes such as the *Diagnostic and Statistical Manual of Mental Disorders* (fifth ed.; American Psychiatric Association, 2013) take an entirely descriptive approach to mental disorders. That is, a clinician will diagnose patients with a depressive, anxiety, or other disorder if patients display a certain number of specific symptoms or signs. However, as we saw with the earlier example, even though Dr. Smith assembled a group exclusively for individuals diagnosed with an anxiety disorder, the group composition was heterogeneous on a variety of factors that predict patient outcomes. For example, Dr. Smith included in the group some people whose level of personality functioning was relatively healthy or mildly impaired and others whose personality functioning was more severely impaired. Research shows that patients at varying levels of functional impairment and personality functioning have different needs and experience different outcomes from treatment (Harwood et al., 2011; Lingiardi & McWilliams, 2017). Similarly, her group might have included those with internalizing coping styles and others with externalizing coping styles. However, patients with varying coping styles respond differently to problem-focused versus insight-oriented interventions (Beutler et al., 2018). By relying on a purely descriptive approach to her patients' problems, Dr. Smith's therapeutic model assumed that all the patients would have similar needs and would respond uniformly. The treatment model did not allow Dr. Smith to draw on a vast body of research to adjust her interpersonal stances and interventions to patient factors (Norcross & Lambert, 2018).

A transdiagnostic approach such as the one we developed in GPIP places more emphasis on the underlying causal and maintenance factors that confer vulnerability for mental disorders, as well as other areas of dysfunction. A group treatment such as GPIP will help therapists to focus on key patient factors and provide therapists with a framework to assess individuals, compose groups, and craft interventions. The GPIP model helps therapists to individualize their interpersonal stances based on patient factors such as attachment style, interpersonal patterns, and defensive functioning. We discuss each of these factors and their roles in case formulation and group treatment in greater detail in subsequent chapters.

A DEVELOPMENTAL APPROACH

In this book, we take a developmental approach, mainly based on attachment theory to conceptualize mental disorders and the underlying patient vulnerabilities. There is a large body of research and theory implicating the role of attachment relationships, childhood maltreatment, and the role of families in adult functioning (see Pinquart et al., 2013; Repetti et al., 2002; Teicher & Samson, 2013). The research is clear that these early experiences have an ongoing impact on adult relationships, coping style, views of self, and psychopathology (Bakermans-Kranenburg & van IJzendoorn, 2009). Beyond that, a developmental model aimed at understanding adult problems in living provides therapists and patients with a way of making sense of the problems and with a means by which patients may begin to gain a more realistic and less self-critical perspective on current difficulties.

For better or worse, early family interactions are our first group experiences and provide us with an implicit template for how individuals behave in groups and what to expect from being in a group. Understanding a patient's attachment history and expectations of relationships provides the therapist with a window into the patient's potential expectations of and behaviors in group psychotherapy (Marmarosh et al., 2013). For example, someone with a *dismissing attachment* style may see relationships as secondary, including with the group, and downplay their own emotions. Therapists treating an attachment-dismissing individual may have to emphasize subtly to the patient the potential importance of relationships and gradually help the patient to become more in touch with their emotional experiences. Someone with a *preoccupied attachment* style tends to be overly anxious about relationship loss, including within groups, and they often up-regulate their emotional experiences. Therapists treating attached preoccupied individuals may have to help them take a more reflective stance with regard to their emotions and to see relationships in a more realistic and less threatening light.

In the earlier example, Dr. Smith found out after the fact that Rob had a "complicated" relationship with his father, whom Rob perceived as critical. It also became clearer to her that Rob was generally unassertive and quiet both in the group and in relationships in general. A comprehensive assessment and individualized case formulation based on an attachment perspective might have helped Dr. Smith understand that Rob's reluctance to participate in the group was a long-standing interpersonal pattern that likely created a sense of safety for him on the one hand but also contributed greatly to problems in his current relationships, his negative view of himself, and his symptoms of anxiety on the other hand. Rob likely had a dismissing attachment pattern in which he downplayed his relational needs and emotions. Hence, Dr. Smith and Rob might have developed treatment goals that included using the group therapy to value rather than avoid his attachment needs, to increase his assertiveness in relationships, and to understand better his feelings about himself and others.

A PSYCHODYNAMIC-INTERPERSONAL APPROACH

The clinical perspective we developed in GPIP is based on psychodynamic and interpersonal approaches to case conceptualization and treatment (see Hewitt et al., 2017; Tasca et al., 2005). Psychodynamic theory has informed clinical practice in psychotherapy for over a century and has provided the foundation for key concepts in psychology such as attachment, defense mechanisms, transference and countertransference, unconscious processes, affect regulation, and relational styles. Contemporary psychodynamic theory emphasizes the nature and quality of relationships both past and present and the internalization of relationships into a self-concept, as well as the role of social and cultural factors. The comprehensiveness of psychodynamic theory, its developmental focus, and its emphasis on interpersonal relations make it uniquely suited to group therapy. After all, group therapy is, at its core, an interactional and relational context for working on problems with living.

For the GPIP model, we modified a classic psychodynamic model (Malan, 1979) so that it incorporates attachment theory (see a full description of the triangle of adaptation in Chapter 1 and Figure 1.2). Early attachment figures may have punished, dismissed, or ridiculed many of our patients' expressions of *attachment needs* (wish to be cared for, need for security). These negative experiences may lead to *affects* such as shame, anxiety, or fear that become automatic and associated with the attachment needs. As a result of the affects, patients engage in *defense mechanisms* to cope, which also denies them the expression of attachment needs. This model is consistent with contemporary psychodynamic treatments that have an evidence base (e.g., McCullough Vaillant, 1997), and it provides a strong and comprehensive understanding of the underlying dynamics of many of our patients' problems.

One of our goals in developing GPIP was to integrate intrapsychic and interpersonal aspects of functioning. Relational patterns have their genesis in early attachment experiences and generalize to other relationships. We illustrate this consistency of relationships across different contexts (from past relationships to current relationships and the therapeutic and group relationship) in our concept of the triangle of object relations (see Chapter 1 and Figure 1.2). In the moment-to-moment interactions that occur in a therapy group, the GPIP therapist and group directly experience the relational patterns evident in each individual's life.

A key task for a group therapist working within GPIP is to reinterpret symptomatic behavior in intrapsychic and interpersonal terms. To achieve this, we describe aspects of interpersonal patterns with the cyclical maladaptive interpersonal patterns (CMIP; Strupp & Binder, 1984) model in some detail in Chapter 1. Elements of the CMIP include (a) the *acts of self*, or one's behaviors, thoughts, and feelings in interpersonal situations to meet relational goals; (b) a client's *expectations of others*, often based on assumptions of others' intentions reinforced by a history of responses by others; (c) the *acts of others*, or how others respond to the person; and (d) the *introject*, which is the internalization of the interpersonal pattern and transactions into a self-concept (see Chapter 1 and Figure 1.3).

The interpersonal aspect of the GPIP model is particularly salient to the group therapy modality. Therapists who are capable of exploring interactions

---

THERAPIST TASK BOX

A TRANSDIAGNOSTIC APPROACH: ATTACHMENT AND PSYCHODYNAMICS

1. Take a transdiagnostic approach to understand the patient's problems.
   - Do not rely solely on descriptions, observations, and stated frequencies of symptoms.
   - Instead, evaluate the patient's level of personality functioning, preferred coping, and interpersonal style.
2. Consider the individual and their presenting problems within their developmental history.
   - What is the quality of the patient's past attachment relationships, current relationships, and romantic relationships, and how might this affect them now?
3. Take an interpersonal perspective on presenting problems.
   - How are current problems related to or maintained by interpersonal problems past and present?
   - How does their relationship to you and the group parallel their relationship to current or past others?

in the group as they occur by using the triangle of object relations and the CMIP can harness a powerful means of understanding and altering interpersonal styles in their patients. Group therapists can make use of therapeutic factors such as interpersonal learning and feedback (Yalom & Leszcz, 2020). And therapists can facilitate these therapeutic factors by encouraging self-disclosure and self-reflection in patients as a means of helping them learn about themselves and others. Segalla (2012) suggested that group therapy recognizes and draws on the embeddedness of individuals within intersubjective and relational experiences, and in so doing, groups serve as vehicles for the individual to find "the self through finding the other" (p. 134). Therapists who enhance interpersonal learning in groups can help patients improve capacities such as *mentalizing*, the ability to understand one's own and others' intentions and behaviors in terms of mental states (Fonagy et al., 2002).

A CASE FORMULATION APPROACH

We are keenly aware that psychotherapy, including group therapy, requires a deep understanding of the individual and what they bring to the therapeutic context. Because of that, we take an idiographic case formulation approach to assessing patients and defining an individualized focus of treatment (Hewitt et al., 2018). To achieve this with GPIP, we describe in Chapter 2 a pre-group assessment process by which therapists and patients collaboratively develop a case formulation that informs treatment goals. We use the principles of interpersonal theory to provide a step-by-step guide to an assessment process aimed at a comprehensive understanding of the patient. The process integrates an awareness of the patient's attachment style and the unique elements of their psychodynamics and interpersonal patterns. This information is central to guiding the therapist to assume an effective interpersonal stance with patients that will facilitate their movement toward their particular goals for group therapy. For example, in Rob's case, a GPIP assessment process would have identified that Rob had underlying needs for self-assertion and self-pride and a need to be cared for. However, his father may have punished or ridiculed any expression of these attachment needs, and so over time, Rob developed automatic affects such as anxiety and shame in relation to these feelings and needs. As a means of coping with the anxiety or shame, Rob minimized his needs and self-pride by self-effacement and avoidance. These defense mechanisms may have been useful at some point in his life but currently were often maladaptive and not always effective to manage his anxiety. His relationships with others in the past and present, including with Dr. Smith, were characterized by passivity, fearfulness, and withdrawal.

Had Dr. Smith engaged Rob in a pre-group assessment process as we illustrate in Chapter 2, she would have been able to describe Rob's mode of adaptation in interpersonal terms using a CMIP. Rob's interpersonal behaviors were evident in his passivity or lack of assertion, his tendency to minimize his needs, and his experience of anxiety (i.e., acts of self). Others in Rob's life may be dominating and perhaps critical of Rob (i.e., acts of others), perhaps provoked by his passivity and self-criticism, which in some ways repeats his unsatisfactory relationship with his father. Rob engaged in avoidance and passivity possibly because he expected that others would ridicule or reject him (i.e., expectation of others). In response, others tended to avoid talking to him or experienced him as forgettable. As a result, Rob may have felt rejected and dismissed, thus repeating the relational issues with his father. Rob may have internalized this failure, which demonstrated yet again to him that he was not worthy and defective (i.e., introject). Rob gave Dr. Smith a hint of this when he referred to himself as a "loser." He likely saw himself as ineffective and not worthwhile, which may fuel depressive affect, anxiety, and passivity in relationships. In a sense, Rob's passivity and negative introject are also reflected in his willingness to go along with the notion that medication is what is needed to "fix" his problems because of his sense that there is something inherently wrong with him or "broken."

Such an assessment and case formulation would have been helpful to Dr. Smith and Rob as they considered how best to approach group therapy. Dr. Smith would have understood Rob not just as shy or quiet, but as someone whose interpersonal behaviors were fundamental to his relational problems, his negative self-concept, and his symptoms. In collaboration with Rob, Dr. Smith would have developed more comprehensive goals for his therapy that also addressed the underlying or maintaining aspects of his problems. She might have decided to help Rob to value rather than be anxious about his attachment needs. She would have alerted him during the assessment to be particularly attentive to his inner experience and reactions when others offer him feedback—specifically, that he might experience anxiety during group interactions in which others affirm or support him. The group's affirmation would stand in marked contrast to Rob's experience of himself and of his father's view of him. Initially, he might dismiss such feedback from the group while selectively attending to or being acutely sensitive to any signs of criticism, disapproval, or neglect.

Dr. Smith would explain to Rob that group therapy might help him understand that his quiet manner and retiring interpersonal style may create an illusion of safety because it allows him not to reveal a self that is open to criticism and rejection. But the cost to Rob is that others may experience him as distant and dismissing of them, rather than seeing him as wanting a connection. During the therapy group, Dr. Smith would focus interventions on Rob's minimizing and avoiding coping style and highlight the cost of these defenses to his relationships, including with the group and to his sense of self.

A GROUP PSYCHOTHERAPY APPROACH

The great potential of group therapy lies in the interpersonal nature of the treatment context. Patients benefit most from groups when a therapist taps into this potential by metacommunicating about interactions in the moment during the group or what Yalom and Leszcz (2020) referred to as the here-and-now processes in the group. A here-and-now focus must have two essential components to be effective: (a) members must experience one another with spontaneity and honesty, and (b) they must be able to reflect on that experience. We developed GPIP as a group therapy precisely because it encourages therapists to make use of the transformative nature of the interpersonal context of the group. One expression of that interpersonal context is group cohesion, or the sense of belonging and attraction to a group. Cohesion is a well-known predictor of patient outcomes and is a precursor to successful groups (Burlingame et al., 2018). However, cohesion requires nurturing and development. And so, as we describe in more detail in Chapter 4, the GPIP model takes a group development approach to treatment in which nurturing and maintaining group cohesion is a key therapist task (Tuckman, 1965; Tuckman & Jensen, 1977).

Successful groups are known to go through stages of development (as do all significant relationships, including one's relationship with oneself), and therapists who are aware of the qualities of these stages and the associated tasks are better able to help the group move forward to achieve its goals. Our research identified stages of GPIP (Tasca, Balfour, et al., 2006), and we incorporate Tuckman's (1965; Tuckman & Jensen, 1977) group development model with evidence of how GPIP works. At the start or *forming* stage, therapists help groups come together to find common cause, and so therapists may knit group members together by focusing on the universality of their experiences. The next *storming* stage is possible after the group successfully negotiates the initial forming stage. Storming involves greater expression of individuation among members. In the *norming* stage, therapists may shape and reinforce positive therapeutic norms such as self-disclosure, self-reflection, and interpersonal feedback. It is during this stage that groups solidify their sense of cohesion, thereby allowing them to move on to the work or *performing* stage. In GPIP, the performing stage focuses on challenging a patient's CMIP and encouraging them to try unfamiliar ways of relating in the group that might generalize to relationships outside the group. The final, *adjourning* stage recognizes the universal importance and anxiety inherent in ending relationships, internalizing the group as an attachment figure, and allowing patients to take stock of their progress and come to terms with the limits inherent to all relationships.

As we illustrate in Chapters 2 and 4, one of the most useful functions of developing a good case formulation is that it allows therapists to anticipate how a client might adapt in the early stages of group and what challenges may emerge in later stages. For example, during the forming stage, a therapist might expect Rob to be quiet, and Rob may feel anxious and wonder whether he belonged in the group. The initial goal of group therapy might be to help Rob examine these feelings, develop a sense of belonging and that he is not alone, and consider that he could be a valued group member. This may require the therapist and other group members to encourage Rob to participate and for Rob to receive feedback that his participation is worthwhile, a task that is likely to give rise to anxiety because it challenges his long-held beliefs about the self. Once Rob experiences a sense of cohesion, alliance, and safety within the group, he may be capable of reducing his minimizing defenses, which may allow him to experience a sense of pride or to express attachment needs that have been dormant. That is, the performing stage of the group might be an important but difficult stage for Rob because the group might challenge him to diminish his maladaptive defenses and expose himself to the potential for shame and ridicule that he expects of others. However, the disconfirmation of this expectation will be key to Rob's future attempts in the group to behave in a way that is different from his usual passive and self-effacing manner. One outcome of this change might be that his self-concept will alter from one in which he experiences himself as a "loser" to one in which he feels more worthy.

Another important consideration of GPIP is the attention paid to group composition. At the outset, we described Dr. Smith as feeling perplexed by the wide-ranging patient characteristics in a group that was supposed to be homogeneous in terms of symptoms. Even if patients share similar symptoms (e.g., anxiety), they may differ in meaningful ways that may make it difficult for them to connect and feel safe with each other and to work productively together. And so, we describe in Chapter 2 a means of assessment that is attentive to group composition to increase the probability that a group will become cohesive and function optimally.

AN EVIDENCE-BASED APPROACH

Dr. Smith, like many practitioners, wants to provide evidence-based treatment to her patients. That is, she wants to practice in a manner that is consistent with and supported by research, that allows her to use her clinical experience to adjust her interventions and interpersonal stances, and that is congruent with her patients' characteristics and preferences. GPIP offers such an evidence-based practice approach to group therapy.

As we highlight in Chapter 5, we completed and have ongoing clinical trials that demonstrate the effectiveness and efficacy of GPIP to reduce symptoms (e.g., Hewitt et al., 2015; Hewitt, Qiu, et al., 2019; Tasca et al., 2013, 2019; Tasca, Ritchie, et al., 2006). In support of the GPIP transdiagnostic model, our research demonstrates that the treatment is effective not only in reducing distress and symptoms but also in reducing the level, intensity, and impact of those patient variables that maintain or cause problems in living, such as attachment insecurity, interpersonal problems, personality and relational styles, depressive affect, maladaptive defense mechanisms, and problems with mentalizing (e.g., Hewitt et al., 2015; Hewitt, Qiu, et al., 2019; Hill et al., 2015; Maxwell et al., 2018, 2014; Tasca, Ritchie, et al., 2006). Finally, our research on group processes in GPIP highlights the importance of increasing group cohesion and therapeutic alliance, the role of interpersonal learning in reducing symptoms, and the importance of developmental stages of group when planning interventions (e.g., Gallagher, Tasca, Ritchie, Balfour, & Bissada, 2014; Gallagher, Tasca, Ritchie, Balfour, Maxwell, & Bissada, 2014; Hill et al., 2015; Tasca et al., 2007; Tasca, Ritchie, et al., 2006).

Our research to date allows the conscientious group therapist to learn and apply GPIP with confidence that the treatment is effective. We geared this book to help the practitioner not only learn the clinical techniques of the psychodynamic-interpersonal approach to assessment, case formulation, and group treatment but also understand the research that supports GPIP. This will help the clinician feel comfortable and confident in the treatment and inform their patients of the treatment's efficacy to increase patients' expectations of a good outcome. Moreover, knowing the research support for GPIP may help clinicians inform administrators, third-party funders, and policy makers about the utility of the approach. With this evidence in hand, Dr. Smith will be able to propose an alternative approach to group therapy in her place of employment.

THERAPIST TASK BOX

GPIP CASE FORMULATION, GROUP PROCESS, AND EVIDENCE BASE

1. Use a case formulation approach to inform therapist interpersonal stances in the group.
   - Consider that symptoms are a manifestation of attachment and interpersonal patterns.
2. Think about group therapy in terms of stages of group development.
   - Different stages of the group require different therapist interpersonal stances and interventions.
   - Early stages of group therapy should focus on developing a sense of cohesion to the group and an alliance with the therapist and group.
3. Know the research evidence for GPIP, and convey this knowledge to your patients and to those who fund your practice.

ORGANIZATION OF THE BOOK

We designed this book for both new and experienced psychotherapists who want to solidify their grounding in psychodynamic or interpersonal psychotherapy theory and its impact on group therapy practice. The book provides a means to advance one's knowledge and skills in these areas and to integrate theoretical perspectives and clinical practice to understand one's patients better and to be a more effective group therapist. Our objectives are to make the content of the book user friendly and to encourage therapists to apply the knowledge and skills outlined in the text. To meet these objectives, we use several pedagogical methods to illustrate the theoretical and practical material and facilitate learning. First, we provide a number of detailed case illustrations as examples of the concepts, assessment process, case formulation, pre-group preparation, and typical group therapy interactions and therapist interventions at each stage of the development of a GPIP group. The case illustrations are composites of many patients that we worked with over the years (and the therapist and patient names are pseudonyms), so the information does not identify any one patient. The cases appear throughout each of the chapters to bring the concepts and practices to life. Second, we provide Therapist Task Boxes that are specific to the topic of each chapter or sections within a chapter. Therapist Task Boxes are designed to be a quick and easy reference for therapists wishing to brush up on the tasks that are germane to the theory, assessment and case formulation, pre-group preparation, and group treatment. Third, each chapter ends with Chapter Review Exercises. These are designed to help the clinician test their understanding and hone concepts or practices that need further review. Finally, we encourage the reader to view the American Psychological Association video on GPIP featuring Samuel F. Mikail and Giorgio A. Tasca (2021). This video provides an example of many of the techniques used in the treatment, as well as a discussion with experts that refers to the therapy session itself in describing the treatment approach.

We start the book in Chapter 1 with a general description of the transdiagnostic approach to understanding patients, their interpersonal world, and the factors that underlie and maintain their problems. This is consistent with our view that, although useful, descriptive diagnoses alone are not enough to inform a clinician on how to be with and how to treat a patient. The chapter then goes into more detail about the theory of GPIP. The psychodynamic model of the triangle of adaptation, the triangle of object relations, the CMIP model, and their integration represent the core guiding framework of GPIP. Understanding these models is crucial to directing a therapist's assessment and interventions. We encourage clinicians to read Chapter 1 first to prepare for the more applied chapters to follow.

Chapter 2 focuses on assessment and case formulation using the GPIP model. In this chapter, we provide a step-by-step approach to assessing interpersonal style by using the interpersonal circumplex, attachment insecurity within a developmental approach, defensive functioning, and level of personality functioning. An idiographic person-centered assessment and case formulation is key to treatment planning, setting treatment goals, ensuring an optimal group composition, and informing the clinician on the most therapeutic interpersonal stances with each patient.

In Chapter 3, we turn to pre-group preparation and treatment planning. In this chapter, we emphasize the importance of preparing patients for group therapy and developing specific treatment goals by using the individualized case formulation for each patient. We provide specific steps and examples of how to prepare patients for group therapy.

In Chapter 4, we highlight therapist tasks and goals during each stage of group therapy. We discuss in some detail how a therapist emphasizes the therapeutic alliance, universality, group norms, and safety in the forming stage; manages needs for patient individuation during the storming stage; solidifies cohesion and authentic engagement in the norming stage; uses group processes and interactions to change CMIPs and maladaptive defenses during the performing stage; and deals with termination during the adjourning stage.

Finally, in Chapter 5, we provide a detailed description of the evidence base for GPIP, including its effectiveness and efficacy, the impact of GPIP on transdiagnostic maintenance factors, and research on group processes in GPIP.

Our intention in writing this book on GPIP is to provide clinicians such as Dr. Smith with an evidence-based treatment option for group psychotherapy that addresses the transdiagnostic factors that maintain or cause problems in living. There is an unfortunate and increasing lack of diversity in treatments offered to patients like Rob, which limits the relevance and effectiveness of psychotherapy in general and group psychotherapy in particular. With GPIP, clinicians are equipped with an intentional, comprehensive, research-informed theory and practice that emphasizes not just symptom reduction but helping the whole person to live a more fulfilling and self-aware life.

1 A PSYCHODYNAMIC AND INTERPERSONAL FOCUS

This chapter presents the theoretical underpinnings of the model we use to inform group psychodynamic-interpersonal psychotherapy (GPIP). We believe it is critical for therapists to have a good knowledge of the theoretical framework of interventions to apply the model effectively in their work with patients. In carrying out our clinical work, we acknowledge the complexity underlying each group member's pain, past experiences, ability, and stylistic approach to managing their exigencies in life, including the nature of their temperament, personality, and relational needs. We rely on a well-developed clinical formulation to guide treatment for a given person rather than focusing treatment predominantly on targeting symptoms or clusters of symptoms (i.e., syndromes or diagnoses). Having a model that incorporates elements of each person's uniqueness helps the clinician to fashion effective and optimally timed interventions that respond to patient and group needs. That is, we do not teach therapists that when X happens, do Y. Instead, we equip therapists with a way of thinking about the specific nature of each patient and his or her struggles that is based on the theoretical framework. This approach offers the clinician intervention options that

https://doi.org/10.1037/0000213-002
Group Psychodynamic-Interpersonal Psychotherapy, by G. A. Tasca, S. F. Mikail, and P. L. Hewitt

are both appropriate for that individual and timed to the patient's particular stage in the change process. In other words, when X happens, there are numerous Y options for the group therapist based on their understanding of the patient or group following from the GPIP theoretical model.

At first, clinicians may find that gaining at least a hypothesized understanding of patients' complexity seems daunting. We use several organizing principles and tools to make this an easier and more manageable task (see Hewitt et al., 2018). These principles include an understanding of transdiagnostic core vulnerability factors and how these factors inform the focus of treatment (see Hewitt et al., 2017). In part, GPIP involves integrating a psychodynamic understanding of the individual's unique issues and needs with interpersonal models of human connection and communication to help the clinician effect change. Thus, the purpose of this chapter is to introduce the reader to this framework and the tools we use to help patients in group therapy. As we illustrate later, group therapy provides a context to view and understand individuals in their interpersonal world, and this understanding allows therapists to formulate and enact change processes within a group context.

A TRANSDIAGNOSTIC APPROACH

Despite recent writing from a cognitive behavior therapy perspective about the importance of approaching treatment of psychological difficulties with a transdiagnostic lens (Mansell et al., 2008), the idea of focusing treatment on underlying causal processes has been a cornerstone of psychoanalytic and psychodynamic treatments since their inception over 120 years ago. Recently, authors have been describing the limitations of focusing only on symptoms and diagnostic entities (i.e., the co-occurring sets of symptoms) for understanding and treating patients. For example, Hewitt and colleagues (2008) stated that "the focus of psychotherapy should be on patient characteristics and personality vulnerabilities that bear directly and indirectly on the psychopathology the patient exhibits rather than on the clinical syndrome or symptoms per se" (p. 116). That is, by focusing treatment only on reducing symptoms, clinicians may not address the predisposing or vulnerability factors that lead the individual to remain at risk of future experiences of symptoms and relapse (Blatt & Zuroff, 2005).

The focus on symptoms to inform treatment derives from early attempts in medicine to understand and diagnose psychological problems based on descriptive features. This way of thinking forms the basis for current diagnostic schemes such as the *Diagnostic and Statistical Manual of Mental Disorders* (fifth ed. [*DSM-5*]; American Psychiatric Association, 2013). For example, in the 19th century, Kraepelin suggested that the focus of diagnostic entities should be on observable signs and symptoms (Zuckerman, 1999). From this Kraepelinian perspective, diagnostic labels reflect the grouping of sets of observable symptoms and signs that appear to co-occur. Under this scheme, the label constitutes the entirety of the psychological problem and focus of treatment. Although the label is simply a name given to a group of symptoms, over time, the label may take on other characteristics, such that the diagnostic entity itself may become mistakenly understood as the cause of the symptoms. For example, one may label symptoms such as difficulty with sleep, appetite disturbance, sad mood, low energy, and memory and concentration problems as major depression. But by applying circular logic, one might mistake the symptoms of the diagnosis as causing the diagnosis (e.g., "He has major depressive disorder because his mood is low, and his mood is low because he has major depressive disorder"). In reality, the grouping of these symptoms is simply something that diagnostic schemes call "major depression." An example of the logical circularity of this descriptive diagnostic approach is provided by Maung (2016), who quoted from a standard psychiatric textbook:

> Depression is more common in older people than it is in the general population. Various studies have reported prevalence rates ranging from 25 to almost 50 percent, although the percentage of these cases that are *caused by major depressive disorder* [emphasis added] is uncertain. (Sadock & Sadock, 2008, p. 215)

We do not imply that nosologies based on descriptive features only are not useful. They represent a first step in attempting to understand human problems; however, they are limited and open to misinterpretation. What is particularly concerning is that the therapies listed as empirically supported by the Clinical Division of the American Psychological Association (Chambless & Hollon, 1998) or recommended by the National Institute for Health and Care Excellence in the United Kingdom (Pilling et al., 2009), for example, were designed largely to focus on symptoms and were evaluated in clinical trials exclusively on the basis of their ability to reduce symptoms.

An alternative approach to understanding and diagnosing psychological difficulties involves focusing on the possible causes of those symptoms and signs. Thus, by analogy, rather than directing clinical attention to treating chest pain (i.e., the symptom) with pain medication, a clinician would determine the differential cause of the pain (e.g., myocardial infarction vs.

acid reflux) and direct treatment toward that cause (heart surgery vs. antacid). Sigmund Freud, who was a contemporary of Kraepelin, took a different approach to define and understand psychological problems by focusing on the putative causes of observable behaviors (Zuckerman, 1999). Freud and colleagues focused efforts on the interplay of internal psychological processes and psychodynamics of individuals to provide a focus for clinical efforts. This approach suggests that ameliorating the cause will result in a reduction of symptoms and the likelihood of relapse. This stance toward understanding psychological problems and suffering has continued in the psychodynamic world ever since.

These two fundamentally different approaches to understanding the problems that people experience result in differing views of the nature of psychopathology and different foci for clinical attention and intervention. From a Kraepelinian perspective, symptoms are alien and problematic, and the focus of treatment is to rid the person of these symptoms. From a psychodynamic perspective, symptoms are markers of an underlying pathogenic process, and so clinicians evaluate symptoms within the entirety of the person.

> John, a White man in his late 20s, became anxious when he was in social situations and worried that he would be embarrassed or humiliated. He avoided such situations much of his life. As an adult, this became a significant problem: He had a limited social life, he wanted to but could not date anyone, and his job as a software developer required him to work in small teams, which made him anxious. John's therapist diagnosed him with "social phobia" and suggested an empirically supported treatment of the symptoms that included graded exposure to feared situations. Several months of this approach helped John tolerate working in small groups, but he continued to harbor self-doubt and to devalue his contributions to team projects. John's efforts to engage with colleagues left him exhausted at the end of the day, and his romantic life remained nonexistent. Although his symptoms improved, he was still unhappy with his life, and over time, he became more and more sad and despondent about his situation. This led him to see another therapist who explored John's developmental history in detail. John was a sensitive child and always found social interactions to be a little overwhelming. During his childhood, peers severely bullied him, and his parents were critical of him for not standing up for himself. He began to think of himself not only as different from other people but also as being flawed and defective. Not surprisingly, he became increasingly anxious around others during his teens, with fears of being ridiculed, taunted, or abused. John sought solace in solitary play and online video games and became quite adept at computer programming.
>
> Once in his early 20s, he was romantically interested in a young woman who was kind to him but not interested in a relationship. This perceived rejection devastated John. The therapist suggested that John did want to

be close to others, but he feared rejection and hurt. John protected himself by walling himself off, avoiding others, and trying not to acknowledge his real needs for attachment. Although this method of self-protection allowed John to feel less fearful, it also created problems of isolation, loneliness, and sadness. His new therapist concluded that John could benefit from group psychotherapy, where he would have an opportunity to experience both his self and others in a manner aligned with his unfulfilled attachment needs.

THERAPIST TASK BOX

A TRANSDIAGNOSTIC APPROACH TO PROBLEMS

1. Consider that a patient's presenting problems or symptoms are a manifestation of an underlying process that should be a target of treatment.

2. Use this way of understanding problems to assess the patient's history of relationships, the nature of their emotional experiences, how they cope with troubling emotions and anxiety, and their current relationship quality and patterns when thinking of what caused what is currently maintaining the symptoms.

TRANSDIAGNOSTIC ISSUES: ATTACHMENT STYLES

A significant shift in psychodynamic thought that occurred in the mid-20th century was to emphasize relational processes that underlie both adaptive and maladaptive behavior. Thus, one of the most fundamental or core transdiagnostic issues involves relational experiences (especially early relational experiences) and the learning that takes place as a function of these experiences. These include interpersonal styles of behaving and the stylistic nature of the relationship between self and others (see Hewitt et al., 2017). Consistent with this interpersonal view of psychodynamics, we emphasize the importance of the relational world of people in terms of causing, maintaining, and exacerbating psychological difficulties and providing the focus and vehicle for change and growth (Sullivan, 1953). The work on attachment theory by John Bowlby and Mary Ainsworth, as well as the work on the self by Heinz Kohut, has been influential in our thinking with respect to GPIP. Investigators have described for decades the importance of early relationships with caregivers and the deleterious effects of the asynchrony[1] or mismatch (Hewitt et al., 2017) between a child's needs and a caregiver's responses (e.g., DeKlyen & Greenberg, 2008; Mills, 2005). Moreover, research has demonstrated that experiences of asynchrony contribute to problematic and inflexible relational styles (Benjamin, 1996; Bowlby, 1980) that remain stable over one's lifetime and influence all relationships (Main & Hesse, 1992; Sroufe, 1996). Zilberstein (2014) noted that "through those experiences, children develop an internal representation or internal working model of the care and protection they have received, which provides a similar regulating and self-comforting role" (p. 93).

Asynchrony and Insecure Attachment

As outlined in Hewitt et al. (2017), insecure attachment stemming from asynchrony between a child's needs and the caregiver's responses gives rise to a variety of affective reactions, most important, attachment insecurity. This, in turn, contributes to the development of behaviors designed to quell the sense of insecurity, as well as mental representations of significant others that ultimately lead to the unfolding of a limited and inflexible inter-personal repertoire. In asynchronous relationships, children may perceive significant others as indifferent, unavailable, critical, frightening, intrusive, or incapable of meeting their needs. The resulting working models of others that these children develop (Bowlby, 1980) are carried throughout their lives and relationships. These working models of others contribute to the development of insecure attachment styles and unmet relational needs, both of which are reflected in the stylistic nature of a person's relating to others and in their affect regulation. Ainsworth and colleagues (1978) initially described a number of attachment styles, and subsequent authors refined, expanded, and elaborated on these (e.g., Cassidy et al., 1992; Crittenden, 1992, 1995; Main & Hesse, 1990; Main & Solomon, 1990).

Broadly speaking, the organized patterns of attachment include secure attachment and two types of insecure attachment: preoccupied and dismissing. Main and Solomon (1990) also described a disorganized attachment pattern. As described by Tasca and Balfour (2014a, 2014b), individuals with *secure* attachments are capable of deep, meaningful, and loving relationships. They can moderate their emotions without becoming overwhelmed or without dismissing them, and they are not overly self-critical (Fuendeling, 1998). Moreover, individuals who are securely attached have coherent

---

[1]Hewitt et al. (2017) used the term "asynchrony" rather than "nonattunement" because they believe the term asynchrony reflects the interplay between the child and caregiver rather than the caregiver solely being nonattuned.

mental states characterized by a consistent, relevant, and contained narrative when discussing attachment relationships (Main et al., 2003) and when discussing the self. Finally, their reflective functioning is adequate. Reflective functioning is a relatively new development in attachment theory and is also known as *mentalizing*. It involves the acquired ability to have an awareness of and appreciation for one's own and others' mental states, such as personal desires, feelings, needs, intentions, and reasons for behavior (Bateman & Fonagy, 2006). It provides the foundation for the ability to appreciate and be informed by another's perspective, which allows for the development of the ability to empathize with others (Crittenden, 2006).

Individuals with a *preoccupied* (or anxious) attachment style tend to be overly concerned with potential relationship loss or abandonment, and they attempt to reduce anxiety by minimizing emotional distance by both demonstrating and soliciting displays of love and support from others (Tasca & Balfour, 2014a, 2014b). Individuals with a preoccupied attachment state of mind easily and repeatedly access painful attachment-related memories, and so they may become overwhelmed by rage and despair in response to perceived or actual separation or rejection (Bartholomew & Horowitz, 1991). Such individuals have emotional systems that tend to be hyperactivated (Mikulincer & Florian, 1995). Because of their anger, those with preoccupied attachments often have a difficult time making orderly sense of their past experiences. Their reflective functioning is impaired by these processes, and so individuals with preoccupied attachments have difficulty keeping in mind the needs and internal experiences of others and themselves.

Individuals with a *dismissing* (or avoidant) attachment style are overly self-reliant and appear indifferent and, in extreme cases, averse to intimate relationships, likely because they learned that reliance on others is at best a source of disappointment and pain (Tasca & Balfour, 2014a, 2014b). They tend to avoid affect that communicates a desire for affiliation, and so they use emotional distancing strategies to create a sense of safety and security (Fonagy, 2001). Moreover, those with a dismissing attachment style tend to either idealize or denigrate attachment figures. Their defensive memory structure results in impoverished narratives about themselves, indicating a mental state that is lacking in coherence. They have a difficult time considering their own or others' internal experiences in a flexible and non-distorted fashion; thus, their reflective functioning and ability to mentalize is compromised (Wallin, 2007).

Disorganized (or fearful) attachment is often associated with childhood adversity, neglect, and abuse. It is unclear whether the disorganized style is a separate category of insecure attachment or whether it exists in addition to either preoccupied or dismissing attachment styles. Those with a disorganized attachment style experience mental states that become disorganized (i.e., mental states characterized by overriding guilt, absorption, or dissociation) when recalling the experience of trauma or loss of an attachment figure (Bakermans-Kranenburg & van IJzendoorn, 2009). As a result, their narratives about their attachment relationships are not coherent, and their ability to reflect on their own and others' internal states (i.e., to mentalize) can be poor.

Asynchrony and Relationship With Self

Although attachment styles and internal working models contribute to the stylistic nature of relating to others, asynchrony of child and parent needs also plays a crucial role in the development of the relationship one has with oneself. For example, Kohut (1971) suggested that the development of a healthy and cohesive self is based on early childhood interactions with caregivers. Consistent child–caregiver interaction patterns that are synchronous help the self to develop as cohesive and allow the self to internalize others as objects that provide care, safety, security, and soothing. Moreover, there is contiguous development of a representation of the self as worthy and deserving of others' care. From this experience, one develops a cohesive self-structure that serves as a foundation for positive self-esteem, personal worth and meaning, autonomy, and a capacity for healthy reciprocal relationships (see Hewitt et al., 2017).

Conversely, Kohut (1971) suggested that exposure to persistent asynchrony compromises the development of a cohesive self and contributes to the formation of a disordered self. Kohut and Wolf (1978) indicated that a *disordered self* is characterized by people who are "focused on their deficiencies, extremely vulnerable to criticism and failure, and overwhelmed by negative emotions, pessimistic thoughts, and feelings of alienation and loneliness" (p. 226). In other words, the asynchronous experiences dampen the possibility of forming a resilient and stable identity and self-concept in which one experiences the self as valuable and valued by others. Thus, the individual may develop a fragile and fragmented view of self. In such instances, one holds the self in low esteem, such that a harsh inner dialogue characterizes one's relationship to the self. That inner dialogue can be reflective of a sense of defectiveness, not fitting in, not mattering, and so forth (Hewitt et al., 2019).

An individual whose self developed from asynchronous experiences with caregivers will have an inflexible interpersonal style (Leary, 1957).

Such styles aim to address longstanding unmet needs for acceptance, love, and esteem and aim to repair or compensate for what they experience to be a flawed self (Stolorow, Atwood, & Orange, 1999). Kohut (1971) referred to interactions stemming from these styles and selves as *transferences*, whereby the individual uses relationships with others to correct missing components of the self and missing elements of early relationships. Kohut argued that individuals may use other people as "selfobjects" in attempts to provide functions that the self has not developed and for other-relational needs.

Understanding the Patient

The combination of thwarted attachment needs, negatively toned or incoherent internal working models, and compromised self-concepts contributes to a distorted perceptual lens through which significant interpersonal encounters are experienced (Kohut, 1971; Lichtenberg, 2013) and influenced (Benjamin, 1996). The principles of attachment theory and theories of the development of the self are generally applicable across individuals as underlying mechanisms of problems in living; however, the manifestation of these mechanisms for a given individual is idiosyncratic. That is, the combination of attachment style and self-concept and their impact on a person's life is unique to each person in that it occurs within the complex and intricate environment of the developmental and relational world of the individual. There is an infinite number of family environments and possible interaction patterns that can contribute to each individual's characteristics. The transdiagnostic approach we describe is one that involves the unique characteristics of the individual, including the self and other relational needs, possibilities for interactions, temperament, and history and nature of the environment in which the person exists. This perspective guides our understanding of each person and, in turn, influences our intervention choices. As we describe throughout this volume, for each patient entering group treatment, we create an individualized working formulation or case conceptualization (see Hewitt et al., 2017, 2018, for specific clinical examples) that determines patients' treatment goals and therapists' interpersonal stances.

In developing and refining GPIP over the years, we incorporated theories from two broad treatment-related theoretical domains: contemporary psychodynamic theory (e.g., Bowlby, 1980; Kohut, 1971; Malan, 1979; Strupp & Binder, 1984) and interpersonal theory (e.g., Benjamin, 1996; Kiesler, 1996), both of which are discussed later. The emphasis of the theory behind

GPIP is on the interplay among relational needs, behaviors, and defensive approaches evoked in response to unmet attachment needs. Moreover, we emphasize developmental aspects of a person's functioning as a way of understanding that defensive patterns in current relationships have both adaptive and maladaptive features. The inclusion of both psychodynamic and interpersonal models provides a unique way of understanding patients and their problems and to guide clinicians in understanding and choosing group interventions at opportune times.

As suggested, a pivotal aspect of GPIP involves establishing a case formulation for each patient (Hewitt et al., 2018). The GPIP case formulation incorporates two key elements of psychodynamic and interpersonal theories (Hewitt et al., 2017). The first element is a modification of a psychodynamic model first described by David Malan (1979). The second element involves incorporating the cyclical maladaptive interpersonal patterns (CMIP) model described by Strupp and Binder (1984). Before discussing our modification of Malan's model, we first briefly review Malan's two triangles. We then describe how we incorporate the CMIP model.

THERAPIST TASK BOX
PATIENT ATTACHMENT STYLE

Consider a patient's attachment style and type of attachment insecurity when trying to understand their presenting problems and symptoms.

- Do they likely have a dismissing attachment style in which they see relationships as secondary and downplay their emotional experiences?
- Might they have a preoccupied attachment style in which they are overly concerned with relationship loss and maintain heightened emotional experiences?
- Or do they display a disorganized attachment related to trauma or abuse, in which they have approach-avoidance behaviors in relationships and experience dysregulation of their emotional experiences?

MALAN'S TRIANGLE OF CONFLICT

Malan's (1979) two triangles represent an important heuristic model for understanding symptoms from a psychodynamic point of view. In this model, the *triangle of conflict* consists of impulse, anxiety, and defense elements (Figure 1.1). The *triangle of person* consists of parallel relationship themes

FIGURE 1.1. Malan's (1979) Two Triangles: Triangle of Conflict and Triangle of Person

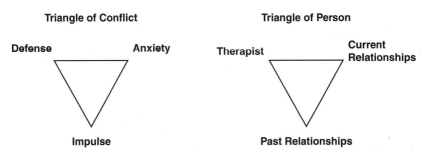

Note. From *Individual Psychotherapy and the Science of Psychodynamics* (p. 80), by D. H. Malan, 1979, Butterworth-Heinemann (https://doi.org/10.1016/C2013-0-06209-3). Copyright 1979 by Elsevier. Adapted with permission.

among relationships with the therapist, current others, and past others, usually parents (Figure 1.1). Malan suggested that the triangles stand on their apex because the element at the apex is historically earlier and more likely out of awareness. In Malan's *triangle of conflict*, the defense is typically a coping strategy, symptom, and/or behavior that is an attempted solution to the problem of unwanted anxiety. Anxiety is often generated by an unconscious impulse that tends to be sexual or aggressive.

Although it is an important heuristic device, Malan's (1979) model is an outdated drive theory or dual instinct theory of psychoanalysis. Drive theory focused on the dual instincts of sex and aggression that people must master by ego development and defenses so they can adaptively relate to each other. In the dual instinct model, relationships and relationship styles are a result of the resolution of inner conflict related to sexual and aggressive drives (Gabbard, 2004). In contrast, relational psychoanalytic theories, such as object relations theory and self psychology, view relationships as the primary psychological elements that move individuals to act and develop (Ornstein & Ornstein, 1990). Thus, writings by Bowlby (1980), for example, underscore the inherently biological and primary nature of the need to have attachments to others to survive and develop.

GPIP TRIANGLE OF ADAPTATION

We modified Malan's (1979) model for the dynamic-relational treatment of perfectionism and of binge eating (Hewitt et al., 2017; Tasca et al., 2005) as a way of incorporating contemporary psychodynamic thinking on the role of one's interpersonal context in psychological development. In the wake of object relations theory and self psychology, psychodynamic theory undertook an evolution that places relationships and attachment at the core of psychological being. Relating is, as Bowlby (1980) stated, hardwired and a central motivating force for human development. To reflect this, we redefined Malan's (1979) triangle of conflict into what we call the *triangle of adaptation* (see the example in Figure 1.2). In our redefinition, attachment needs take the place of sexual and aggressive impulses as the primary and often unconscious movers of human thoughts, emotions, and behaviors. In the case of maladjustment or psychopathology, attachment needs are often historically rooted and may not have been met adequately throughout one's life starting in childhood. Attachment needs may also represent one's needs for security in relation to individuals currently in one's life or needs stemming from relationships with internalized attachment figures.

Often, patients who seek treatment have histories in which their attachment needs were punished, ridiculed, shamed, or neglected. As a result, these attachment needs became paired with automatic responses in the form of affects, including anxiety. Affects may take various forms, such as fears of rejection or abandonment, concerns with not mattering, aloneness in the world, anxiety, and shame. Should attachment needs begin to emerge into conscious awareness, they may trigger automatic aversive affects. We represent the affects as a pole in the triangle of adaptation similar to Malan's (1979) anxiety pole (Figure 1.2).

As a result of the negative or noxious experiences of the affects, individuals develop defense mechanisms to cope and maintain their psychological

FIGURE 1.2. GPIP Triangle of Adaptation and Triangle of Object Relations

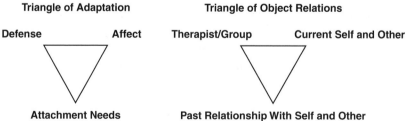

Note. From "Group Psychodynamic Interpersonal Psychotherapy: Summary of a Treatment Model and Outcomes for Depressive Symptoms," by G. A. Tasca, S. F. Mikail, and P. L. Hewitt, in M. E. Abelian (Ed.), *Focus on Psychotherapy Research* (p. 165), 2005, Nova Science. Copyright 2005 by Nova Science. Adapted with permission.

equilibrium and self-esteem. Moreover, defenses can include not just ego defenses but also defensive positions or enduring defensive "ways of being in the world" (Hewitt et al., 2017), such as characterological aspects of personality (e.g., perfectionism, dependency, not trusting). Defense mechanisms may vary in terms of how effective and adaptive they are. As we indicate throughout this text, defense mechanisms and defensive positions were likely the best psychological solutions possible during an earlier time in one's life but often are no longer adaptive or appropriate in current contexts. Defenses not only manage affects but often they also complicate one's striving to meet attachment needs and one's ability to access adaptive feelings and interactions. Defenses tend to be relational, or they have interpersonal consequences, and they help define relationship styles that are more or less consistent across situations. Because the focus is on the responses to thwarted relational needs, we call this model the triangle of adaptation (see Figure 1.2).

GPIP TRIANGLE OF OBJECT RELATIONS

The second triangle central to our conceptualization is an extension of Malan's (1979) triangle of person. Malan's triangle helps one to understand the importance of examining how relational styles evident in past and current relationships, as well as with therapists or groups, are parallel or consistent. However, an important element that is missing from Malan's model is the implication for one's sense of self (i.e., introject) or the relationship with self. There has been interest in the self in other psychoanalytic theories, such as Sullivan's (1953) interpersonal theory or Kohut's self psychology (Baker & Baker, 1987). Because we incorporate the relationship with self in the triangle and because we incorporate relational schemas and mental representations in the triangle, we have extended Malan's triangle of persons and now refer to it as the *triangle of object relations*.

The triangle of object relations involves three domains, all of which are relevant to our understanding of an individual (see the example in Figure 1.2). The past relationships vertex reflects the early learning for which children are prepared and at which they are exceedingly successful. Recall that asynchrony in early relationships is often evident in those who have problems in living. Early relationships provide opportunities for the child to learn what they can do to feel safe and secure and reduce negative affective states (e.g., hunger, pain, fear), and children also learn to form an understanding of self through the responses of caregivers. This provides children with a sense of whether they are worthy, loved, and lovable and matter to others and whether others are trustworthy, supportive, caring, and so forth. Not only do children experience these states, they also learn ways to deal with them motivated by needs for survival. Recall also that asynchronous relationships with caregivers in the past influence current affective experiences and patterns of relating to others to meet relational goals. Early relationships with siblings, peers, and important adult figures are central to contributing to affective experiences and interpersonal styles as the child learns to navigate the world in as safe and secure a manner as possible. Moreover, within the past relationships domain of the triangle of object relations, the self evolves from the early relational experiences in terms of how the person felt about him- or herself during their childhood (i.e., whether the person felt esteemed, lovable, defective).

The relational styles and attempts to meet relational needs established early on are evident in current interpersonal interactions, as represented by the current relationship vertex of the triangle of object relations (Figure 1.2). That is, styles identified in past relationships find their parallel in current relationships. Identifying these patterns in current relationships provides information about the stylistic nature of the patterns and the importance of these patterns to meet relational needs in one's present. Moreover, identifying a patient's patterns of relating can solidify for the clinician an understanding of the person's relational needs and styles to regulate affect that arises when current relationships do not meet their needs.

Finally, one can expect that the relational styles identified in the triangle of object relations will arise in the therapeutic context either with the therapist or with others in a therapy group (Figure 1.2). This is one manifestation of transference, or what Sullivan (1953) termed *parataxic distortions*, whereby patients relate to the therapist or group in a similar stylistic manner as they relate to current other relationships and/or past relationships. The expression of the styles within the therapy context allows the therapist to work with these relational needs and defensive responses as they occur immediately in the group (i.e., in the here-and-now), which is a powerful process facilitating change and growth for the person.

Thus, interpersonal styles have their beginnings in past relational experiences. Understanding the genesis and the purpose of the defensive behaviors aids therapists in working with the relational needs and dynamics of a person, and therapists can expect these patterns to show up in current relationships, including the therapeutic context. Knowing these patterns helps clinicians and patients understand how and why interpersonal defensive styles arose, what purpose they served in the past, and whether they are still useful in the present.

As an example of the triangles, consider an individual whose underlying attachment need is characterized by one of intense longing for connection, mattering to others, and the need to be taken care of (i.e., someone with a preoccupied attachment). This constellation of attachment needs can underlie numerous *DSM-5* disorders, including major depression, various somatoform disorders, avoidant or dependent personality disorder, social anxiety, or eating disorders. This was evident in the example of John described earlier, whose first therapist diagnosed him with social anxiety disorder. John had an unexpressed need for connection with others, a longing for a romantic relationship in which he could feel cared for or protected, and a desire to ultimately experience himself as lovable and worthwhile. Yet, John's needs remained unconscious because early caregivers did not meet them or rejected them. John's parents offered little solace or protection from bullies whose taunting and verbal attacks contributed to John viewing himself as defective. John protected himself by trying to fade into the background in social situations, expecting that if others did not notice him, he would not likely face derogating and humiliating comments. Although this form of adapting brought some reprieve to John, it also meant that most people in his life failed to notice him or consider his needs.

As so often happens, John's chosen solution served to perpetuate the pattern that was at the core of his pain. The affects generated in this context included anxiety, shame, and potentially anger, although despair may also accompany the expectation of rejection. In John's case, he expected rejection and derogation, which then gave rise to persistent anxiety and fear in most social situations. Following from the triangle of adaptation, John's defenses to deal with the anxiety and shame included attempts to distance himself from others or avoidant withdrawal. Other patients with similar histories of relationships may engage in a *denial of anger* by being too sociable and drawing attention away from themselves, and in so doing, they maintain an emotional distance intended to protect the self. With a psychodynamic-interpersonal framework, defenses and attendant symptoms can be understood as failed or maladaptive solutions to an experience of internal turmoil, interpersonal conflict, and fear of impending rejection and disappointment. Thus, patients such as John may enact in current relationships similar behaviors that were established in earlier relationships to deal with the anxiety of their expectation of rejection or bullying. When first enacted, such defenses may have offered John a degree of solace, but when indiscriminately applied over the course of his life, they exacted a considerable cost. We also note that defense mechanisms that emerge in childhood or adolescence in response to a particular set of life experiences are limited by the emotional and intellectual maturity of the individual at the time, as well as the environmental demands. So, not only are defense mechanisms self-limiting by virtue of perpetuating the difficulties one is trying to overcome but they also fail to draw on latent resources of the individual.

A group therapist can expect that defensive behaviors developed early on and used currently will show up in a therapeutic context. For example, John might have difficulty expressing genuine needs and emotions in the group, keeping the therapist or group members at a distance and not revealing himself to others. Further, John may experience as an attack the genuine feedback the therapist or group intended as an expression of caring and a desire to connect.

A therapist might also expect that at the start of group therapy, John will remain silent and withdrawn, thus reenacting a familiar though maladaptive interpersonal pattern. The work of Strupp and Binder (1984) on the CMIP, which we discuss next, gives an interpersonal account of how these relationship patterns develop and their impact on the self-concept. In addition, the principle of complementarity from interpersonal theory, which we describe in more detail later in this chapter, indicates how these interaction styles are reinforced and perpetuated through the effect they have on others.

THERAPIST TASK BOX

A PSYCHODYNAMIC FOCUS: THE TWO TRIANGLES

1. Triangle of object relations: Listen to the patient's narrative for consistency in their relational style and relationship themes in their past relationships, current relationships, and with the therapist.

2. Consider how these relationship patterns and themes affect the patient's self-concept and their self-evaluation.

3. Triangle of adaptation: Conceptualize the patient's maintenance and causes of symptoms in terms of their underlying dynamics.
   - What are the attachment needs that remain unexpressed or unconscious for the patient?
   - What affects, such as shame, anxiety, and fear, occur when attachment needs might make it to the patient's consciousness?
   - What is the nature of the patient's defenses to manage affects? Consider how the defenses manifest in relationships and may affect behaviors related to symptoms.

CYCLICAL MALADAPTIVE INTERPERSONAL PATTERN

The triangles provide a starting point for clinicians to understand the patient's developmental history, vulnerabilities, predominant affective experiences, and defenses. They also help clinicians make sense of patients' interpersonal patterns in past, current, and therapeutic relationships. However, adding another heuristic to the triangles will aid clinicians in elaborating the patient's relational pattern, particularly because the pattern is enacted during periods of heightened anxiety. The CMIP in GPIP is a conceptual framework of the psychodynamic-interpersonal cycle that describes patients' prototypic relational patterns that perpetuate their relational difficulties. The CMIP is a hypothesis or heuristic that guides the therapist's understanding of the patient's behavior in and out of the therapy and, in turn, informs the therapist's choice of interventions.

One metaphor to understand the role and variations of individual CMIPs in a therapy group is the musician's use of music notation systems and culturally based musical styles. Two composers in the baroque or jazz style can create very different melodies and harmonies using the same music notational system. Further, each composer can create distinct melodies and harmonies within each musical style. For example, both Bach and Vivaldi composed in the baroque period, yet their music is quite different, as is the jazz music of Oscar Peterson and John Coltrane. Thus, although the CMIP is a framework built on specific principles, individual CMIPs differ from person to person in a group as a function of their idiosyncratic histories and experiences.

The CMIP is not a substitute for a comprehensive psychological assessment (although a clinician may use validated assessment instruments to complete the CMIP), nor is it an immutable truth carved in stone. Rather, it describes a hypothesized process whereby an individual experiences affective states that may be disquieting, distressing, overwhelming, or chaotic. These states and the defensive operations to manage them come to define the individual's behaviors and experiences, expectations of others, and view of the self in relation to others. In elaborating the CMIP model, we incorporated concepts from brief psychodynamic psychotherapy, interpersonal models of psychotherapy, and the psychopathology literature. We derived the components of the CMIP from Strupp and Binder's (1984) work. Components of the CMIP include behaviors in which the patient engages (acts of self), expectations of others' reactions to the patient (expectations of others), others' overt behavior (acts of others), and finally, the patient's incorporation or internalization of these three interpersonal components into of a model of the self (introject).

For several reasons, it is paramount for GPIP clinicians to establish the CMIP for each patient. First, the individualized CMIP provides therapists with a framework or explanatory model to illuminate the patient's recurrent interpersonal patterns that contribute to and sustain the patient's difficulties. Second, a well-constructed CMIP provides therapists with a means of understanding a patient's interpersonal intent, underlying motivation, and affective communication as they emerge in a therapy group. Third, the CMIP provides therapists with an important therapeutic tool that guides their selection of interventions. Fourth, clinicians may discuss the CMIP with the patient at the conclusion of the assessment process for group therapy (discussed in greater detail in a later chapter). This provides patients with more insight into and control of the dynamic processes that drive their behaviors.

The CMIP describes facets of patients' behavior that fall into four categories outlined by Strupp and Binder (1984; Strupp and Binder refer to this as the *cyclical maladaptive pattern*). These four components (acts of self, expectations of others, acts of others, introject) work in a dynamic and interactive fashion, with each having an influence on the other rather than being static or independent parts (see Figure 1.3).

FIGURE 1.3. Illustration of the Cyclical Maladaptive Interpersonal Pattern

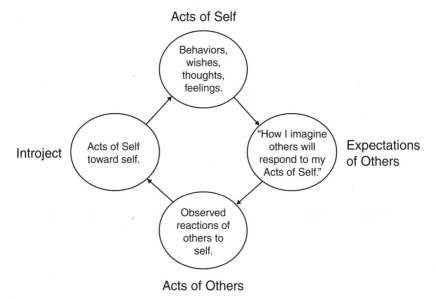

Note. From *Perfectionism: A Relational Approach to Conceptualization, Assessment, and Treatment* (p. 163), by P. L. Hewitt, G. L. Flett, and S. F. Mikail, 2017, Guilford Press. Copyright 2017 by Guilford Press. Adapted with permission.

Acts of Self

This facet of the CMIP includes all behaviors in which the individual engages covertly and overtly. It can involve needs, wishes, desires, affective states, cognitions, and perceptions. It refers to all domains of behavior, including public and private (e.g., feeling angry and expressing anger), and the behaviors may be more or less available to consciousness. Examples of acts of self might include taking a particularly passive interpersonal stance with others, engaging in nondisclosure of personal information, and ruminating about the self. Another individual might behave in a particularly compliant, ingratiating, or obsequious manner with others, not expressing his or her demands. A third individual might express hostility and vindictiveness in interacting with others, believe people to be dangerous, and express sadness over not having a close intimate relationship.

Expectations of Others

This facet involves what the patient expects or imagines other people will experience (i.e., think, feel, perceive) in response to the patient's acts of self. This can include the imagined reactions of others that are fully available to the patient's awareness or that may be at a less-than-conscious level. The verbalizations that characterize this facet often involve if–then statements, whereby there is an expected inner experience of the other person based on the patient's acts. For example, individuals may express the following: "If I reveal my inner self to another person, they will feel disgusted or repulsed" or "If I am compliant or submissive, others will think me weak and take advantage of me" or "If I do not take care of others' needs, people will have no use for me or will not love me."

Acts of Others

This component of the CMIP involves the actual observed reactions of others that the patient reports or the therapist sees. These are observed acts of others that can occur in relation to or as a response to the patient's acts of self. The patient may unconsciously "pull for" or "evoke" these responses from others (i.e., complementary interpersonal responses, as defined later). Acts of others can include all domains of behavior described within the acts of self. For example, individuals may describe situations wherein others may reject (e.g., avoiding interactions, not including the patient, not paying attention to or acknowledging the patient's utterances, looks of disgust) the patient when the patient exhibits passivity or aggression. Likewise, others may respond with anger or fear when the patient exhibits hostility. Similarly, others may take advantage of the helpfulness or good-natured behaviors of the patient or not allow the focus of disclosures to be on the patient. The patient may interpret the observed acts of others as evidence of others' evaluation of the patient's self-worth rather than as a complementary response to the patient's behavior. That is, the patient may not see the responses of others as resulting in part from or in reaction to his or her behavior. For example, a patient may be quite hostile in relating to others, and when the others respond in kind or with avoidance, the patient may understand this as evidence of how unlovable he or she is or may understand this as evidence of how horrible and predictably mean other people are.

Acts of Self Toward Self (Introject)

This is an important facet of the CMIP that involves the patient incorporating the acts of self, expectations of others, and acts of others into their self-system or self-concept. That is, it describes how patients treat themselves in relation to the other components of the CMIP, particularly the behavior in which others engage. It often takes the form of "When X occurs, I [am, feel, think, experience, etc.] Y." For example, a patient may indicate that she tends to be passive (act of self) in an attempt to avoid rejection or avoid annoying others. She expects others will not be hostile to her or reject her because of her passivity. However, as a result of her passivity, others may take advantage of her (acts of others). As a result, she views herself or comes to believe herself to be weak, ineffective, or defective (introject). Similarly, a patient might respond to an interpersonal situation by "blending into the woodwork" (act of self) and might expect others not to notice him (expectations of others). The acts of others might involve ignoring or not noticing him. As a result, he may view himself as irrelevant and unimportant (introject). Another person might express that when others respond in frustration toward him (acts of others), he experiences self-reproach and defines himself as worthless (introject). Finally, a patient may express aggressiveness or hostility to others (acts of self), to which others respond with anger (acts of others). As a result, the patient may experience confirmation of their sense of weakness, helplessness, or powerlessness (introject) that drove the hostility in the first place.

These categories of the CMIP synthesize into a transactional pattern whereby each component influences or reinforces other components. The synthesis of components provides the clinician with an initial focus of a patient's CMIP, which is the framework for understanding the patient's interpersonal and intrapersonal behaviors, reactions, and symptoms. The pattern does not meet the needs of the individual and can take the person far afield from having his or her needs met. Hence the pattern is maladaptive, but we recognize that at some point in the patient's development, when the pattern was first established, this style of behavior may have been adaptive or the best possible relational solution given the circumstances. For example, if a patient has a history in which caregivers physically or verbally abused her during childhood (acts of others), the response of blending in with the woodwork (acts of self) could have been effective in avoiding the abuse. However, as developmental and social demands shift with age, the cost of blending into the woodwork became high. Patients frequently have the feeling that there has always been something wrong with them. Or they may express that their behavior, although troublesome, has served them exceedingly well in the past. However, currently, these defensive interpersonal behaviors come at a cost, which is an important message for the therapist to convey to the patient.

THERAPIST TASK BOX
CYCLICAL MALADAPTIVE INTERPERSONAL PATTERN

1. Use the CMIP model to understand the components of a patient's interpersonal pattern and its relation to their self-concept.

2. Help the patient to see the seemingly confusing or self-limiting interpersonal behaviors as understandable within the CMIP.

3. Expect the CMIP to manifest itself in the patient's interactions with the group.

4. Consider the changes in components of the CMIP as treatment goals for individual patients.

INTERPERSONAL THEORY

A crucial aspect of our model is the interpersonal expression of attachment needs and defenses, which are a focus of GPIP interventions. Although the CMIP model that Strupp and Binder (1984) proposed does incorporate interpersonal components, we include a more explicit involvement of defensive interpersonal styles. This is not particularly innovative on our part; numerous writers from psychodynamic and interpersonal circles have underscored the importance of interpersonal styles based on anxiety (e.g., Benjamin, 1996; Kiesler, 1996; Leary, 1957; Luborsky, 1984; Strupp & Binder, 1984). To appreciate this synthesis, a brief description of interpersonal theory is in order.

Interpersonal theory is a model of behavior that arose from a psychoanalytic framework but focused on the interpersonal domain. Sullivan (1953), who understood human behavior in relation to past and current interpersonal contexts, pioneered the work. An important tenet of the interpersonal paradigm is that interpersonal behavior involves both the relationship one has with others as well as the relationship one has with oneself. This is what Sullivan described as the *self system*, whereby how an individual experiences their "self" develops through the reflected appraisals of others. Thus, interpersonal behavior encompasses relations between self and others and between self and self.

Psychologically healthy people can respond to sundry interpersonal situations with appropriate interpersonal behavior. For example, a healthy person in a situation involving a coveted job interview with an executive of the business can engage in friendly but neither overly dominant nor overly submissive behaviors. That same person may take a more dominant interpersonal stance in a context in which they must discipline an insubordinate worker. Likewise, a healthy person can express caution or lack of trust in interacting with certain individuals but may express complete trust in interacting with others. That is, the healthy individual demonstrates flexibility in interpersonal responding based on the requirements of the current relational environment.

Individuals tend to have "preferred" interpersonal styles or general styles in which they automatically engage. However, those with problems in living or relating often lack flexibility in interpersonal responses and also tend to engage in rigid and intense interpersonal behaviors in a stylistic manner (Leary, 1957). For example, an individual who trusts no one responds to nearly all people in most interpersonal situations with caution and suspicion. This person does not have the flexibility in interpersonal behavior to trust some people and not others.

INTERPERSONAL CIRCUMPLEX MODEL

One can represent interpersonal styles on the interpersonal circumplex, or interpersonal circle, as illustrated next. We use the circumplex developed by Leary (1957) and elaborated by Kiesler (1996) in Figure 1.4 in which interpersonal behaviors and styles are ordered along two continua

FIGURE 1.4. The Interpersonal Circumplex

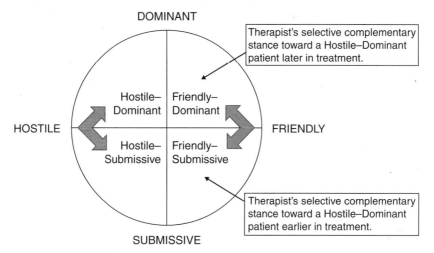

Note. Quadrant version of the interpersonal circle. Dominant-submissive and hostile-friendly represent orthogonal dimensions. Quadrants represent elements of each dimension. Double headed arrows indicate complementary interactions such that friendly-submissive and friendly-dominant interactions are complementary, as are hostile-submissive and hostile-dominant interactions. From "Group Psychodynamic Interpersonal Psychotherapy: Summary of a Treatment Model and Outcomes for Depressive Symptoms," by G. A. Tasca, S. F. Mikail, and P. L. Hewitt, in M. E. Abelian (Ed.), *Focus on Psychotherapy Research* (p. 165), 2005, Nova Science. Copyright 2005 by Nova Science. Adapted with permission.

or dimensions that reflect power (or status) and affiliation. The poles of the power axis (the vertical axis) have *dominant* at one end and *submissive* at the other. The poles of the affiliation axis (horizontal axis) have *hostile* at one end and *friendly* at the other. Due to the orthogonality or independence of the two dimensions, they can be depicted as two independent axes of a circle.

Interpersonal behaviors that are located close to each other on the circumplex are positively correlated or closely related to each other. Those behaviors that are at a 90-degree angle from each other are not correlated (independent), and those that are at extreme points of each dimension are negatively correlated or opposite. Figure 1.4 also depicts the quadrants of an interpersonal circle, which represent aspects of both the status and the affiliation dimensions.

One can order or locate any interpersonal behavior around the circumplex. For example, the behavior of an individual who listens carefully and empathically to others' problems and provides helpful advice can be seen as both dominant (i.e., takes a helper role) and friendly. Thus, the behavioral style is located in the upper right quadrant of the circumplex (i.e., friendly–dominant; Figure 1.4). However, the behavior of an individual who listens carefully to what others say about their problems and provides advice (dominant) but also expresses blame toward the person with the problem (hostile) is located in the hostile–dominant quadrant (Figure 1.4).

Interpersonal theory assumes that individuals with psychological difficulties exhibit these interpersonal styles in a rigid fashion and that these interpersonal styles initiate and perpetuate interactional patterns with others. This description is the confluence of the interpersonal circumplex and the *interpersonal transaction cycle* (ITC; Wagner et al., 1995), whereby two individuals reciprocally influence one another's behavior. Kiesler (1996) described the ITC as representing the relationship between the overt interpersonal behavior of one individual and the covert reactions of the other individual. Each person's behavior is both a cause and result of the other's behavior. Individuals with problems in living or relating tend to enact the same ITC over and over again and can shape others' responses to them. This reinforces the perceptions, feelings, and needs that underlie the maladaptive behavior. Thus, beliefs about one's self and others go unchallenged, and the interpersonal interaction cycle repeats in a self-confirming and self-perpetuating manner (Kiesler, 1996).

COMPLEMENTARITY

A pivotal component of the interpersonal perspective is the principle of complementarity in interactions. Complementarity suggests that an individual's interpersonal behaviors can evoke or pull a restricted set of interpersonal responses from another. For example, the individual who is ready for an important date after primping and preening for several hours and asks his roommate, "How do I look?" is pulling for a particular response. The behavior compels the roommate to answer, "Wonderful." This is an example of complementarity whereby the roommate responds to the "pull" for a positive affirmation from the individual. Carson (1969) used the interpersonal circumplex to define *complementarity* as (a) an opposite or reciprocal response on the control/status dimension and (b) a corresponding response on the affiliation dimension. *Reciprocity* refers to a stance of dominance in response to an individual who is submissive or vice versa. *Correspondence* means that friendly behaviors tend to beget friendly responses, and hostile behaviors tend to beget hostile responses. Thus, an individual behaves in a particular fashion with his or her preferred interpersonal style, and this will likely produce a predictable response in others. Hence, with the circumplex, one can predict that hostile–dominant behavior tends to evoke hostile–submissive behaviors and vice versa (Figure 1.4). Concurrently, friendly–dominant behavior tends to evoke friendly–submissive behavior and vice versa.

Complementary interactions tend to continue unchanged because they are reinforcing to the self-systems of both parties. When one person does not behave in a complementary manner, it creates tension and anxiety in one or both participants because noncomplementarity challenges the self-systems of one or both participants. The interaction then must change to a complementary one in which one of the participants alters their behaviors to complement the other. Alternatively, the interaction could terminate if the level of anxiety caused by the noncomplementarity is too high.

Thus, an important facet of the CMIP is the interpersonal style and the complementary responses the individual's manner of relating evokes in others. Moreover, the interplay of others' complementary responses and the patient introjecting others' behaviors into a self-view provides the therapist with a further understanding of the dynamic processes involved in the patient's psychological difficulties.

THE IMPORTANCE OF THE INTERPERSONAL STYLE TO PSYCHOTHERAPY

Understanding and illuminating the interpersonal style of the patient is extremely important in GPIP. First, because of the inflexibility of the patient's defensive interpersonal style, a clinician can assume that the interpersonal style will show itself in the group therapy situation as it does in other interpersonal situations. Second, not only does the interpersonal style inform the therapist of the expected interpersonal behavior of a patient but it also allows the therapist to choose to engage in a way that either supports the patient's behavior (complementary therapist response) or provokes change in the patient's behavior (noncomplementary therapist response).

> In the pre-group assessment, Jane had considerable difficulty providing details of what brought her to therapy. She admitted to various symptoms but often spoke in generalities, which made it difficult for her therapist to clearly understand the social, family, or interpersonal context of her problems. She complained that others were not interested in her problems, and they either became irritated with her or neglected her (acts of others). For example,

her relationship with her adult children had become increasingly distant. She concurrently reported significant low self-esteem, feelings of worthlessness, and poor self-evaluation when she compared herself with others (introject). She was concerned that her problems were not significant enough to warrant being in group therapy, and she expected that others in the group would not be interested in her (expectations of others). She also expressed concern that she was taking up the therapist's time (acts of self). Her walling-off and avoiding manner resulted in the complementary response in the therapist of being less directive than was typical for an assessment, and he found himself feeling uncharacteristically irritated with her.

After some reflection, the therapist took a selectively complementary stance with her (i.e., he complemented her dominance with a measure of submissiveness in his overall approach, but he did not complement her hostility with counter-hostility or disengagement). He suggested to her that if she agreed to join the group, it would be useful to her. However, he suggested that she might feel unworthy and might not want to take up much of the group's time at first, and this may lead her to feel disappointed and angry (acts of self). She may also experience others in the group as neglectful of her (acts of others). He took a more dominant, though friendly stance when he suggested that one of her goals for therapy might be to feel that she could take her rightful place in the group. This would be a sign that she saw herself as worthy of self-care and worthy of the care of others.

As this example suggests, clinicians can use the patient's interpersonal style to understand components of the CMIP and the dynamic interplay therein. The CMIP reflects not only the acts of self within the interpersonal domain but it also influences the reactions and behavior of others through the principle of complementarity. These complementary interactions may create difficulties for the person's view of him- or herself (introject) and of their interpersonal world (expectations of others).

THERAPIST TASK BOX
THE INTERPERSONAL CIRCUMPLEX

1. Use the interpersonal circumplex to help understand the patient's interpersonal behavior and how others are likely to respond.

2. Understand how the principle of interpersonal complementarity works (reciprocity on the power and status dimension of the circumplex and correspondence on the affiliation dimension).

3. Use your knowledge of complementarity to predict how others in the group, including the therapist, are likely to respond to a patient's specific interpersonal style.

ESTABLISHING AN INTERPERSONAL FOCUS IN GROUP PSYCHOTHERAPY

Establishing an interpersonal focus in group therapy is a multilayered task. It involves careful observation of the patient and his or her behavior with the therapist and group and carefully obtaining information from the patient regarding their other relationships. This can involve a patient's descriptions of relationships with significant others in the past and present, acquaintances, coworkers, and so forth. The patient's explanations and views of others' behaviors also are useful to understand their interpersonal style and CMIP. Because group psychotherapy is an intensely interpersonal enterprise, perhaps the most important task for the therapist is to establish and fine-tune the CMIP by observing his or her responses to the patient. What affective, cognitive, or behavioral responses are evoked in the therapist in relation to a particular patient? That is, what complementary behaviors are "pulled from" the therapist? This is a question that therapists have to ask themselves repeatedly during the therapy process. The therapist must pay attention to his or her affective and cognitive responses. Also, and perhaps more important, the therapist must be aware of the complementary pulls for the group to respond in a particular manner.

> Jane, an African American woman in her 50s, tended to pull for caring and support from the therapist and the group. This, in a way, was a repetition of a long-standing maladaptive interpersonal pattern in which others treated her as incompetent, which negatively affected her self-worth. The therapist and group members felt strongly compelled to give Jane support and not to challenge her behaviors. Although Jane felt supported, her behaviors and the group's responses reinforced her interpersonal transactional cycle, whereby she pulled for support (acts of others) by communicating her general ineffectiveness (acts of self). The therapist's and group's unconditional support (acts of others) may reinforce Jane's self-view of being a dependent and ineffective person (introject).

However, there may be times when a complementary response from the therapist is necessary, especially in the early stages of the group when developing a sense of safety may be most important to the group. We discuss the optimal timing of complementary and noncomplementary responses in a subsequent chapter on stages of group therapy.

Young and Beier (1982) described the importance of understanding interpersonal pulls in psychotherapy by stating that at times the most therapeutic stance for the therapist is to be asocial. That is, the therapist may have to become aware of the interpersonal pulls of the patient and then choose whether to respond in a complementary or an asocial (noncomplementary) manner. Behaving in a complementary fashion means that the therapist responds to the patient's interpersonal pulls in the same way as other people in the individual's world. However, at the right time, the therapist may choose to respond in a noncomplementary way, in effect inducing the patient to change his or her behavior to one that is complementary to the therapist.

> Michael, a White man in his late 40s, initially behaved in a hostile–dominant manner toward the group. He gave categorical advice and was critical of other group members if they did not follow the advice. The therapist's response was marked by noncomplementary friendliness—that is, she reframed Michael's behaviors as good intentions to help other patients. In other words, she rephrased what Michael said by focusing on the intent of his communication and not on the explicit criticism. She resisted her complementary urge to be passively hostile toward him, which would have reinforced and perpetuated the interaction. Michael did not expect the therapist's behavior toward him (his expectations of others was that they would respond with hostile–submission). This resulted in some anxiety and mild confusion in Michael. To manage the anxiety in the face of the therapist's friendliness, Michael had to alter his behavior to be less intensely hostile and own the helpful intent behind his advice.

Therapists behaving in an asocial fashion at the right time in the group's development can be a pivotal feature of interventions that produce change. The therapist's noncomplementary response, in effect, "disarms" the patient's hostility and halts the maladaptive interpersonal exchange. Key to this therapeutic aspect is that the therapist must then engage in the process of meta-communicating about the transaction by providing the patient with an understanding of how the patient's interpersonal behavior evokes predictable responses in others. The therapist may then further explore this understanding in terms of the patient's introject, whereby the therapist can ask the individual how their interpersonal behaviors and others' responses impact their sense of self.

> Toward the middle of the group's life, Alice (a group member) commented to Jane (a second group member) that although Jane spoke from time to time in the group, Alice had no sense of what Jane's personal life and relationships were like (acts of others: friendly–dominant). Jane snapped back that had she been listening more carefully, Alice would know how lonely she was (acts of self: hostile–dominant). Alice looked irritated and withdrew (acts of others: hostile–submissive), and after a brief silence, Bob (a third group member) began to describe his weekend. Had the therapist not intervened at this point, Jane would have gotten confirmation that others were not interested in her despite saying how lonely she was, thus reinforcing an introject of being unworthy of caring. However, the exchange proceeded as follows:

THERAPIST: Alice, what were you hoping for by asking Jane about herself?

ALICE: I noticed that she didn't talk much about herself. I thought that she wanted to, and I'm interested in knowing about her. But she seemed angry, so I got the sense that she really didn't want to talk about it.

THERAPIST: Jane, what was it like for you when Alice asked you about yourself?

JANE: Well, I'm glad somebody took an interest, but then Bob changed the subject.

THERAPIST: You were glad that Alice took an interest in you, which makes perfect sense. But she experienced your reaction as you being angry with her, and as a result, she stopped asking you. You've described a few times how this happens in your life with your kids as well and how that makes you feel awful about yourself. Is there another way you would have liked it to go with Alice? Is there anything different you could do to get what you want here and feel like people genuinely care for you?

This interactional sequence allowed the patient to focus on her defensive behaviors, how these behaviors affect others in predictable ways, and then how the person attributes meaning to others' behavior and incorporates that meaning into her self-concept. It is pivotal for therapists to focus on the need for affiliation that underlies the defensive interpersonal style of the hostile patient (e.g., Jane: "I'm glad someone took an interest"). The therapist's stance must be friendly and either dominant or more submissive, depending on the context and desired outcome. The whole process rests on understanding each patient's CMIP and especially the interpersonal style as defined by the interpersonal circumplex. Thus, an interpersonal focus is extremely important to inform the therapist of appropriate responses when the CMIP is evident in the group's interactions.

Overall, we have covered a lot of ground with the theoretical models discussed. We hope the reader will have an appreciation of the theoretical perspectives that have influenced the development of GPIP and their practical implications. These perspectives influence how a therapist can view the functioning of individuals seeking help and the kinds of therapeutic experiences that can aid the individual in their growth within a group psychotherapeutic experience. In the next chapters, we outline the use of these heuristics (triangles of adaptation and object relations, CMIP, the interpersonal circumplex, and attachment theory) as they apply to assessment and case formulation of individual patients and the principles of group treatment.

THERAPIST TASK BOX
ESTABLISHING AN INTERPERSONAL FOCUS IN THE GROUP

1. Focus on immediate interactions in the group (i.e., using a here-and-now focus) as a way of helping patients learn about themselves and their problems in living.

2. Use the interpersonal circumplex and the CMIP to understand interpersonal interactions in a therapy group.

3. Use metacommunication (therapist statements about the interpersonal impact of what someone says or does in a group) to help to unpack the relational effects of how people relate and communicate with each other.

CHAPTER 1 REVIEW EXERCISES

Exercise 1.1

Relationship patterns will be evident in which elements of the triangle of object relations?

A. Current relationships
B. Therapeutic relationships
C. Past relationships
D. All of the above

Exercise 1.2

Please indicate which element of the CMIP the following behaviors would fall in:

A. Act of self   B. Expectations of others
C. Acts of others   D. Introject

_____ 1. Believing that others will respond positively to one's non-disclosures of shortcomings

_____ 2. Feeling inadequate and self-denigrating after being rebuffed

_____ 3. Being coy in interacting with another person

_____ 4. Observing that others respond negatively to one's self

Exercise 1.3

Answer true (T) or false (F) to the following statements about descriptive nosologies, such as the *Diagnostic and Statistical Manual of Mental Disorders (DSM-5)*.

1. Issues underlying diagnoses and problems in living are not the focus. T/F
2. Observable signs and reported symptoms are the focus of interest. T/F
3. Putative causes of symptoms or problems in living are incorporated into the diagnostic categories of *DSM-5*. T/F
4. Diagnostic labels are simply names given to a group of symptoms. T/F
5. The diagnostic labels themselves give rise to or cause the symptoms. T/F

Exercise 1.4

Please select the best answer. The transdiagnostic elements in GPIP include

A. Relationship styles with others
B. Relational styles with the self
C. Attachment anxieties and behaviors
D. All of the above

Exercise 1.5

Think of a person with social phobia and complete a hypothetical triangle of adaptation for the person. What are the attachment needs and activating feelings, inhibiting affects, and defense mechanisms? Give some examples.

Attachment need. _____

Inhibiting affect. _____

Defense mechanism. _____

CHAPTER 1 REVIEW ANSWERS

Exercise 1.1

D. All of the above.

Exercise 1.2

1. B. Expectations of others
2. D. Introject
3. A. Acts of self
4. C. Acts of others

Exercise 1.3

1. True
2. True
3. False
4. True
5. False

Exercise 1.4

D. All of the above.

Exercise 1.5

Attachment need. Need for others to care about and accept me and not abandon, ridicule, humiliate, abuse, or neglect me; activating feelings of pride in self or assertiveness.

Inhibiting affect. Anxiety and fear of being seen as stupid, being judged, being vulnerable; shame over not being good enough or being different or defective.

Defense mechanism. Avoiding interactions, focusing on own behaviors in interactions, containing displays of anxiety, thinking about ways not to come across as anxious, trying not to come across as stupid.

2 ASSESSMENT AND CASE FORMULATION

In this chapter, we describe a comprehensive assessment process that leads the group therapist to a case formulation of the individual based on the group psychodynamic-interpersonal psychotherapy (GPIP) model. As we indicate throughout the chapter, understanding the intrapersonal and interpersonal dynamics of each individual allows the clinician to determine appropriate treatment goals for the patient, informs the clinician about the most effective interpersonal stances to take with a patient, and can direct a therapist to make informed decisions about whether a patient will "fit" with a particular group. We review the process of taking a developmental history, focusing on attachment internal working models, assessing elements of the triangles of adaptation and object relations, and determining the maladaptive interpersonal patterns using the cyclical maladaptive interpersonal patterns (CMIP) model as a framework. Consistent with the transdiagnostic approach, we use a theory-driven idiographic method in the assessment of the individual for group therapy.

Several writers have been critical of psychotherapy research trials because this research typically does not rely on a theory-driven idiographic

https://doi.org/10.1037/0000213-003
Group Psychodynamic-Interpersonal Psychotherapy, by G. A. Tasca, S. F. Mikail, and P. L. Hewitt

assessment and treatment focus for patients (Persons, 1991; Silberschatz, 2017). Because of this, psychotherapy outcome studies may not accurately represent current models of psychotherapy that tend to engage in individualized assessments of patients and tailor interventions according to patient factors. In fact, ample research has indicated that patient factors such as coping style, attachment style, interpersonal problems, preferences, culture, and outcomes expectations are by far the largest predictors of patient outcomes (Norcross & Wampold, 2019). Nevertheless, the training of psychotherapists often focuses on standardized and atheoretical assessments of patients to derive diagnoses and describe symptoms. However, diagnosis accounts for little of patient outcome variance, whereas patient, therapist, and therapeutic relationship factors account for much more (Duncan & Reese, 2015). This is probably because of the great variability of patient qualities within diagnostic categories (Blatt et al., 2006). Psychotherapy research and training often ignore the important link between idiographic assessment and the treatment that psychotherapists inevitably practice (Persons, 1991; Silberschatz, 2017).

Patient assessment for group psychotherapy should be multifaceted to account for those patient factors that affect the therapist, the therapeutic relationship, and group processes. In other words, assessment should not limit itself to identifying a diagnosis. Individuals considered for GPIP, for example, may have a variety of interpersonal patterns in which they engage, and so they will have diverse CMIPs. A GPIP assessment provides the therapist and patient with a basis for an idiographic case formulation that defines the process and goals of group therapy for that patient (Persons, 1991; Silberschatz, 2017). In light of this, our approach to pre-group assessment focuses on identifying core dimensions of the individual's relational patterns, including relationship with self, intimate others, and attachment figures who have assumed a significant role in the individual's development.

Our treatment approach emphasizes changing self-limiting to more adaptive relational patterns as an important outcome, along with symptom reduction. This perspective is foundational to pre-group preparation for GPIP, discussed in the next chapter. According to existing research, the pre-group assessment of patients and their preparation for GPIP is essential to a positive therapeutic outcome (Bednar & Kaul, 1994; Swift & Callahan, 2011). In effect, GPIP begins with the assessment of the individual patient. In this chapter, we discuss the process by which therapists can assess a patient's interpersonal style, psychodynamics, and maladaptive interpersonal patterns. One of the key processes of this assessment is for the clinician to take a comprehensive developmental and attachment history.

TAKING A DEVELOPMENTAL AND ATTACHMENT HISTORY

Individuals' relational style, methods of managing emotions, expectations of receiving love and care from others, ability to give love and care, and sense of self or identity as coherent and continuous across time and contexts are in part determined by their early experiences with attachment figures (Amianto et al., 2016). Attachment theory has emerged as one of the most important theories of human development over the past 60 years (Bowlby, 1988). The theory indicates that individuals develop internal working models of attachments on the basis of early experiences with attachment figures such as parents.

Securely attached adults often had parents who were optimally available and responsive. Securely attached individuals tend to grow up expecting care and love from others, can provide caring to others, have adequate emotion regulation skills, and can reflect on their own and others' experiences. However, almost 45% of the adult population experiences an insecure attachment characterized by dismissing, preoccupied, or disorganized states of mind (van IJzendoorn, 1995). Individuals with a *preoccupied attachment* (i.e., those who are anxiously attached) are highly sensitive to abandonment and relationship loss and tend to up-regulate their emotions so that they focus on negative affect and easily recall difficult emotional situations (Mikulincer & Shaver, 2007). Others experience individuals with preoccupied attachments as sometimes overwhelming and needy. Those with *dismissing attachments* (i.e., avoidant attachment) often see relationships as secondary, are sensitive to others placing emotional or interpersonal demands on them, and tend to down-regulate their emotions so that they have difficulty identifying or expressing their feelings (Mikulincer & Shaver, 2007). Others experience individuals with dismissing attachments as distant and aloof. Finally, those with *disorganized attachments* (i.e., those who are fearfully attached) show profound disorganization in emotion, behavior, and cognition, usually related to traumatic experiences, and they are both needy and fearful of close relationships (Mikulincer & Shaver, 2007). Others might experience them as confusing or discombobulating. Generally, it is people with attachment insecurity that present for psychotherapy, partly to work on their interpersonal problems and emotion regulation.

Taking a developmental and attachment history is key to understanding the patient that one is assessing for group therapy. It also allows the clinician to put some context to a patient's interpersonal style and the current CMIP, and it allows one to understand better the triangle of adaptation and triangle of object relations. For example, one can conceptualize the affect pole of the triangle of adaptation as learned affective responses to criticism, humiliation, or punishment by parental figures of a child's attachment needs. Also, research indicates that those who have a preoccupied attachment style tend to demonstrate problems on the friendly–dominant part of the interpersonal circle, those who have a dismissing attachment demonstrate problems on the hostile side of the interpersonal circle, and disorganized attachment is often associated with the submissive and hostile–submissive part of the interpersonal circle (Horowitz et al., 1993). Hence, understanding a patient's attachment style gives one a window into their expectations of interpersonal encounters. For example, the patient with preoccupied attachment often wishes for a close relationship but is expecting abandonment, the patient with dismissing attachment often maintains greater interpersonal space in relation to others to protect themselves from being overrun in relationships, and the individual with a disorganized attachment may wish for closeness but fears that closeness will result in being retraumatized.

A developmental history starts with asking some key questions about past and current relationships. It is important for clinicians to listen for patient relationship episodes, including formative attachment relationships, how clearly and coherently the patient remembers and describes these episodes, how willing or able patients are to talk about their history of relationships, and their emotional state during their responses to specific questions. Each of these provides a window into the patient's internal experiences of themselves and their relationships, both past and present.

- What was it like growing up in your family?
- Describe your relationship with each parent. What about currently?
- Describe your relationship with your siblings and peers. What about currently?
- How did your family deal with conflict or strong emotion?
- Tell me about your most important past and current romantic relationships. How did they end?

Questions based on the Adult Attachment Interview (AAI; George et al., 1985) may be useful in this regard as well. These questions can prime the attachment system by focusing on memories of attachment, separation, and loss. They include, for example:

- Provide a few adjectives to describe your relationship with your mother/ your father as a young child.

- Give specific instances from your childhood to illustrate why you chose that adjective.

- When you were upset as a child, what would you do?

- When you were sick or hurt as a child, how would your parents respond?

- Did you or your family experience any adversity (death of a loved one, abuse, substance dependence, mental illness, bullying)? How did your family respond to the adversity? How did you respond? How do these experiences affect you now as an adult?

For a more formal assessment of attachment, the clinician can use several available psychometric measures. The following is not an exhaustive list of measures but includes ones that we find useful in assessing a patient's attachment style. The Experiences in Close Relationships scale is a patient self-report measure that comes in a 36-item (Brennan et al., 1998) and a 12-item (Lafontaine et al., 2015) version. Another short patient self-report method is the Relationship Questionnaire (Bartholomew & Horowitz, 1991), a brief single-item measure made up of four short paragraphs, each describing prototypical attachment patterns. The AAI is the gold standard for assessing attachment internal working models (George et al., 1985), but it requires extensive training to administer and score reliably. Another clinician-rated scale is the Attachment Questionnaire (Westen & Nakash, 2005), which has 37 items completed by the therapist about the patient.

THERAPIST TASK BOX
TAKING A DEVELOPMENTAL AND ATTACHMENT HISTORY

1. Ask about the quality of early relationships in the family of origin.

2. Ask about the specifics of early adversity and how the family and patient reacted.

3. Ask about the quality of current and past romantic relationships.

4. Assess patient insecure attachment style:

   - preoccupied (anxious)—up-regulates emotions and is preoccupied with relationships

   - dismissing (avoidant)—down-regulates emotions and is dismissing of relationships

   - disorganized (fearful)—disorienting affect and is fearful in relationships

ASSESSING INTERPERSONAL STYLE

Interpersonal style refers to the current relationship style as plotted on the interpersonal circumplex (see Figure 1.4). As indicated in the previous chapter, one can rate interpersonal behavior on two independent dimensions of affiliation (with friendliness and hostility at opposite poles) and status (with dominance and submission at opposite poles). Depending on where one falls on each of these dimensions, one can plot typical interpersonal behaviors around the circle as either friendly–dominant, friendly–submissive, hostile–submissive, or hostile–dominant. Such classification around the interpersonal circle is useful to broadly describe a patient's interpersonal behaviors, provide a context for the individual's CMIP, and predict others' responses to the patient.

As described previously, one can predict complementary responses to certain interpersonal stances (see the two-headed arrows in Figure 1.4). For example, friendly–dominance tends to pull for a complementary friendly–submissive response and vice versa. Similarly, hostile–dominance tends to evoke a complementary hostile–submissive response and vice versa. These complementary interpersonal behaviors and responses may help a therapist during the assessment phase to begin to predict with the patient how others in the group might respond to the patient's interpersonal pulls.

THERAPIST: It seems that you tend to take a more passive role when you allow your wife, for example, to drive the conversation or tell you what to do. Although you sometimes appreciate that she takes control, there are other times when it frustrates you so that you do not feel that you have a voice in the decision making in your family. Also, you said that your wife has complained that you tend to be too passive in many aspects of your marriage. I wonder if your passivity pulls her into being more dominant and active, which then rubs you the wrong way. I also wonder if that might come up in the therapy group— if you remain unassertive and quiet, will other group members fill the void? Perhaps an early goal for you in therapy will be to try out more active and assertive behaviors in the group and see how that fits for you.

The classification around the interpersonal circle may also help one to conceptualize a goal of therapy for a particular patient. That is, how and to what part of the circle can the patient shift their interpersonal behaviors to be more adaptive. Whittingham (2018) suggested that the interpersonal goal for patients in group therapy is to move one quarter turn around the interpersonal circle and toward the friendly half of the circle. A quarter turn in one, but not both, of the interpersonal dimensions (affiliation or dominance) is more achievable than trying to effect change on both dimensions of the circle at the same time. For example, a therapist might encourage a patient with problems of being predominantly hostile–dominant to be less angry but remain relatively assertive (i.e., a quarter turn to friendly–dominance). Similarly, a therapist might encourage a patient with problems predominantly in the friendly–submissive quadrant to get their needs met in the group by speaking up more, while remaining an empathic and good listener (i.e., a quarter turn to friendly–dominance).

The most common way to assess a patient's interpersonal style is to use a validated measure, such as the Inventory of Interpersonal Problems–32 (Horowitz et al., 2000). This is a relatively easy to use 32-item patient self-report scale with eight subscales that plot interpersonal problems around the circle. Alternatively, a clinician can ask during an assessment interview that patients carefully describe interpersonal episodes. A clinician might ask about current important relationships with colleagues, romantic partners, parents, children, and friends. The clinician must listen to the nature of the patient's behavior in the interpersonal narrative (i.e., were they dominating, submissive, friendly, or hostile?). Getting a sense of how others behave toward the patient may also provide one with clues about others' complementary responses to the patient. Another source of information might be the patient's response and interpersonal interactions with the clinician during the assessment interview itself and the clinician's experience of the interpersonal complementary pull in response to the patient. Here, it is worth noting that interactions with the therapist during assessment are somewhat unique. The patient may view the therapist as an authority figure. At the same time, the context of the assessment is one in which the patient is seeking help or support at a time of heightened vulnerability, which may activate attachment strivings and patterns.

In the following example, the therapist asks for more detail about an interpersonal episode previously described by this characteristically hostile–submissive patient. In brackets after each speaking turn, we indicate the placement around the interpersonal circle of the speaker's (therapist or patient) statement or question.

THERAPIST: You seem disappointed that your husband planned the vacation by himself and did not ask you where you wanted to go. [*Friendly–dominant to the patient*]

PATIENT: He should have known that I didn't want to go to Florida again. [*Hostile–submissive regarding the husband*]

THERAPIST: So, you never actually expressed your preference to him. [*Dominant but neutral affiliation*]

PATIENT: No, I didn't—he should have known. [*Hostile–submissive toward the therapist and regarding the husband*]

THERAPIST: What do you mean he should have known—how could he possibly have known? [*Hostile–dominant, uncharacteristic for this therapist*]

THERAPIST: (Later and after some thought) You and I seem to be getting into this tug of war. I wonder if this is how it feels with your husband when he doesn't seem to understand what you need? [*Friendly–dominant to the patient*]

PATIENT: Yah, I know, we're always sniping at each other. [*Friendly–submissive to the therapist*]

We see in this example how the patient pulled the therapist into an uncharacteristically complementary hostile–dominant/hostile–submissive interaction sequence. This might indicate that the patient tends to have a hostile–submissive interpersonal style. However, this therapist was able to reflect on and recognize his countertransference reaction and

---

THERAPIST TASK BOX
ASSESSING INTERPERSONAL STYLE

1. Elicit and listen carefully to the patient's relationship episodes.
2. Assess whether the patient is mainly dominant or submissive in important relationships.
3. Assess whether the patient is mainly friendly or hostile and disengaged in relationships.
4. Consider the complementary interpersonal pull that the patient evokes in you, the therapist.
5. Plot the patient's typical interpersonal style around the interpersonal circle.

immediately invited the patient to step back and consider their interaction as an exemplar of the problematic interpersonal process between the patient and her husband. This therapist's reflective stance (friendly–dominant) pulled the patient a quarter turn away from her typical style of interacting (Whittingham, 2018) and into a friendly–submissive response to the therapist.

ASSESSING THE TRIANGLE OF ADAPTATION

As previously discussed, one can understand symptoms as a maladaptive solution to an experience of internal turmoil and interpersonal conflict. Recall that within the triangle of adaptation, symptoms often sit at the defense pole (Figure 1.2). A symptom may be a means of coping with problematic and often unintegrated affect that has become associated with unmet attachment needs or adaptive feelings (attachment needs). The CMIP and the triangle of object relations are the interpersonal manifestation of the triangle of adaptation that frequently perpetuates a manner of relating so that those attachment needs continue to remain unfulfilled, and activating feelings remain unexpressed or unprocessed. Because of asynchronous or negative responses by attachment figures, patients' attachment needs may generate intolerable affect that gives rise to coping behaviors (defense), some of which may be highly self-limiting.

Assessing the components of the triangle of adaptation requires that the clinician listen to the patient's relationship episodes, identify the different elements of the triangle, and use the triangle to guide questions (McCullough et al., 2003). We list these elements of the triangle in Table 2.1, which provides some, but not an exhaustive list, of examples from each pole. In the following example, the therapist asks three types of questions to understand the patient's anger at his husband, where the patient's anger is related to feeling anxious about his husband's safety.

1. Question about an attachment need that is hidden or not accessible.

   THERAPIST: What was going through your mind when you didn't hear from him?

   PATIENT: I was worried that he was drinking and driving again; I don't want to lose him.

The underlying attachment need is tenderness and need for closeness.

TABLE 2.1. Examples of Elements Related to Each Pole of the Triangle of Adaptation

Attachment need	Affects	Defenses
Self-assertion	Fear and panic	Minimizing, dismissing
Sexual desire	Anxiety	Blaming, defensive anger
Need for closeness	Shame, guilt, humiliation	Defensive humor
Need for self-differentiation	Emotional pain, misery	Self-punishing, defensive sadness
Need for security	Contempt, disgust	Self-limiting behaviors
Need for intimacy	Contempt, disgust	Avoiding, repressing
Self-pride	Anger	Intellectualizing
		Acting out, defensive excitement

2. Question about the affect that resulted in the attachment need being inaccessible.

   THERAPIST: How were you feeling when you were worried?

   PATIENT: I was really getting worked-up . . . more and more anxious.

   The affect is anxiety or fear.

3. Question about how the patient managed the affect.

   THERAPIST: Sounds like you were pretty angry at him. What happened to your worry and anxiety about losing him when you were angry?

   The therapist is probing the nature and function of the defense, which in this case is defensive anger.

ASSESSING THE TRIANGLE OF OBJECT RELATIONS

The triangle of object relations speaks to the consistency with which interpersonal patterns that first developed in formative or attachment relationships are reenacted in current relationships and therapeutic relationships. In addition, the triangle of object relations takes into account the relationship of the self with the self, or the introject. Hence, the triangle has three domains: past relationship with self and other, current relationship with self and other, and relationship with the therapist and group (Figure 1.2).

To assess for the domains of the triangle of object relations, the clinician must ask questions that elicit relationship episodes from the patient. Questions about past relationships can focus on attachment figures, peers, and early romantic partners. These early relationships often form a template for current interactional patterns and views of self. For example, patients might describe that in their early interactions with peers, they were shy and anxious about being manipulated or bullied and experienced themselves as outcasts. A clinician might expect and listen for a similar pattern of social withdrawal and anxiety in current relationships with romantic partners, friends, and coworkers. This might involve therapists asking specific questions about what the patient said or did, how the patient expected others to respond, how others actually responded, and how the patient felt about themselves following this interaction. During the assessment interview, the therapist may experience the patient as anxious, fearful, and withdrawn. The astute therapist will pay attention to their reactions to the patient as a barometer for the interpersonal pulls that this patient may evoke in others, including in the group. Patients may have a varying capacity to identify and comment on the similarities of their interpersonal styles and interaction patterns across times and situations. Nevertheless, therapists may suggest to patients that their relational patterns across times and situations have some similarities. In doing so, the therapist can assess whether the patient can see the parallels, identify their roles in relationship interactions, speculate on their own and others' interpersonal intentions, and understand the impact on their self-concept.

USING THE TRIANGLES TO FORMULATE THE CASE

To communicate to the patient about the triangle of adaptation and triangle of object relations and to develop the case formulation, the clinician could use a blackboard or clipboard to draw the triangles. This may be an effective means of illustrating the relationship among the patient's attachment needs, affects, and defenses and the parallel structure of interactional patterns across time. The therapist should seek the patient's input into the formulation's veracity or utility. In the following example, a therapist provides an idiographic case formulation to a patient who has a friendly–submissive interpersonal style. Here the therapist describes two formulations for this patient. In the first, the therapist uses the triangle of adaptation and triangle of object relations to make sense of the patient's sexual acting out. In the second, the triangles help the therapist to formulate the patient's tendency to over-accommodate.

> You described very clearly that typically you seek out anonymous sexual encounters through dating sites when you feel insecure or sad [*attachment needs*], likely because these feelings make you feel anxious or shameful [*affects*]. Sexual encounters may be a way of soothing yourself and managing your anxiety [*defense*], and this may be a long-standing pattern. Maybe this way of coping was adaptive at some other time in your life [*past relationships*]. Perhaps earlier in your marriage when you and your wife fought, your sexual relationship was a way of reconnecting. But now, this pattern is causing you grief [*current relationships*]. You have also discussed how, despite the fact that you are married and working, you feel very much alone, and this increases your sadness [*current relationships*]. It seems to me that your sadness and anger come from this sense of being alone and not cared for by others the way that you might need [*attachment needs*]. This reminds me of how you described feeling as a child in relation to your mother [*past relationships*]. Nevertheless, this pattern may be the start of a downward spiral that leads to the sexual acting out. You have a strong need to be cared for, which you feel is unmet [*attachment needs*]. You may feel angry or sad about this, but these feelings are shameful or intolerable to you [*affects*], and so the sexual encounters may be a means of taking care of your needs and avoiding your anxiety and other painful emotions [*defense*]. It follows a common pattern of coping that may look something like this (Figure 2.1).

> There also seems to be a second way you use for coping that has implications for your relationships. What you described in your marriage, in your relationship with your parents, and even at work, is that you tend to really put

FIGURE 2.1. Example Triangle of Adaptation and Triangle of Object Relations for a Friendly-Submissive Patient Who Sexually Acts Out

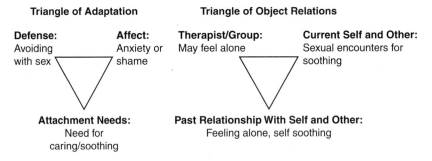

Note. From "Group Psychodynamic Interpersonal Psychotherapy: Summary of a Treatment Model and Outcomes for Depressive Symptoms," by G. A. Tasca, S. F. Mikail, and P. L. Hewitt, in M. E. Abelian (Ed.), *Focus on Psychotherapy Research* (p. 165), 2005, Nova Science. Copyright 2005 by Nova Science. Adapted with permission.

yourself out for others—you are too accommodating [*defense, current relationships*]. Even if you need others to care for you [*attachment needs*], you tend to focus on their needs instead [*defense*]. Maybe you learned early on that expressing your needs was futile and painful because your most important needs were ignored, leaving you feeling lonely, and so you became afraid that you might be abandoned [*affect*] if you did express your needs. So, to keep the pain of loneliness at bay, you responded by maintaining your mom close to you in the one way that was available to you at the time—you took care of her needs, and you let your needs fade into the background [*defense, past relationships*]. That way of coping might have been effective at one time in your life, but it also makes it hard for you to express your needs when they are not met [*attachment needs*]. That also follows a common pattern of coping that may look like this (Figure 2.2).

In these examples, the therapist began to identify for the individual their triangle of adaptation, including the role their attachment needs and affects play in maintaining their defenses and symptoms. Also implied in this description is the notion that patients' relational patterns are inflexible such that they find themselves faced with the very outcome they are trying to avoid. The model defines this patient's typical ways of relating as a means of defending against problematic affect. His friendly–submissive style was a means of defending against shame, anxiety, and fear of abandonment caused by affect associated with attachment needs to be cared for.

Hostile–dominant individuals may also defend against shame or anger related to attachment needs for intimacy. These individuals may engage in intellectualization, projection, or denial as defense mechanisms in which

FIGURE 2.2. Example Triangle of Adaptation for a Friendly-Submissive and Overly Accommodating Patient

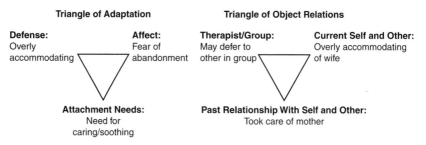

Note. From "Group Psychodynamic Interpersonal Psychotherapy: Summary of a Treatment Model and Outcomes for Depressive Symptoms," by G. A. Tasca, S. F. Mikail, and P. L. Hewitt, in M. E. Abelian (Ed.), *Focus on Psychotherapy Research* (p. 165), 2005, Nova Science. Copyright 2005 by Nova Science. Adapted with permission.

they blame or lash out at others for their anxiety or attribute to others the very attachment needs they find unacceptable in themselves.

> You described that as a child you were ridiculed or beaten for expressing any needs, and so you figured out that wanting love and closeness [*attachment need*] was shameful [*affect*] and should be kept to yourself [*past relationships*]. Now you shame people who express similar needs [*current relationships*], like you did with your wife when she wanted to be close to you [*defense*]. I think that perhaps you still need to be cared for [*attachment need*] and to have a companion who looks up to you and makes you feel good about yourself. But you learned pretty early on that such needs could be shameful and that others were not up to the task [*affect*] (Figure 2.3).

Hostile–submissive individuals may defend against the anxiety they experience related to their attachment needs for acceptance or adaptive feelings of assertiveness. Unlike the hostile–dominant individual who directly expresses anger as a defense, the hostile–submissive patient is indirect in their expressions of hostility by using defense mechanisms such as passive-aggression or perhaps reaction formation.

> I can understand that being direct with your wish for acceptance in your family [*attachment needs*] was met by them with ridicule, which made you angry [*affect, past relationships*]. If you expressed how you felt, you were often punished or humiliated by your family or bullied by peers. So, you had to keep to yourself any legitimate anger that you felt [*defense, past relationships*] for fear of reprisals. Even now, it seems that if you have any feelings like anger or even love, it makes you anxious [*current relationships*], and those old fears come up again [*affect*]. So, it makes sense to me that you would be indirect with your anger by being sarcastic or by telling your husband that

FIGURE 2.3. Example Triangle of Adaptation for a Hostile-Dominant Patient

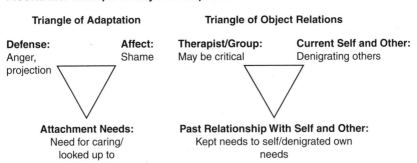

Triangle of Adaptation		Triangle of Object Relations	
Defense: Anger, projection	**Affect:** Shame	**Therapist/Group:** May be critical	**Current Self and Other:** Denigrating others
Attachment Needs: Need for caring/ looked up to		**Past Relationship With Self and Other:** Kept needs to self/denigrated own needs	

Note. From "Group Psychodynamic Interpersonal Psychotherapy: Summary of a Treatment Model and Outcomes for Depressive Symptoms," by G. A. Tasca, S. F. Mikail, and P. L. Hewitt, in M. E. Abelian (Ed.), *Focus on Psychotherapy Research* (p. 165), 2005, Nova Science. Copyright 2005 by Nova Science. Adapted with permission.

FIGURE 2.4. Example Triangle of Adaptation for a Hostile-Submissive Patient

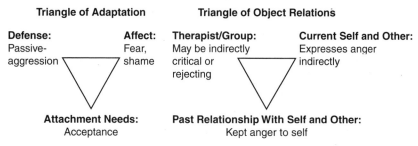

Triangle of Adaptation   Triangle of Object Relations

Defense: **Affect:**   **Therapist/Group:**   **Current Self and Other:**
Passive-   Fear,   May be indirectly   Expresses anger
aggression   shame   critical or   indirectly
     rejecting

Attachment Needs: **Past Relationship With Self and Other:**
Acceptance   Kept anger to self

Note. From "Group Psychodynamic Interpersonal Psychotherapy: Summary of a Treatment Model and Outcomes for Depressive Symptoms," by G. A. Tasca, S. F. Mikail, and P. L. Hewitt, in M. E. Abelian (Ed.), *Focus on Psychotherapy Research* (p. 165), 2005, Nova Science. Copyright 2005 by Nova Science. Adapted with permission.

you will do something knowing that you won't follow through [*defense, current relationships*] (Figure 2.4).

Friendly–dominant individuals may defend to ward off shame related to the disapproval of others when the individual has attachment needs for intimacy, attention and caring, or security. The view of the self is negative and unworthy of genuine caring from others. Defense mechanisms might include repression, intellectualization, undoing, and reaction formation that services their controlling behaviors.

> I understand that you had to take care of your younger siblings from a very young age [*past relationships*], and so you felt you had to set aside your own needs in order to make life manageable for everyone else in the family [*defense*]. If you felt sad, you had to "suck it up." Today, you are very helpful to others, like your siblings and coworkers, though you have gotten some feedback about being intrusive and controlling [*defense, current relationships*]. When you were younger, you had excellent school grades, and you were able to keep your siblings in line, and those were an important source of attention and acknowledgment [*attachment needs, past relationships*]. But sometimes others accused you of showing off if you boasted or if your siblings felt you were being bossy [*past relationships*]. Even now, you feel anxious when you are the center of attention [*affect*], and so you focus your energies on helping others, sometimes to your own detriment [*defense, current relationships*]. When you feel insecure or sad [*attachment need*], you have no one to turn to because no one has a clue of what you are feeling and what you need [*current relationships*] (Figure 2.5).

These descriptions are prototypes related to the four quadrants of the interpersonal circle. However, one should keep in mind that there will be variations in these broad themes within each prototype, hence the need for the idiographic case formulation.

FIGURE 2.5. Example Triangle of Adaptation for a Friendly-Dominant Patient

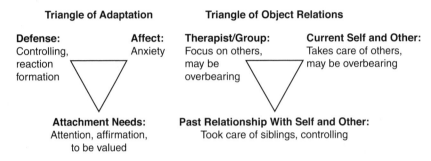

Triangle of Adaptation | Triangle of Object Relations

Defense: Controlling, reaction formation   **Affect:** Anxiety   **Therapist/Group:** Focus on others, may be overbearing   **Current Self and Other:** Takes care of others, may be overbearing

Attachment Needs: Attention, affirmation, to be valued   **Past Relationship With Self and Other:** Took care of siblings, controlling

Note. From "Group Psychodynamic Interpersonal Psychotherapy: Summary of a Treatment Model and Outcomes for Depressive Symptoms," by G. A. Tasca, S. F. Mikail, and P. L. Hewitt, in M. E. Abelian (Ed.), *Focus on Psychotherapy Research* (p. 165), 2005, Nova Science. Copyright 2005 by Nova Science. Adapted with permission.

THERAPIST TASK BOX
ASSESSING THE TWO TRIANGLES

1. Assess the predominant attachment needs of the patient.
2. Assess the affects in reaction to attachment needs.
3. Identify the predominant defense mechanisms the patient uses to manage affects.
4. Communicate to the patient the components of their triangle of adaptation.
5. Look for consistent or parallel interpersonal patterns and self-concept in current and past relationships.
6. Consider how these patterns may repeat themselves in the therapy group.
7. Modify this part of the case formulation on the basis of a collaborative discussion with the patient.

ASSESSING THE CMIP

The CMIP is the interpersonal manifestation of the triangle of adaptation. And the CMIP can be superimposed on each apex of the triangle of object relations to understand the patient's relationship patterns in past and current relationships, including their manner of relating to the therapist and group.

Following Strupp and Binder (1984), the clinician can assess these four elements of the CMIP of each patient.

Acts of Self

Acts of self may include *needs* ("I wish my husband would take care of me," "I wish my parents would notice my accomplishments"), *self-perceptions* ("I feel fat and ugly"), *affects* ("I get so angry when she doesn't do what I want her to do"), and *overt behaviors* ("I usually get critical and sarcastic when I get angry," "I am often the one arranging social events for people at work and my family and friends," "I just give up and veg out in front of the TV"). Assessing the acts of self is usually straight forward because it includes a patient's overt behaviors, conscious feelings, and thoughts. The interviewer must listen to a patient's relationship narratives and then ask about and reinterpret the narrative in interpersonal terms. The following is an example of evaluating the acts of self for Phil, a 48-year-old White man.

PHIL: I'm here mainly because I'm depressed. I'm sad all of the time, and I hate myself.

THERAPIST: When was the last time that you felt really sad and that you hated yourself?

PHIL: Well, all of the time. (Pauses) Yesterday, for example.

THERAPIST: Tell me about yesterday—who you were with, and what was going on?

PHIL: I had a report to complete at work. And when my boss read it over, she found a number of problems with it and made suggestions to fix it. I felt so stupid—they were so obvious. Then when I got home, I could barely function. I helped out my wife by feeding the kids and putting them to bed, but I was exhausted and passed out on the couch.

THERAPIST: So, what did you share with your wife about what had happened and how you were feeling?

PHIL: Nothing. I was too tired.

In this brief narrative, the therapist was not satisfied with Phil's simple description of the symptom ("I'm depressed, and I hate myself"). So, the therapist asked Phil for a specific relationship narrative ("When did you last feel that way? Who were you with? What was going on?"). These questions gave the patient an opportunity to provide a relational context to his depressive affect and self-loathing and provided the therapist with a number of clues to the acts of self ("I could barely function. I helped out my wife. I didn't talk to my wife about what happened"). In conjunction with information gleaned from a relational and attachment history and psychometric assessment of interpersonal problems, the therapist might develop a clearer picture of the acts of self. For example, Phil might have high standards for himself, be highly self-critical when he does not meet self-imposed standards, be supportive of others, but not seek support and nurturance from others when he is in pain.

Expectations of Others

Expectations of others are reactions that one imagines will be forthcoming from others that are directly tied to the acts of self. ("If I tell her what I need [*act of self*], I'm afraid she won't or can't respond [*expectation of others*]"; "I get angry [*act of self*] because my kids just won't listen to me otherwise [*expectation of others*]"). Expectations of others are based on previous experiences of others' reactions, attributions made about what others might be thinking or feeling, and predictions of others' responses. These expectations are powerful reinforcers of the CMIP and are excellent opportunities for disconfirmation by other patients in group therapy. Assessing expectations of others is especially critical to group therapy because therapists can target the expectations directly using interventions in which patients are encouraged to express their reactions to the acts of self exhibited by others in the group. In the example, Phil provided clues, but the therapist must ask more questions to assess expectations adequately.

THERAPIST: Looking back on the situation, was there anything you could have done differently with that report?

PHIL: Probably. But my boss is so busy, she doesn't have time for that. I should be able to handle it on my own. She would probably just tell me to deal with it.

THERAPIST: What about with your wife? I know you felt depleted, but why not tell her what was going on and how you were feeling?

PHIL: She had a hard day with the kids. She doesn't need to be taking care of me too.

THERAPIST: What do you worry might have happened if you asked her for help?

PHIL: I don't know. She wouldn't really understand the situation, so it's up to me to take care of it.

In his responses, Phil provided clues as to why he feels so alone and helpless—he expects others to be unable or unwilling to provide guidance or to care for him. His attachment history may help to clarify why he developed this expectation of others. He may have experienced his parents as ineffective, unresponsive, or uncaring. He may have developed a need to be highly effective and productive as a means of gaining attention and caring, and he may have carried this internal model into his adult relationships. So now, when he needs help, he expects others (boss, wife) to be too busy, not useful, or not interested in caring for him. This patient may expect the same from fellow group members and the therapist. Therapists must help to uncover and challenge these expectations in the group by drawing Phil's attention to instances in which other members of the group acknowledge his need, offer empathy, or affirm his worth by expressing their desire to connect with him. Typically, these are simple but meaningful exchanges that a therapist can easily miss, yet they need to be underscored.

Acts of Others

Acts of others are behaviors of others that may be a direct result of acts of self ("I sort of told him a while ago what I really wanted for my birthday [*act of self*], but he didn't remember [*act of others*]"; "I think my kids aren't calling me anymore [*acts of others*] because I'm so critical and angry [*act of self*]"). Acts of others is the easiest aspect of the CMIP to assess because it is based on a description of how others behave toward the client. These are often responses by others that are complementary to the patient's acts of self (Figure 1.4). However, as with the acts of self, the interviewer must ask specific questions and listen carefully to the patient's relationship narratives to get a sense of how others typically respond to the patient's acts of self.

THERAPIST: It seems that you kind of shut down with your wife [*act of self*]. I wonder if she sensed that something was wrong?

PHIL: Yah, I think so. It was pretty obvious.

THERAPIST: What did she do?

PHIL: She just left me alone [*acts of others*]. I don't think she knew what to do [*expectations of others*]. Plus, she was pretty tired herself.

This brief narrative suggests that shutting out his wife (act of self), which is typical behavior for Phil, resulted in the complementary behavior of her leaving him alone (act of other). This is likely a persistent pattern in their relationship that is based in part on his expectation that she is not capable or emotionally available to respond to his needs (expectation of other). The acts of others reinforce his acts of self and also his expectations that people in his life are unavailable. This self-limiting pattern can become self-reinforcing and self-perpetuating.

Introject (Acts of Self Toward Self)

Introjects are self-statements, feelings, behaviors, and core beliefs about one's self that form enduring aspects of one's self-experience. The introject represents what many commonly referred to as self-concept, but it also includes self-esteem, self-evaluation, and self-care. One can conceptualize the introject as the end product of the CMIP, but it also provides the fuel that drives the relational pattern inherent in the CMIP: "I feel like such a shit [*introject*] whenever I yell at my kids [*act of self*]—no wonder they avoid me [*acts of others*]"; "I am such an idiot [*introject*] because I lose control over my eating [*act of self*]"; "I want to be loving [*act of self*], but I don't think she'll care [*expectation of other*], so I end up withdrawing and seeking sexual encounters with strangers [*act of self*], and then I feel even more worthless [*introject*]."

Because introjects are composed of private self-evaluations and self-concepts that are the outcome of the CMIP, they may be more difficult to evaluate. Patients who are less psychologically minded and more concrete may have difficulty identifying internal states and feelings about the self. Introjects require therapists to ask about the experience of the self. Introjects may be obvious ("I'm such a loser"), but sometimes they are subtle ("I don't know why I do that; I always end up feeling bad about it").

PHIL: Sorry, I don't think I answered your question properly.

THERAPIST: I'm not sure why you are apologizing—you gave a pretty thoughtful answer.

PHIL: I don't know—it sounded dumb.

THERAPIST: This reminds me of when you said that you felt stupid at work. It seems like this is a common experience for you. You feel that you have to perform well, but you worry that you will come up short, and then you are automatically self-critical.

PHIL: Yah, all the time. It's exhausting.

THERAPIST: I bet. What do you think this says about how you feel about yourself?

PHIL: I really think I'm a loser. I have to work so hard to keep up the appearance that I'm capable; otherwise, I'm useless.

We illustrate Phil's CMIP in Figure 2.6.

One of the goals of the assessment is to collaborate with the patient in the task of developing a case formulation that brings coherence to seemingly disparate parts of their experience. Thus, giving feedback to the patient about the CMIP in a way that makes sense and invites the patient to modify aspects of the formulation is an important clinical function of the pre-group assessment. For example, the complete CMIP for Phil, the friendly–submissive patient described earlier, is as follows:

> You described your relationship with your parents as having been difficult. They were often too busy just trying to make ends meet. It seemed that you adapted as well as you could to that situation by being the "good son"

FIGURE 2.6. Cyclical Maladaptive Interpersonal Pattern Model for Phil

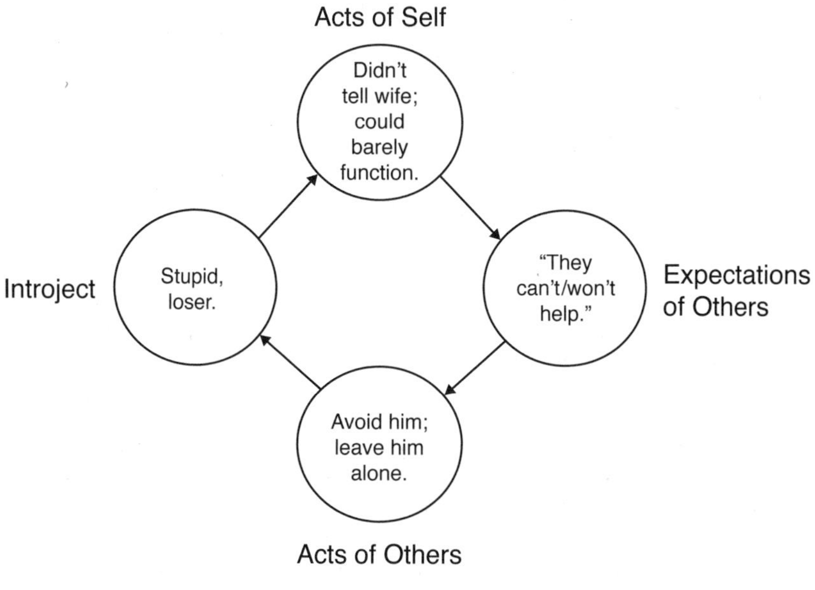

Note. From *Perfectionism: A Relational Approach to Conceptualization, Assessment, and Treatment* (p. 163), by P. L. Hewitt, G. L. Flett, and S. F. Mikail, 2017, Guilford Press. Copyright 2017 by Guilford Press. Adapted with permission.

who did well in school and didn't add to their burden [*acts of self*]. But that meant that you didn't have much support or caring when you needed it [*acts of others*]. This may have left you wondering if you were lovable [*introject*], and this left you feeling sad and hopeless. I see a similar pattern playing itself out with your wife. You are worried about overburdening her, and so you keep your troubles to yourself [*act of self*] because you feel that she can't manage your problems as well as taking care of the kids [*expectations of others*]. It might be that she senses that there is something wrong when you go quiet, but she may not know what to do, and so she leaves you alone [*acts of others*]. I'm wondering if this reinforces your sense that you are not lovable because no one is there for you when you really need help [*introject*]?

Similarly, one could construct a CMIP for a patient who is hostile–dominant and who struggles with depressive symptoms.

If we take your relationship with your ex-wife as an example, what you seem to be saying is that you really wanted to be close to her [*attachment need*], and at the same time, you were afraid of losing your autonomy. You wanted her to be interested in you and responsive to your needs [*acts of self*], but whenever she asked about your day or became amorous, you felt closed in, as if she was being intrusive and trying to control you [*expectation of others*]. It seems that at those times, your tone became sharp, and you withdrew both physically and emotionally [*acts of self*]. My understanding is that, initially, she doubled her efforts by asking more questions and being solicitous but then got angry and critical when you continued to keep her at arm's length [*acts of others*]. Now that she's left the relationship and is fighting you over custody and alimony, you are increasingly angry with yourself and her [*acts of self*] and questioning whether you are capable at all of having a satisfying intimate relationship [*introject*].

For someone with a friendly–dominant interpersonal style, the CMIP may resemble the following:

Often, your parents were unavailable to you and your younger brother [*acts of others*], and so you took charge by caring for your brother [*acts of self*]. This has served you well in your life—you've been very successful in your work as a nurse. It brings you a lot of self-esteem to be in charge and to take care of others, even if it has led to misunderstandings with your coworkers. You describe the same thing happening with your husband, and this has caused some problems between the two of you—sometimes you have felt overburdened [*acts of self*]. You also spoke about worrying that if you did not do so much for others, then they might not like you or want to be with you [*expectations of others*]. This makes me wonder if, deep down inside, you feel worthless unless you are in charge and taking care of others [*introject*] whether they feel they need it or not.

Finally, a CMIP for a hostile–submissive patient may have the following components and qualities:

> You have had many experiences in which people took advantage of you, hurt you, or exploited you [*acts of others*]. I can see how you have learned to protect yourself by not being direct about your feelings or your intentions, especially if you were angry or annoyed at someone [*acts of self*]. You worry that if you are honest about how you feel, then others might attack you or use it against you [*expectations of others*]. So, your annoyance might come out indirectly, like when you give your husband the silent treatment or when you make sarcastic remarks to your sister [*acts of self*]. I also wonder if, deep down, you see your own anger as shameful or unacceptable [*introject*], and so you do your best to keep it to yourself, even if it comes out indirectly with those with whom you are close.

THERAPIST TASK BOX
ASSESSING THE CMIP

1. Listen carefully to patient relationship episodes and translate symptoms in relational terms.
2. Assess the patient's prominent acts of self (feelings, thoughts, behaviors, wishes).
3. Assess the patient's expectations of others (attributions or predictions of others' behaviors, feelings, thought toward the self).
4. Assess the acts of others in relation to the acts of self (actual behaviors of others, often complementary behaviors).
5. Assess the patient's self-concept or introject as a culmination of acts of self, expectations of others, and acts of others.
6. Communicate this part of the case formulation with the patient. Make alterations to the cyclical maladaptive interpersonal pattern on the basis of the patient's feedback.

ASSESSING FACTORS RELATED TO GROUP COMPOSITION

In addition to obtaining a developmental and attachment history, assessing interpersonal style, and developing a case formulation based on the triangle of adaptation, triangle of object relations, and the CMIP, one must consider at least two other factors when evaluating a patient for GPIP: the patient's level of functioning and its impact on group composition. Many group therapies are centered on specific diagnoses. In these groups, diagnosis serves as the primary dimension of assessment and patient selection. However, there is ample evidence that patient diagnosis is not a strong predictor of treatment outcomes or patient functioning (Caspi et al., 2014; Duncan & Reese, 2015) and that patients with the same diagnosis can vary greatly on a number of dimensions critical to treatment outcome. For example, in reviewing over 30 years of research, Blatt (2004) defined two dimensions of depressive experiences that have an impact on therapeutic processes and outcomes: one based on feelings of loneliness and abandonment, the other based on feelings of failure and worthlessness. Consideration of factors such as self-concept and core affective experiences as they relate to patient selection and treatment outcome is consistent with the transdiagnostic nature of GPIP.

McCullough and colleagues (2003) suggested that the level of patient functioning should determine the focus of individual psychodynamic psychotherapy. They argued that patients at higher levels of functioning could likely tolerate more emphasis on changing defenses and exposure to activating feelings, whereas those at lower levels of functioning may need more supportive interventions to shore up adaptive defenses. In the group therapy context, Yalom and Leszcz (2020) argued that therapists should base assessment for group composition on the overall quality of patient functioning. That is, members of a group that function at a similar level with regard to interpersonal effectiveness and affect regulation will likely remain in group therapy longer, and the group will function better. There is now emerging evidence to support this view that person–group fit is a key variable to a successful outcome in group therapy. Paquin and colleagues (2013) found that if a patient is not a good fit with the rest of the group, the patient is likely to drop out, and the impact on group cohesion will be negative.

Following from these clinical and research examples, we believe that it is essential to consider the level of patient functioning and its impact on group composition when assessing a patient for the group. Thus, a question that should be top of mind for the therapist is, Will this patient fit with this group given their overall level of functioning and that of the group? If the results of the assessment and case formulation suggest the patient is likely to be an outlier or misfit in a given group according to the level of functioning, therapists should consider such a patient for another treatment.

Broadly speaking, level of patient functioning refers to ego functions, such as the nature of reality testing, judgment, regulation of impulses and emotions, quality of relationships, cognitive abilities, and predominant defenses. Adaptive ego functions are important for mental health and overall quality of life and relationships. One can assess ego functioning in a number of different ways, but we briefly review the assessment of the level of defensive functioning (Perry et al., 1998) and the profile of mental functioning within levels of personality organization from the *Psychodynamic Diagnostic Manual* (*PDM-2*; Lingiardi & McWilliams, 2017).

Defensive Functioning

Common measures of defensive functioning list the defense mechanisms in a hierarchy from most to least adaptive (Table 2.2; Bond, 2004; Perry, 1990; Perry & Henry, 2004). More adaptive defense mechanisms are developmentally more mature, prosocial, and aligned with reality; allow the individual to manage inhibitory affects; and permit the individual to function well in work, play, and relationships. Less adaptive defenses tend to be associated with more severe psychopathology and lower developmental maturity and cause problems in relationships and affect regulation. Høglend and Perry (1998) found that higher adaptive defenses were related to better treatment outcomes in individual psychotherapy. In a study of GPIP for binge-eating disorder, Hill and colleagues (2015) found that defensive functioning became significantly more mature as the group treatment progressed from early to late stages.

The clinician should consider the impact on group functioning if a patient with predominantly low-adaptive defenses, such as major imaging distorting or action defenses, is placed within a group of individuals who use primarily more adaptive obsessional and other neurotic defenses. A gross mismatch between the individual and the rest of the group on the dimension of defensive functioning could result in the patient dropping out or could have a negative impact on group cohesion.

Overall Mental Functioning

One means of assessing overall mental functioning is to use the framework described in the *PDM-2* to describe levels of personality organization and the capacity for mental functions within each level. The levels of personality organization exist on a continuum from relative health to neurotic to borderline to psychotic (Clarkin et al., 1999; Table 2.3). Lingiardi and McWilliams (2017) reviewed the substantial research supporting the notion of levels of personality organization, which suggests that genetic vulnerability, temperament, early life experiences, and attachment influence personality

TABLE 2.2. Defense Levels and Examples of Individual Defenses

Level	Example defense	Description
7. High adaptive	Altruism	Neutralizes an anxious situation by an act of goodwill to another
	Humor	Finds a funny aspect of a difficult situation to help self or other endure it
	Sublimation	Converts an unacceptable impulse to an acceptable form
	Suppression	Consciously and temporarily forces feelings or thoughts from awareness
	Self-observation	Deals with emotional conflict by reflecting on own feelings, thoughts
6. Obsessional	Isolation of affect	Recalls a painful event without experiencing the associated emotion
	Intellectualization	Uses abstract thinking to minimize emotional discomfort
	Undoing	Negates or makes amends for unacceptable thoughts or feelings
5. Other neurotic	Displacement	Transfers feelings or responses from an appropriate person to a less threatening person
	Reaction formation	Substitutes actual thoughts and behaviors for their opposite
	Repression	Removes unpleasant wishes or thoughts from consciousness, but the emotions remain
4. Minor image distortion	Omnipotence	Responds to emotional conflict by acting superior to others
	Idealization	Grossly exaggerates positive qualities of self or others
	Devaluation	Grossly exaggerates negative qualities of self or others
3. Disavowal	Rationalization	Illogical justification of one's behaviors or feelings
	Projection	Attributes unacceptable characteristics in self to others
	Denial	Completely unable to acknowledge unpleasant reality, thoughts, or feelings
2. Major image distortion	Projective identification	Must protect self from bad others
	Splitting	People are only either good or bad
1. Action	Help-rejecting complaining	Elicits help but then rejects it
	Passive-aggression	Indirectly expresses of anger
	Acting out	Is driven to act out impulsively

Note. From "Studying Defense Mechanisms in Psychotherapy Using the Defense Mechanism Rating Scales," by J. C. Perry and M. Henry, in U. Hentschel, G. Smith, J. G. Draguns, and W. Ehlers (Eds.), *Defense mechanisms: Theoretical, research and clinical perspectives* (p. 167), 2004, Elsevier (https://doi.org/10.1016/S0166-4115(04)80034-7). Copyright 2004 by Elsevier. Adapted with permission.

TABLE 2.3. Levels of Mental Functioning

Total score	Level of mental functioning	Description
		Healthy
54–60	Healthy/optimal	Optimal or very good functioning in all or most mental capacities, with modest, expectable variations in flexibility and adaptation across contexts.
		Neurotic
47–53	Good/appropriate	Appropriate level of mental functioning with some specific areas of difficulties (e.g., in three or four mental capacities). These difficulties can reflect conflicts or challenges related to specific life situations or events.
40–46	Mild impairment	Mild constrictions and areas of inflexibility in some domains of mental functioning, implying rigidity and impairment in areas such as self-esteem regulation, impulse and affect regulation, defensive functioning, and self-observing capacities.
		Borderline (higher level)
33–39	Moderate impairment	Moderate constriction and areas of inflexibilities in most or almost most domains of mental functioning, affecting quality and stability of relationships, sense of identity, and range of affects tolerated.
		Borderline (lower level)
26–32	Major impairment	Major constriction and alteration in almost all domains of mental functioning (e.g., tendency toward fragmentation and difficulty in self-object differentiation), along with limitations in experience of feelings and/or thoughts in major life areas (i.e., work, love, play).
19–25	Significant deficits	Significant deficits in most domains of mental functioning, along with problems in the organization and/or integration-differentiation of self and objects.
		Psychotic
12–18	Severe deficits	Major and severe deficits in almost all domains of mental functioning, with impaired reality testing; fragmentation and/or difficulties in self-object differentiation; disturbed perception, integration, regulation of affect and thought; deficits in one or more basic mental functions (e.g., perception, integration, motor, memory, regulation, judgment).

Note. From "Profile of Mental Functioning—M Axis," by V. Lingiardi and R. F. Bornstein, in V. Lingiardi and N. McWilliams (Eds.), *Psychodynamic Diagnostic Manual: PDM-2* (2nd ed., pp. 118–119), 2017, Guilford Press. Copyright 2017 by Guilford Press. Adapted with permission.

pathology. There are 12 capacities of mental functioning within each of the personality organization levels: (a) regulation, attention, and learning; (b) range and communication of affect; (c) mentalizing; (d) differentiation or integration necessary for identity; (e) relationships and intimacy; (f) regulating self-esteem; (g) impulse control; (h) defensive functioning; (i) resilience and adaptation; (j) psychological mindedness or self-observation; (k) internal standards or ideals; and (l) meaning or purpose in one's life. The model suggests that these 12 capacities will be lower or more compromised as one moves from healthy to neurotic to borderline to psychotic personality organization levels.

People with a *healthy level of personality organization* generally function at a high level in terms of affect regulation, emotional range and control, ability to mentalize, resiliency, use of flexible coping strategies, a coherent sense of self, and purpose or meaning in their lives. Such individuals may seek treatment if they experience a significant amount of situational stress in their lives or in the face of trauma or loss.

Those with a *neurotic level of personality organization* generally are at a good level of functioning and/or have mild impairments in mental capacities. They tend to respond to stress with some rigidity in coping styles, their defense mechanisms are not optimal but do not result in a distortion of reality, their relationship problems tend to be specific or circumscribed and not generalized to all relationships, they can tolerate negative emotions without becoming impulsive, their sense of identity is relatively coherent, they can observe themselves and others from multiple perspectives (e.g., they can mentalize), and their self-esteem may be mildly impaired.

People with a *borderline level of personality organization* are susceptible to disorganization caused by high levels of overwhelming affect. Their coping is moderately to severely compromised, and so they may be impulsive with intense episodes of anger, anxiety, or depression. Because of the intense emotions and difficulty regulating their affect, they tend to have recurring problems with intimate, social, and work relationships. Their impulsivity may lead to problem behaviors, including gambling, sexual acting out, binge eating, substance abuse, and self-harm. Their defense mechanisms tend to be in the less adaptive range. Individuals with a borderline personality organization have a sense of self that is often disorganized, and so their identity may not be coherent, and their self may not be sufficiently differentiated from others. As a result, their values and goals are often unstable. Problems with impulsivity and identity are exacerbated in these patients when an attachment relationship is threatened. Lingiardi and McWilliams (2017) made an important distinction between higher and lower levels of mental functioning among those with a borderline personality organiza-tion. The higher level describes individuals whose functioning is closer to those at the neurotic level of personality organization. That is, they have a moderate level of impairment in many of the 12 capacities of mental functioning described previously. However, those in the lower level of borderline personality organization have significant impairments in most, if not all, of the 12 capacities of mental functioning. They show major limitations in their experiences of emotions, a higher propensity toward impulsivity, lower level defense mechanisms, poor differentiation of self, lower capacity to mentalize, and significant problems in all areas of life, including intimate relationships, social functioning, and work.

Those at the *psychotic level of personality organization* tend to have severe deficits in most or all capacities of mental functioning, including problems with reality testing and disturbed perception. Their thinking may be concrete or bizarre, and their behaviors are usually socially inappro-priate. They may have a diagnosis of psychosis, or they may have episodes of psychotic-like thinking from which they recover quickly. Some with severe personality pathology may report delusional thinking, an inability to sepa-rate their thoughts and feelings from others, or the conviction that their attributions about others are correct regardless of the reality or evidence. The latter cognitive aspects indicate severe identity diffusion, poor differen-tiation between self and others, and difficulty with differentiating fantasy from reality.

We encourage clinicians to make broad decisions about the overall level of personality organization and mental functioning to facilitate treatment decisions, including for group composition (Table 2.3). Clinicians must keep in mind that in the early stages of group development, patients are often apprehensive and, in some cases, ambivalent about group therapy. The anxiety and doubt that is common at this point in the group are often expressed by patients by comparing their struggles with the concerns being expressed by other members of the group. Patients who are most anxious about entering group therapy will be most attentive to perceived differences between themselves and others. It is for this reason that group therapists must be particularly attentive to group composition, particularly on dimensions such as defensive functioning and personality organization.

Broadly speaking, patients with major deficits in mental functioning (i.e., lower levels of functioning in the borderline personality organization range; Table 2.3) may work best in a group that is homogenous on this dimension. These are groups that might be more typical of partial hospital programs or inpatient mental health programs. Such patients likely have less adaptive defense mechanisms, including acting out and major image distortion (Table 2.2). The GPIP therapist's stance in a group of patients with major deficits in mental functioning should be more directive and supportive of adaptive coping. In regard to the CMIP, the therapist might focus on encouraging patients' acts of self that are appropriate for different social contexts. The group therapy might be particularly helpful in modifying misattributions in the patient's expectations of others and also checking possible misinterpretations of the acts of others. Hence, group therapy for patients with major deficits in mental functioning capacities and less adaptive defensive functioning should take more of a social skills approach to modifying interpersonal patterns and a supportive approach to shoring up adaptive defenses to reduce impulsive acting out or gross misattributions. Feedback from other group members will be important, but therapists have to manage these carefully so that therapists contain the anxiety in the group at a manageable level.

Therapists must help patients to express affect in a moderated manner and encourage patients to step back and take an ego-observing perspective on their emotions, rather than taking an expressive or exclusively insight-oriented approach. Therapists will do well to actively manage levels of emotions in the individual and the group so that emotional arousal remains at an optimal level. As such, therapists should structure interactions among group members and act as a go-between for those who may be too anxious to discuss moment-to-moment group interactions directly with each other. Countertransference in therapists may be characterized by intense emotions that may be difficult to manage and are disruptive. There may be a strong pull for therapists to do something, to reject the patient or group, or to over-accommodate patients. Such reactions are sources of important information about the patient, their relational world, their attachment needs, and the responses they expect and receive from others. Here-and-now interventions by therapists may be useful if the comments focus on the individual patient and their experience of the therapist. Therapists should be cautious about focusing on member-to-member interactions and relationships.

By contrast, patients who, broadly speaking, have moderate impairment in mental functioning (i.e., at the higher level of the borderline personality organization; Table 2.3) are likely to work well in a group with patients who have a mild impairment (i.e., neurotic or healthy patients; Table 2.3). That is, some heterogeneity in group composition for patients with mild to moderate impairment in mental functioning is likely beneficial for these patients. Mildly and moderately impaired patients will have in common an adequate ability to consider mental states in themselves and others (i.e., to mentalize). Typically, they have other neurotic, obsessional, or high adaptive level defense mechanisms; adequate control of their impulses; and ability to tolerate anxiety and express their emotions and be reflective about their relationships and relational style. Therapists will be able to make full use of the CMIP, including examining and altering the introject. Therapists can also emphasize the here-and-now process as it occurs among group members and encourage members to discuss their experiences with each other in the group directly. However, therapists must keep in mind that patients with moderate impairment in mental functioning may be somewhat less capable of self-reflection and will need more support and guidance in exploring their emotions, defenses, and CMIP. Patients with mild impairment are likely good candidates to be the emotional leader of the group (see Chapter 4, this volume). Such patients will have the capacity to move the group forward by accessing difficult feelings and attachment needs, relinquishing less adaptive defenses, and altering their CMIP. Therapeutic relationships with mildly and moderately impaired individuals tend to be collaborative, and countertransference in therapists tends to be mild, easily observed, and not disruptive to the therapist's functioning or judgment.

Lingiardi and McWilliams (2017) suggested a few ways of assessing the level of personality organization on the basis of capacities of mental functioning. For example, they provided a rating scale from 1 (*severe deficit*) to 5 (*optimal capacity*) for each of the 12 capacities of mental functioning we listed earlier. One can derive a total score from the ratings (ranging from 12 to 60), indicating a summary of overall mental functioning and personality organization (see Table 2.3). Higher scores indicate healthy to neurotic personality organization, whereas lower scores indicate borderline to psychotic levels of personality organization.

CONCLUSION

The assessment process is key to developing individualized treatment goals for each member of the group and making decisions about the person–group fit or group composition. Clinicians looking for assessment tools to evaluate attachment, interpersonal problems, readiness for group therapy, group cohesion, and outcomes will find the American Group Psychotherapy Association CORE Battery to be a useful resource (Burlingame et al., 2006). As indicated, the *PDM-2* also provides a useful resource for assessing capacities and levels of mental functioning (Lingiardi & McWilliams, 2017), and the Defense Mechanisms Rating Scales (Perry et al., 1998) is helpful to evaluate the level and quality of defensive functioning. Some authors have written about the role of assessment in establishing a therapeutic alliance (Ackerman et al., 2000). The pre-group assessment process is the first phase of developing a therapeutic alliance in which the therapist and patient come to an agreement about treatment goals. Key to the GPIP assessment is an understanding between therapist and patient that symptoms or presenting problems are manifestations of intra- and interpersonal dynamics and that these dynamics are the key targets of the treatment. For that reason, communicating the case formulation and modifying it according to patient feedback is important to this model. Hence, the assessment process not only functions to help the therapist understand the patient but also functions to define how and what is targeted by the therapy.

The fundamental building block of the assessment is the therapist's ability to help the patient provide an interpersonal narrative that includes aspects of self-concept. Although this sounds straightforward, it requires the therapist to let go of a strictly symptom-focused assessment mind-set and embrace a developmental, interpersonal, and dynamic assessment approach. This means therapists must listen carefully when taking a developmental history, ask about attachment relationships and trauma, evaluate the nature and role of defensive functioning, look for consistencies in relationship episodes in the past and currently, and clearly delineate components of interpersonal functioning and their impact on the self. The end goal is to predict as accurately as possible the patient's interpersonal approach to the group, their expectations of the group, how the group might respond, and how these interactions may affect the individual's sense of self. We take up this element of predicting patient behavior in the group in the next chapter on pre-group preparation.

THERAPIST TASK BOX
ATTENDING TO GROUP COMPOSITION

1. Assess the level of the patient's typical defense mechanisms and defensive functioning.
2. Assess the level of the patient's personality organization and mental functioning.
3. Consider the patient-to-group fit according to the level of defensive functioning and level of personality organization.
4. Compose the group of relatively homogenous patients with regard to personality organization.

CHAPTER 2 REVIEW EXERCISES

Exercise 2.1

Read the following statements that might be made by a patient. Identify which attachment style is best represented by each of the statements.

Secure   Preoccupied   Dismissing   Disorganized

1. If there is one thing I have learned, it is that you have to rely on yourself; others just aren't going to be there for you. _____
2. I'm worried that he is going to leave me. I ask him about it all the time, and I think it's starting to really annoy him. _____
3. I don't know how I feel about it. It really doesn't matter how I feel. _____
4. I love my parents. I mean, they weren't perfect, but they did the best they could. _____
5. I can't talk about what happened to me. If I do, I'm afraid I'll lose it. What was your question? _____
6. I get so angry. I can't stop thinking about how she just left me like that and how she won't return any of my text messages. _____

Exercise 2.2

• Which quadrant of the interpersonal circle best represents each of these patient statements?

• Identify the complementary response quadrant from the interpersonal circle for each statement. Which interpersonal response around the interpersonal circle is most likely to be evoked in another person by the patient's behavior? Refer to Figure 1.4.

Friendly–dominant   Friendly–submissive
Hostile–submissive   Hostile–dominant

1. He really could use my help, and I know what's best for him in that situation.

   Quadrant _____   Complementary _____

2. Yes, I did go along with her. It's what she wanted, and it made her happy.

   Quadrant _____   Complementary _____

3. I really resented it, but I did it anyway.

   Quadrant _____   Complementary _____

4. I had to put him in his place. It was for my own sanity.

Quadrant _____   Complementary _____

Exercise 2.3

In the following patient narrative, underline and identify the elements of the triangle of adaptation (attachment needs, inhibitory affects, defense).

> John spent a lot of money on that car, and I'm worried that we can't afford it. I need him to be responsible and take care of the family. I kept thinking, "If you really loved me and the kids, you wouldn't do that." I wish I could just tell him to take the car back and get a refund, but then I'd feel guilty for depriving him—who am I to place such restrictions on him? So, I ended up giving him the silent treatment. We barely talked this morning, and I just went to work. Then, at work, one of my employees made a mistake with the billings, and it annoyed me, but again, I felt guilty for being annoyed, so I didn't say anything about it. I ended up fixing it myself. I don't want to be seen as "that bitch." It's so hard to find dependable people. By afternoon, I was so wound up and felt so awful that I went to the drive-through, ordered a bunch of food, and binged in the car.

Exercise 2.4

Review the narrative in Exercise 2.3. Underline and identify the elements of the cyclical maladaptive interpersonal pattern (acts of self, acts of others, expectations of others, introject).

Exercise 2.5

Identify which of the seven defense levels from the Defense Mechanisms Rating Scale are best represented by each of the following patient statements. Use Table 2.2 as a reference.

High adaptive   Obsessional   Other neurotic   Minor image distortion
Disavowal   Major image distortion   Action

1. I was angry at my boss, but I ended up taking it out on my children when I got home. _____
2. I think you are the best therapist in the world. _____
3. How do I feel about losing my job? In the context of things like chaos theory and the globalization of money markets, it was inevitable. _____
4. It's her fault that I stole the money. She shouldn't have had it out in the open like that. _____

5. I need to put it out of my mind for the time being so that I can write the exam. _____
6. He is such an angel, and I can't believe that he's going out with that evil woman. _____
7. They wouldn't give me the remote control, so I started throwing furniture around. _____

Exercise 2.6

The following are descriptions of four patients. Rate their level of personality organization using the descriptions in Table 2.3 (i.e., healthy, neurotic, borderline, psychotic).

1. Jack is a father of two and married to Clarissa for 12 years. They had difficulty in their marriage several years ago but have been trying to work things out with moderate success. He works at a local high-tech firm but has not been promoted, and this affects his self-esteem. Once a month, he meets his only long-term friend for drinks. Every couple of months, he experiences low mood and difficulty sleeping, but after a week or so, the symptoms seem to get better.

   Level of personality organization: _____

2. Frank regularly thinks about suicide since the breakdown of his marriage several years ago. He binge drinks on the weekend. He lost his job last year and has not regained employment. He has no close friends and does not return phone calls from family members. He spends his days at home, alone, surfing the internet.

   Level of personality organization: _____

3. Joanne is a university student who has had a good circle of friends since early high school. She is dating Keya and describes the relationship as close and supportive. Joanne reports some arguments with her mother that have been occurring on and off since Joanne left for university, but they seem to remain close despite the occasional conflict. Joanne reports some anxiety before exams, which she appears to be managing relatively well.

   Level of personality organization: _____

4. Helen is 35 years old and recently broke up with a boyfriend, which was stressful for her. Her longest romantic relationship lasted 6 months.

She works as a barista at a local coffee shop and is dissatisfied with the job. She cannot afford to live on her own and so is living with several roommates with whom she often gets into heated arguments. She has student debt that she does not intend to repay, and she did not complete her college degree. Helen has panic attacks about once a week, which make it difficult for her to leave the house and get to work when they occur.

Level of personality organization: _____

CHAPTER 2 REVIEW ANSWERS

Exercise 2.1

1. Dismissing
2. Preoccupied
3. Dismissing
4. Secure
5. Preoccupied
6. Disorganized

Exercise 2.2

1. Quadrant: Friendly–dominant; complementary: Friendly–submissive
2. Quadrant: Friendly–submissive; complementary: Friendly–dominant
3. Quadrant: Hostile–submissive; complementary: Hostile–dominant
4. Quadrant: Hostile–dominant; complementary: Hostile–submissive

Exercise 2.3

John spent a lot of money on that car, and I'm worried that we can't afford it. I need him to be responsible and take care of the family [*attachment needs*]. I kept thinking, "If you really loved me and the kids, you wouldn't do that" [*attachment needs*]. I wish I could just tell him to take the car back and get a refund [*activating feeling*], but then I'd feel guilty for depriving him [*inhibitory affect*]—who am I to place such restrictions on him? So, I ended up giving him the silent treatment [*defense*]. We barely talked this morning, and I just went to work. Then, at work, one of my employees made a mistake with the billings, and it annoyed me, but again, I felt guilty [*inhibitory affect*] for being annoyed [*activating affect*], so I didn't say anything about it [*defense*]. I ended up fixing it myself [*defense*]. I don't want to be seen as "that bitch." It's so hard to find dependable people [*attachment needs*]. By afternoon, I was so wound up and felt so awful [*inhibitory affect*] that I went to the drive-through, ordered a bunch of food, and just binged in the car [*defense*].

Exercise 2.4

John spent a lot of money on that car [*acts of others*], and I'm worried [*acts of self*] that we can't afford it. I need him to be responsible and take care of the family [*acts of self*]. I kept thinking, "If you really loved me and the kids, you wouldn't do that." <u>I wish I could just tell him</u> [*acts of self*] to take the car back and get a refund, but then <u>I'd feel guilty</u> for depriving him [*acts of self*]—<u>who am I to place such restrictions on him</u> [*introject*]? So, I ended up <u>giving him the silent treatment</u> [*acts of self*]. <u>We barely talked this morning</u> [*acts of self, acts of others*], and I just went to work. Then, at work, <u>one of my employees made a mistake</u> with the billings [*acts of others*], and <u>it annoyed me, but again, I felt guilty for being annoyed, so I didn't say anything about it. I ended up fixing it myself</u> [*acts of self*]. <u>I don't want to be seen as "that bitch"</u> [*expectations of others, introject*]. It's so hard to find dependable people. By afternoon, I was so wound up and felt so awful that I went to the drive-through, ordered a bunch of food, and just <u>binged in the car</u> [*acts of self*].

Exercise 2.5

1. Other neurotic (displacement)
2. Minor image distortion (idealization)
3. Obsessional (intellectualization)
4. Disavowal (rationalization)
5. High adaptive (suppression)

Exercise 2.6

1. Neurotic
2. Borderline
3. Healthy
4. Borderline

3

PRE-GROUP PREPARATION

This chapter describes a method of pre-group preparation for group psychodynamic-interpersonal psychotherapy (GPIP) based on the case formulation of the individual we introduced in Chapter 2 and on the practice of group therapy in the early stage of GPIP that we describe in Chapter 4. The pre-group preparation includes a discussion of the goals for a pre-group preparation session. These might include sharing with the patient their case formulation based on the triangles of adaptation and object relations and the cyclical maladaptive interpersonal patterns (CMIP), providing the patient with information on how the group works and what to expect and troubleshooting potential issues that may arise that may be consistent with the interpersonal and intrapersonal dynamics identified in the patient's case formulation.

For some time now, researchers have demonstrated that preparing patients for treatment has a positive impact on successful outcomes in individual and group therapy (Bednar & Kaul, 1994; Swift & Callahan, 2011). Researchers have also documented the positive effects of pretreatment preparation for medical patients. For example, preparing medical patients

https://doi.org/10.1037/0000213-004
Group Psychodynamic-Interpersonal Psychotherapy, by G. A. Tasca, S. F. Mikail, and P. L. Hewitt

for invasive medical procedures, chemotherapy, and HIV medications results in patients reporting decreased anxiety, more accurate expectations, less pain, quicker recovery, fewer side effects, better medication adherence, and shorter length of hospital stay (e.g., Balfour et al., 2006; Cornoiu et al., 2011; Schofield et al., 2008). Prepsychotherapy training of patients is associated with better rates of attendance (Swift & Callahan, 2011), likely because it improves or clarifies patient expectations of treatment and outcomes (Constantino et al., 2018). In group therapy, pre-group preparation of patients is associated with better attendance (France & Dugo, 1985), increased positive attitudes toward group treatment (Budman et al., 1984; Ogrodniczuk et al., 2005), and positive change on measures of symptom outcome (Budman et al., 1984; Muller & Scott, 1984; O'Farrell et al., 1985; Steuer et al., 1984). In an early extensive review of the topic, Bednar and Kaul (1994) concluded that pre-group training and preparation "may well prove to be the most important single consideration in effective group treatment" (p. 647).

Research on pre-group preparation is consistent with the common clinical practice of a number of group treatment approaches. Yalom and Leszcz's (2020) classic textbook and the American Group Psychotherapy Association Clinical Practice Guidelines (Bernard et al., 2008), for example, devote a significant amount of attention to the assessment and preparation of patients for group therapy. These practice-oriented writings emphasize clarifying misconceptions about group therapy, establishing a therapeutic alliance, and generating positive and realistic expectations. Similarly, in his individual treatment manual, Luborsky (1984) included a verbatim script on how to socialize a patient for supportive-expressive psychotherapy. In their treatment manual, Strupp and Binder (1984) encouraged the therapist to assess the patient's cyclical maladaptive pattern and then articulate this pattern to the patient before treatment as a way of establishing goals for treatment and forestalling problems in the therapy associated with transference. This provides the patient and therapist with an initial focus for therapy, which may be modified as more information comes to light during the treatment. Piper's early work on pre-group preparation indicated that experiential rather than didactic approaches were more effective in preparing patients for group (Piper et al., 1982).

The pre-group preparation for GPIP typically takes place in one or two meetings that may be combined with the pre-group assessment described in the previous chapter. Depending on the practice setting, a clinician other than the group therapist may conduct the pre-group assessment and preparation. Using that structure, the clinician conducting the assessment would then provide the group therapist with a report that includes the client's developmental history, case formulation, goals for group treatment, and the patient's attitude toward and demeanor during the pre-group preparation meeting. Appendix 3.1 provides a written group therapy description that therapists can modify and give to prospective clients. This description also provides a group agreement that outlines the individualized goals of group therapy for the patient based on the pre-group assessment of the CMIP and triangles of adaptation and object relations. The emphasis of the pre-group preparation is for the therapist or cotherapists to apply the idiographic case formulation developed during the assessment and use the patient's individualized CMIP as an initial focus for GPIP. However, therapists should understand that this focus is an initial working hypothesis that both patient and therapist may alter during the course of group treatment. On the basis of Piper's work (Piper et al., 1982), the pre-group preparation might include role plays, discussions of scenarios that may occur in a group, therapist trial process comments or metacommunications during the pre-group interview, and trial interpretations of the patient's CMIP. These more experientially based components may lead the patient to a better sense of what to expect during the therapy group. Next, we outline the six aspects of the pre-group preparation for GPIP.

THERAPIST TASK BOX
GOALS FOR PRE-GROUP PREPARATION

1. Reduce the patient's anticipatory anxiety about starting group therapy.
2. Help establish a good therapeutic alliance with the therapist.
3. Educate about and clarify any misconceptions regarding group therapy.
4. Increase the patient's realistic outcome expectations.
5. Increase the patient's engagement with the group they are about to start.

PROVIDE A RATIONALE FOR GPIP

Providing patients with a rationale for GPIP and group therapy accomplishes a number of goals. First, it educates the patient about what to expect in the group, including the time and day at which the group will occur, the number of other participants, the therapists' and patients' role in the group, how the group proceeds, and the norms one might expect (we discuss group therapy norms in the next chapter). Therapists who provide patients with an understanding of what they are about to encounter in the GPIP process help to reduce patients' anxiety about the group. Second, providing a rationale might clarify some misconceptions about group therapy. For example, patients might consider group therapy to be a second-rate or inexpensive form of therapy, and they may be concerned about its effectiveness. It may be helpful for the therapist to talk about the existing research on the efficacy of group psychotherapy for a wide range of disorders and how group therapy is equally effective as individual therapy (see Burlingame et al., 2016; Burlingame & Jensen, 2017). A later chapter in this book reviews the research evidence for GPIP in particular. Third, providing a rationale and discussing how and why group therapy such as GPIP works is one of the building blocks of a therapeutic alliance. The therapeutic alliance is the collaborative agreement between therapist and patient on the tasks and goals of therapy and the emotional bond (Flückiger et al., 2018). A well-articulated rationale provides the foundation to an agreement on the tasks of group therapy. Finally, patients will understandably be anxious about how the therapy is conducted, what may be exposed about themselves in group that they may find shameful, and whether they will feel accepted or rejected by the group, among other issues. Giving a clear rationale about GPIP and discussing the role of safety and security in the group will help to reduce some of these anxieties.

A therapist's explanation to the patient of how GPIP works could be as follows:

> Group psychotherapy of the type we have been discussing is a useful and powerful way of achieving the change you want. Many problems, such as the ones you have described, have had an unwanted impact on your relationships. These relationship problems then affect how you feel about yourself. The struggles and painful emotions you have endured often result from negative feelings related to relationship problems and your feelings about yourself. Having more secure and supportive relationships will help to make you feel less isolated, less angry or sad, and feel better about yourself in general.
>
> Group therapy is a place where you can talk about yourself, your problems, and your relationships. In so doing, you will be relating to others in the group. The therapists will encourage you and the other group members to talk to each other in the group about yourselves and give each other feedback. Even though it is a therapy group, you can expect that you will behave and interact in ways that are similar to the way you are in your everyday life. Your usual way of interacting with people day-to-day will be similar to the way you interact with people in the group. The feelings you will have in the group and related to some group members and therapists will be similar to feelings you generally have. The big difference is that usually in life outside the group, you are not expected to talk about the way you interact, how it makes others

feel, and how it makes you feel. But in the therapy group, we will encourage you to talk about these aspects of your experience and interactions. By doing this, you will get a better understanding of how others experience you, what your expectations are, how you react to people, how this makes you feel about yourself, and how this plays a role in the struggles you've shared with us during the assessment. The therapists will encourage you to start perceiving and doing things differently with others. The first step is to make changes in the group, and the next step is to transfer this new knowledge and ways of relating to the rest of your life outside the group. So, not only will group therapy provide you with a new understanding of yourself and your relationships but also with a new experience of relationships in the group. Understanding and changing the way you interact within the group will have a positive impact on you and your relationships outside the group.

ILLUSTRATE HOW THE CMIP IS MANIFESTED IN THE GROUP

An important part of the pre-group preparation is for the therapist to predict and sensitize the patient to how their CMIP will manifest in the group. Therapists do this after the assessment of the CMIP for the individual, which is outlined in the previous chapter. The importance of this part of the pre-group preparation lies in conveying to the patient that the emergence of the CMIP in the group will be a frustrating experience but also one that holds the potential for personal transformation. The role of the clinician at this juncture is to help the patient assume a stance of self-observation. In other words, the therapist's objective is to allow for the emergence of the patient's observing ego to help the patient gain insight into their unique CMIP and how the pattern is likely to play out in group sessions. This also serves the purpose of collaborating with the patient to establish clear goals for treatment, which is a key aspect of the therapeutic alliance. In addition, this process may mitigate the likelihood of premature termination that may result from feelings of frustration, self-criticism, and anger when patients feel stuck reenacting with other group members the self-limiting patterns that compelled them to seek group treatment in the first place.

The following is an example of how to discuss a case formulation based on the CMIP and triangles of adaptation and object relations and their possible manifestation in the group therapy with a hostile–dominant patient.

> According to what you said earlier, my guess is that you might expect, even now, that as group members begin to ask you questions and express curiosity about aspects of your life, you may see them as nosey or intrusive [*expectations of others*]. And even though you would really like them to like you and accept you [*attachment needs, act of self*], their questions might trigger feelings of anger or annoyance and the sense that you are being controlled [*affect*]. In the

past, you reacted either by being stern and pushing others away or withdrawing into silence with one-word responses [*acts of self*]. What's your sense of how folks in the group might respond in the face of that stance? [*The therapist is inviting the patient's observing ego to consider possible acts of others in the group in response to the patient's acts of self.*]

Another helpful prediction at this point is for the therapists to suggest that the patient may experience someone else in the group who they do not like, with whom they do not get along, or with whom they feel they have a special bond. The therapist in this scenario is predicting a transference reenactment based on the patient's CMIP and the triangles. Rather than seeing this as a problem, the therapist can frame it to the patient as an opportunity to understand their relational patterns and to make changes in the group.

> It is possible that you may find someone in the group who you do not like, who rubs you the wrong way, or with whom you feel that you have a special connection. This will be an important person for your therapy. They will likely remind you of someone in your life with whom you have some unresolved feelings and with whom your relational patterns get activated. It is important to remember that some of your feelings toward this person involve your unresolved feelings from other relationships in your life. This is especially true if other group members do not respond as strongly as you do to this person. In any case, this will be an excellent opportunity for you to work out these feelings and to get a better sense of them and better control over them. This may give you a better understanding of your relational patterns and provide you with an opportunity to do something different in the group that you can then apply to important relationships in your life.

EXPLAIN HOW GROUP THERAPY CAN CHANGE CMIPs

It is important to give the patient a sense of how change may occur in group therapy. That is, group therapy will provide patients with a new understanding of themselves and give them a new experience of relationships (Levenson, 2017). For some patients, this has to be a somewhat concrete description, whereas, for others who are more psychologically minded, this will be more evident to them. The important aspect of describing how change occurs in GPIP is for the patient and therapist to agree on the tasks of therapy. That is, therapists and patients should agree on how group therapy proceeds, how it works, and how it will be helpful. This agreement is fundamental to the therapeutic alliance and, for some patients, must be revisited regularly during the therapy if and when the patient is unclear as to how or why group therapy is proceeding as it is.

This part of the interview typically occurs in a later session of the pre-group assessment and preparation meetings. At this stage, the therapist must have a clearly articulated idiographic case formulation of the patient based on the triangles and the CMIP. That is, the therapist must individualize this part of the pre-group preparation to each patient. Once the therapist has a good understanding of the patient's case formulation, the therapist will be able to describe how change might occur for the specific patient. For example, a patient may have attachment needs that they experience as shameful and which they have to defend (a formulation from the patient's triangle of adaptation). For such a patient, one goal might include allowing them to articulate the attachment need in the group and allowing the group to respond supportively, thus reducing the shame related to the need. A second goal of the group therapy may be to help the patient to understand clearly how this dynamic has an impact on their behaviors in relationships and their view of themselves as articulated by their triangle of object relations and CMIP. A third goal may be for the patient to change their typical pattern of behaving in the group (i.e., change their CMIP as expressed in the group) so that their attachment needs can be expressed without shame or maladaptive defenses.

Although in the following example text, we present the therapist as giving a monologue, we encourage therapists to treat this part of the interview as more of an interactive process in which they continually clarify the formulations, get feedback from the patient, and answer questions about how and why GPIP might work. Keep in mind that this is, in part, a collaborative discussion of how group therapy will work for a particular patient. Therapists will also find it important to gauge the patient's reactions and responses to the formulation: Is the patient able to discuss it collaboratively, do they reject it out of hand, are they puzzled by it, do they simply accept it without comment? These responses may give the therapist more information about the patient's potential interpersonal stance in the group therapy. The following is an example of how a therapist might describe the process of change to a hostile–dominant patient.

> In the group, you will not want your feelings of anger and your critical behaviors [*acts of self*] to go too far because of the impact they will have on how you end up feeling about yourself [*introject*]. The job of the therapists is to be attentive to when and if this happens in the group to try to help you stop it from going too far. We can do that by helping you and the group to take a step back and talk about what is happening. For example, we may help you focus on what you need from the group [*attachment needs*] as opposed to responding with the anger [*defense*] or shame [*affect*] that has had a hold on you for so long. By helping you change the focus from your reaction to

what you need, we may be able to help you with some real change in yourself and in how people in the group, as well as others in your life, interact with you. We will help you to tell the group members that what you really need is to feel accepted and understood and, at the same time, autonomous [*attachment needs*]. You may have to explain to the group that you only get critical and angry [*defense and acts of self*] when you feel others might be controlling you [*expectations of others*] or shaming you [*affect*], only then to reject you [*expectations of others*]. I think you will be surprised by how gratifying it is to form relationships in the group where there is a give-and-take and mutual acceptance [*acts of others, acts of self*]. You will see that this will soften your anger toward others [*acts of self*], change your future expectations of how other people will behave toward you [*expectations of others*], and make you feel better about yourself [*introject*]. Most people find that if they can do this with people in the group, they often can make similar changes in the relationships in their lives.

DESCRIBE THE PROCESS OF GROUP THERAPY

To reduce some of the patient's anxiety regarding the early sessions of the group, it is useful to describe how the group will work. Again, this should be approached as a discussion with the patient, not as a monologue. If necessary, the therapist should address any misconceptions about group therapy (e.g., that it is second rate, cheap therapy and not as effective or as valued as individual therapy). Patients may also have concerns about contagion (e.g., I may feel worse if I hear someone else's problems). In that case, therapists should reassure patients that is unlikely to happen and that the therapist will help maintain the patient's emotional boundaries and those of the group. In addition, some patients are highly concerned about shame, embarrassment, and judgment should they reveal too much about themselves. Therapists should conceptualize these concerns within the patient's case formulation. Often, issues of shame and embarrassment are affects that have developed over the years because of unfortunate or asynchronous responses by parental figures to attachment needs or various experiences of trauma. If that is the case, reducing concern about shame and embarrassment should be a goal of group therapy that may be achieved by the safety and security the patient experiences in the group.

The following is a typical description to a patient of how GPIP works:

There will be about eight men and women, all of whom are working to address challenges they've experienced in their relationships. The therapist will be a psychologist (or other professional) with considerable training and experience in group therapy. In the first session, the therapist will go over some of the basic rules: that you come to each session, stay for the full session, be on time, be respectful, and maintain the confidentiality of the other group members.

Then the group will start. The therapists won't have a particular agenda for any of the sessions, and nobody in particular will be asked to start or talk. People will start talking at their own pace when they are ready. This means that there may be some uncomfortable silence at the beginning. In subsequent sessions, unless there is a matter of business to attend to, the therapist won't start the sessions but will wait for someone to begin. At first, people tend to talk about what brings them to therapy, what relationship problems they have, or what they would like to work on.

Therapists will leave the focus of each session open so that people in the group can be free to be fully themselves and interact with other members of the group in much the same way they interact with other people in their lives. This is important to get a good sense of how you and others in the group experience your relationships and how each of you would like to be different. The therapists will encourage you to talk to each other as much as possible, give each other feedback, and talk about yourselves. The group is not a forced confessional, but we find that the more people use the group, the more they will get out of it.

The job of the group members at the beginning is to come together and start working together. This isn't always easy, but the therapists will help you become a working group. They will help you find similarities and common goals. The fact that all of you face some struggles or dissatisfaction with aspects of your relationships will provide common ground for you to share your goals and experiences.

The job of the therapists is to make sure you and others are on track and work on those aspects of your relationships that have been most troubling for you. At times, the therapists will reflect back to you and others the feelings that you might express subtly or indirectly but that aren't being voiced overtly. At other times, the therapists will encourage several group members to go deeper to explore a feeling or an interaction that is taking place between them. In this and other ways, the therapists' most important task is to help point out and make clear those relationship patterns that are being played out between group members and the impact that these patterns have in the group. Later on in the group, therapists will encourage you to try out new ways of behaving with fellow group members. The therapists will not give you advice on what to do or not do; most people can recognize what they have to do. The real challenge is for you to get beyond your fears and expectations and try out the new ways of relating to others in the group and elsewhere.

IDENTIFY POTENTIAL PROBLEMS AND PITFALLS

Therapists should discuss with the patient problems related to the emergence of the CMIP in the interactions among group members to sensitize them to potentially antitherapeutic events. For example, therapists could caution friendly–dominant patients about focusing on others' needs at the expense of not dealing with their own issues or being overly controlling in group interactions, which may limit others' expression of negative emotions. Such patients have to strike the right balance between being helpful without being dominating and with allowing themselves to be vulnerable. Friendly–submissive patients may be overly accommodating by always allowing others to go first, feel that their problems are not as important, and then have a familiar feeling of being left out of the group. This would be an unfortunate reenactment of their self-effacing roles in their relationships outside the group. Therapists must warn these patients that not asserting their needs and feeling dismissed is potentially a problem for them in the group that the therapists will help them identify and talk about. The hostile–submissive patient may feel resentful in the group and indirectly critical of the therapists and group members. It may be helpful to predict their frustration with the group, which they may signal by missing sessions or having an increased desire to drop out of therapy. Therapists must encourage such patients to talk about their emerging anger and their wish to withdraw from the group. For hostile–dominant patients, therapists could warn them against their overexpression of anger and criticism toward others and the potential countertherapeutic results of this. That is, therapists should encourage these patients to take an observing-ego perspective on their anger. A therapeutic focus on the defense pole or the attachment needs pole of the triangle of adaptation will be important to contain their anger and understand its roots. It may be useful for therapists to role play with patients some interactions that may occur in the group or talk through the patient's potential responses to scenarios that may provoke anxiety in the patient.

The following is an example of how one might discuss potential problems and pitfalls with a hostile–dominant patient:

> There may be times when you may become angry or critical [*defense*] with something or someone in the group [*acts of self, acts of others*]. At those times, the therapists will ask you to take a step back to look at what is happening inside you that may be triggering the anger. As we discussed during the assessment feedback, your anger may be not only related to the person you are talking to but also to your own needs [*attachment needs*] that cause you discomfort [*affect*]. We will encourage other group members to share their reaction to your anger—the impact it's having on them and what it evokes in them. At those times, it will be important for you to listen to their responses and learn how your anger impacts others. It may be difficult to reflect on all of that in the moment when your anger is so close to the surface. But the therapists will help you step back and focus on emotions [*affects*] and needs [*attachment needs*] that may be buried beneath the anger so that you can gain greater clarity on the role that anger plays in your life and the group.

INOCULATE AGAINST EARLY TERMINATION

The pre-group preparation process we have described serves two important functions. First, it reduces patients' anticipatory anxiety to a manageable level to facilitate their willingness to commit to joining the group. Second, a thorough and well-executed pre-group preparation can also reduce the risk of early attrition from the group. Yalom and Leszcz (2020) noted two group therapeutic factors, universality and instillation of hope, that foster engagement in the therapeutic task and go a long way toward reducing the risk of early termination. Therapists can reassure patients that the anxiety they are experiencing is natural and common among those who are considering group therapy. Some patients find solace in the knowledge that this anxiety will be a shared experience with other group members, and this will help them to feel less isolated in their concern about starting the group. Along with this initial anxiety, other universal themes include feelings of shame, struggles with low self-esteem, fear of rejection and criticism, and relationship difficulties. Highlighting these common themes among group members may help foster cohesion with the group even before group sessions start. In addition, instilling a sense of hope and optimism can help with the natural ambivalence that sometimes accompanies a new therapeutic venture. While acknowledging the ambivalence, the therapist should indicate that this form of therapy will be helpful to reduce symptoms, establish more fulfilling relationships, and develop a more positive sense of self. Increasing the patient's realistic expectations of a good outcome will start their group therapy on the right foot (Constantino et al., 2018).

BE ATTENTIVE TO DIVERSITY AND GROUP COMPOSITION

Individual diversity, including age, culture, ethnicity, race, gender, sex, socioeconomic status, sexual orientation, language, and others, are key aspects of people's identity that have an impact on their relationships, their sense of self, and perhaps their reasons for seeking help (Hays, 2009). Many individuals from ethnic and racial minorities might have experienced outright prejudice and exclusion or more subtle forms of indirect discriminatory messages, such as microaggressions (Owen et al., 2014). Managing these diversity issues in individual psychotherapy is complex, especially when the therapist and patient are from different backgrounds. Therapists must honestly examine their implicit biases and values related to the minority group with which the patient identifies. Group therapy magnifies the complexity because of the number of individuals who interact, some of whom may be from different minority groups. Microaggressions are particularly problematic because of their subtler nature and the negative impact they have on the therapeutic alliance. However, research has indicated that successful discussion and resolution of a microaggression may result in a heightened therapeutic alliance (Owen et al., 2014).

One of the key issues in the assessment and pre-group preparation phase is to consider the impact of minority status on an individual's work and demeanor in a therapy group and on the composition of the group. Therapists can engage in a systematic cultural assessment of potential group therapy patients by asking about the patient's cultural identity (e.g., cultural or ethnic reference groups, degree of involvement with the culture of origin), the role of the cultural context in the presenting problems (e.g., the perceived source of distress), and the impact of cultural differences on the therapist–patient relationship (Chen et al., 2008). Therapists must be particularly sensitive to cultural norms and not overinterpret an interpersonal behavior that is culturally bound (e.g., deference to authority) with a problematic interpersonal pattern (e.g., overly submissive).

Cone-Uemura and Suzuki Bentley (2018) cautioned group therapists who are considering including only one member from a minority group in a therapy group because of the potential for explicit or implicit prejudice or insult that may recapitulate past injustices. However, the authors also conceded that, in practice, it might not be possible to compose groups with more than one member from a particular underrepresented population. Cone-Uemura and Suzuki Bentley suggested that a single minority participant may do well in a therapy group if their primary presenting problem is not tied to their minority status (e.g., an LGBTQ member whose primary reason for group therapy is not related to concerns about coming out). Similarly, minority group members whose identity development is advanced (e.g., who feel secure in their cultural identity and value their cultural group) are more likely to feel included in a therapy group as long as others in the group do not express discriminatory attitudes. Therapists must be sensitive to the potential for clashing values of existing and prospective group members (e.g., religious beliefs and sexual orientation). It is important that the group not become a place in which harmful discriminatory experiences might reoccur.

Cone-Uemura and Suzuki Bentley (2018) suggested that therapists consider exploring specific topics as part of the pre-group preparation for some prospective group members. These topics might include providing information about diverse backgrounds and values of other group members, asking whether any offensive stereotypes concern the individual, exploring whether some values held by others might offend them, and asking how they feel about being the only minority member in the group. In addition, it may be prudent in the pre-group preparation phase to have a discussion with any prospective group member, including those from the dominant cultural group, about the need to be respectful of individual differences, even if the values and beliefs expressed by others clash with those of the prospective patient.

As we outlined, pre-group preparation plays an important role in getting a patient ready for GPIP. Patients learn what to expect from group therapy, including the potential challenges and benefits. The pre-group preparation is meant to encourage patients and therapists to develop a collaborative agreement regarding how the therapy will function for the patient—which is the basis for a therapeutic alliance. Therapists achieve this, in part, by aligning the pre-group preparation with the dynamic-interpersonal case formulation, as discussed in Chapter 2 and using the case formulation to define the goals of therapy for the patient. In the next chapter, we outline how the case formulation and pre-group preparation begin to inform the practice of group therapy at the different stages of GPIP.

THERAPIST TASK BOX
PRE-GROUP PREPARATION

1. Provide the patient with a rationale for GPIP and group therapy.

2. Explore with the patient how their CMIP is likely to manifest in the group.

3. Discuss with the patient ways in which their CMIP may change by being in the group.

4. Explain to the patient the process of group therapy and GPIP in particular.

5. Identify with the patient potential problems and pitfalls that the patient may encounter in a group setting due to their CMIP or triangle of adaptation.

6. Help to inoculate the patient against potential early termination.

7. Consider any patient cultural diversity when considering group composition. Assess the patient's cultural identity security, immediately manage any microaggressions among group members, and be aware of your implicit biases.

CHAPTER 3 REVIEW EXERCISES

Exercise 3.1

Identify the cyclical maladaptive interpersonal pattern (CMIP) components in this therapist's description of how a patient's CMIP may manifest in group therapy.

> Given what you have said so far about your relationships, it is possible that you may feel fearful about talking in the group, and you may manage your fear by being silent or expressing your feelings indirectly. It sounds like, in the past, you were ridiculed when you tried to express your needs for caring, and this made you both sad and angry. So, it wouldn't surprise me if you might worry that others in the group will make fun of you if you express what you need or how you feel. Because of your fear of being humiliated, you may not easily express these needs or your anger directly, and so people in the group may not know how to respond to you because they will not know exactly what you are feeling or that you need anything from them. One outcome that has come from all this is that it reinforces your view of yourself as unworthy of attention and love.

Write down the phrases that represent the components of this patient's CMIP.

Acts of self: _____

Acts of others: _____

Expectations of others: _____

Introject: _____

Exercise 3.2

Read the therapist's description in Exercise 3.1 of how a patient's patterns may manifest in the therapy group. Write down the phrases in the description that represent the poles of the triangle of adaptation for this patient.

Attachment needs/activating feelings: _____

Inhibiting affect: _____

Defense: _____

Exercise 3.3

Match the interpersonal style in the following list (defined by the interpersonal circle) with the most likely common pitfall or challenge for a group therapy patient with that interpersonal style.

A. Friendly–dominant B. Friendly–submissive
C. Hostile–submissive D. Hostile–dominant

_____ 1. The patient may indirectly express their frustration with the group or therapist.
_____ 2. The patient may be unassuming and let others in the group speak ahead of them.
_____ 3. Group members may experience the patient as intrusive.
_____ 4. The patient may easily express annoyance at other group members.
_____ 5. Group members may experience the patient as intimidating.
_____ 6. The patient may think of dropping out of group instead of expressing anger with the group.
_____ 7. Group members may experience the patient as shy.
_____ 8. Group members may experience the patient as not having any problems.

Exercise 3.4

Identify the statements or words in this pre-group preparation script that will (a) reduce the patient's anxiety, (b) help establish a therapeutic alliance, (c) educate them about and clarify any misconceptions regarding group therapy, (d) increase their realistic outcome expectations, and (e) increase their engagement with the therapy group that they are about to start.

> It is pretty normal for people to be anxious before they start therapy, including group therapy. I encourage you to talk about feeling anxious because you will find that other group members likely feel the same way. This might help you feel less anxious and more connected to the group. Our goal today is to tell you more about how the group works and to define the goals you would like to work on during the therapy. We encourage you to ask questions about how the group might be helpful. By the end of these sessions, you should have a good idea of what to work on and how the group will help you. There is a lot of excellent research showing that group therapy is effective in treating the issues you described. In some ways, group therapy is very well suited to help you with your relationship issues because we get to see, understand, and work with you while you are interacting with others.

Write down the statements from the script that

1. Reduce the patient's anxiety: _____
2. Help establish a therapeutic alliance: _____
3. Clarify misconceptions regarding group therapy: _____
4. Increase realistic outcome expectations: _____
5. Increase their engagement with the therapy group: _____

CHAPTER 3 REVIEW ANSWERS

Exercise 3.1

Acts of self: "you may feel fearful about talking in the group," "this made you both sad and angry," "you may not easily express these needs or anger directly"

Acts of others: "you were ridiculed when you tried to express your needs," "people in the group may not know how to respond to you"

Expectations of others: "you might worry that others in the group will make fun of you"

Introject: "your view of yourself as unworthy of attention and love"

Exercise 3.2

Attachment needs/activating feelings: "your needs for caring," "sad and angry"

Inhibiting affect: "fearful about talking in the group," "fear of being humiliated"

Defense: "being silent or expressing your feelings indirectly," "not easily express these needs or anger directly"

Exercise 3.3

1. C Hostile–submissive
2. B Friendly–submissive
3. A Friendly–dominant
4. D Hostile–dominant
5. D Hostile–dominant
6. C Hostile–submissive
7. B Friendly–submissive
8. A Friendly–dominant

Exercise 3.4

1. Reduce the patient's anxiety: "normal for people to be anxious before they start therapy," "talk about feeling anxious because you will find that other group members likely feel the same way"

2. Establish a therapeutic alliance: "define the goals that you would like to work on," "should have a good idea of what to work on and how the group will help"

3. Clarify any misconceptions regarding group therapy: "tell you more about how the group works," "ask questions about how the group might be helpful," "because we get to see, understand, and work with you while you are interacting with others"

4. Increase realistic outcome expectations: "excellent research showing that group therapy is effective," "group therapy is very well suited to help you with your relationship issues"

5. Increase their engagement with the therapy group: "more connected to the group"

APPENDIX 3.1: WRITTEN DESCRIPTION OF GPIP FOR PATIENTS, INCLUDING GROUP THERAPY AGREEMENT, AND GOALS

WHY GROUP THERAPY?

Group psychotherapy is a useful and powerful way of achieving the change you want. Many problems that bring you to therapy may have a negative impact on relationships that affect how you feel about yourself, which may worsen your problems. Group therapy can help you achieve more secure and supportive relationships, which will help to make you feel less isolated, angry, anxious, or sad and better about yourself in general.

Group therapy is a place where people talk about themselves, their problems, and their relationships. Group members will be encouraged to talk about themselves and give each other feedback. You will find that your relationship patterns (your usual way of interacting with people, the feelings you often have, and your ways of coping with feelings) will be reflected in your ways of relating in the group. In contrast to "real life," in which you are not often expected to talk about how you interact, how you feel, and how it makes others feel, in the group, you will be encouraged to talk about these feelings and patterns. In this way, you will get a better understanding of how you are in relationships, how others experience you and react to you, what your expectations are, and how this makes you feel about yourself. You will be encouraged to start perceiving and doing things differently with others—first, in the group and then transferring this new knowledge and behaviors to relationships outside the group.

WHAT TO EXPECT

There will be about eight patients in the group, and some will have similar problems to yours. The two therapists are trained and experienced in providing group therapy. There will not be an agenda for each session, and nobody in particular will be asked to start or to talk in any session. People will talk about themselves at their own pace when they are ready. This means that there may be some uncomfortable silence at the beginning, but soon people start the group with more ease. At first, patients talk about what brings them to therapy, what relationship problems they have, or what they would like to work on. The agenda is left open so that people can approach the group in the way in which they approach their lives in general and in a way that is most comfortable for them. Therapists will encourage group members to talk to each other as much as possible, give each other feedback, and talk about themselves. The group is not a forced confessional, but we find that the more people use the group, the more they get out of it.

The job of the group members at the beginning is to come together and start working together. The therapists will help you become a working group. They will help you find similarities and common goals. The job of the therapists is to make sure you and others are on track and working on your relationship problems, and the therapists will reflect on your interactions with other group members. Therapists will help to point out and clarify relationship patterns in the group and help you find out how these patterns affect your relationships outside the group and your ability to cope with emotions. Later on in the group, you will be encouraged to try out new ways of behaving with fellow group members and in your life outside of the group. The overall objectives are (a) that you gain a new understanding of your relationship patterns and feelings and (b) that the group provides you with a new experience of relationships in a safe environment.

Your first few sessions in the group will be the most anxiety provoking for you, and this is normal. You might wonder how this group will be helpful or whether the group is right for you. It is important to talk about these feelings in the group so that you can receive encouragement from others or try to understand whether these feelings are related to what brought you to therapy in the first place. In fact, you and the group will benefit from discussing any reactions or feelings you have during the group and about the group.

It is possible that you might feel strongly about a group member who reminds you of someone in your life. This person and your feelings about them could represent an opportunity for you to work on an important relationship pattern. The therapists will help you understand your reactions, your relationship with group members, and your relationship patterns in general.

GUIDELINES FOR GROUP THERAPY

Group therapy has some basic rules: You (a) come to each session; (b) stay for the full session; (c) be on time; (d) be respectful even if you disagree with someone's opinions or values; (e) be respectful of others' religion, sexual orientation, gender, race, ethnicity, or culture; and (f) maintain the confidentiality of the other group members. If you must miss a session, please call beforehand to inform the therapists so they can inform the group. Finally, we discourage members from socializing with each other outside the group. It is difficult for people to be open and honest in therapy with someone who has become a friend outside the group. If you happen to run into another group member outside of therapy, we encourage you to talk about that at the next session. We ask that you wait for your membership in the group to end before you start a friendship with someone who was in the group with you.

GROUP THERAPY AGREEMENT

1. I will come to each session, be on time, and stay for the full session. If I must miss a session, I will call to inform the therapist and group.

2. I will be respectful to other group members even if I disagree with them or feel negative toward them.

3. I will maintain the confidentiality of the other group members (i.e., not discuss their personal circumstances, names, or identifying information with anyone outside of the group).

4. I will not start a social friendship with another group member while I am a member of the group.

MY GOALS FOR GROUP THERAPY

You and your therapist will discuss your goals for group therapy. These goals are usually related to changing relationship patterns, managing emotions better, changing how one feels about oneself, and becoming more authentic in relationships. The following is a list of goals you and your therapist have agreed on:

1. _____
2. _____
3. _____
4. _____
5. _____

Patient name and signature   Date

_____   _____

Therapist name and signature   Date

_____   _____

4

GROUP THERAPY THEORY AND GROUP PSYCHODYNAMIC-INTERPERSONAL PSYCHOTHERAPY STAGES OF DEVELOPMENT

In this chapter, we review some of the factors that directly inform the practice of group psychodynamic-interpersonal psychotherapy (GPIP). We review the therapeutic alliance, its importance to patient outcomes in groups, and how therapists can develop, maintain, and repair the alliance in group therapy. We also review key concepts in group therapy, such as cohesion, adaptive norms, the use of metacommunication, and working with individuals, dyads, and the group as a whole. We then turn to the theories described in Chapter 2 and how therapists can use concepts from these theories deliberately and in a timely manner to help individuals and the group change. We describe in some detail the stages of development in GPIP groups and how therapists can apply concepts such as the triangle of adaptation, the triangle of object relations, and the cyclical maladaptive interpersonal pattern (CMIP) to inform their work with the group at each stage and structure interventions to the tasks required by the stage. We start by briefly reviewing some concepts of interpersonal theory to set the stage for this practice-oriented chapter on clinical interventions.

https://doi.org/10.1037/0000213-005
Group Psychodynamic-Interpersonal Psychotherapy, by G. A. Tasca, S. F. Mikail, and P. L. Hewitt

INTERPERSONAL THEORY AND GROUPS

Interpersonal theory is based on a number of assumptions, all of which revolve around understanding and working with the patient's relational patterns. At the heart of interpersonal theory is Sullivan's (1953) construct of the self-system. Sullivan conceptualized the *self-system* as an antianxiety system, having as its primary objective the maintenance of "felt interpersonal security" (p. 109). In more contemporary terms, the self-system refers to an individual's self-concept and the unconscious mechanisms that maintain it (Talley et al., 1990). Interpersonal theory posits that each of us is drawn to relationships that confirm our self-concept. Thus, an individual's pattern of communication and style of relating evoke responses from others that are congruent with his or her view of self (i.e., they are complementary). The self-concept has its foundations in early interactions with significant attachment figures, be they parents, grandparents, siblings, teachers, coaches, or peers. The responses of these figures to one's behaviors are influential in shaping one's view of self and, ultimately, the introject, or one's relationship with the self (Bratton, 2010; Bretherton & Munholland, 1999; Pincus et al., 1999). Cooley's (1908) concept of the "looking-glass self" emphasizes that the self-concept stems from the individual's image of how one is viewed by others, particularly those who are significant in one's life. Throughout one's life, the self-concept is maintained through a process of selective attention and interpersonal engagement. Thus, experiences and interpersonal encounters that are congruent with the evolving self-concept are more likely to be noticed and internalized, whereas those that are incongruent evoke a state of dissonance and thus remain either unnoticed or are actively dismissed and discounted.

Although the responses of others are critical, they are not the sole contributor to the development of the self-concept. Theorists such as Rothabart (2011) and Kagan (1994) underscored the importance of temperament in the formation of self-concept. Kagan (2003) conceptualized *temperament* as "a particular physiology and an envelope of potential behavioral phenotypes whose final form depends on the rearing environment" (p. 8). These theorists suggested that personality formation is a product of the interaction between a child's inherent disposition and the unique responses of caregivers to the child's behaviors (i.e., emotional expression, affect regulation, awareness of and expression of needs, reactivity, need for and tolerance of stimulation). As the child's social universe expands, interpersonal encounters that fall outside of what is familiar may evoke feelings of insecurity and anxiety. Thus, each of us strives to create an interpersonal world that is familiar and predictable, even when doing so creates problems in living and relating. It is this striving for a stable and predictable means of relating that lends GPIP such potential as an effective therapeutic tool yet also creates challenges for the clinician.

Specifically, GPIP requires the therapist to enter into and ultimately facilitate a shift in the patient's CMIPs, part of which involves helping the individual reimagine and revise self-limiting components of the self-concept (Strupp & Binder, 1984). For the patient, this task is fraught with anxiety and feelings of heightened vulnerability because it requires viewing the self within the context of one's relational world in unfamiliar ways. In particular, the patient is charged with relinquishing ways of being, coping, and relating to the self and others that have provided a felt sense of predictability despite being self-limiting. It is the enormity of this task that makes psychotherapy so challenging and group psychotherapy, in particular, so anxiety provoking for patients. To facilitate the patient's ability to tolerate such an undertaking, GPIP requires the therapist to create a secure environment in the pre-group assessment phase, as well as during group therapy, that is characterized by mutual trust and respect. This is a key element of the therapeutic alliance with the therapist that facilitates the process of engagement with the group. Although all psychotherapeutic modalities share this requirement for trust, it can be especially challenging in the context of group therapy. Group therapists are tasked with engaging six or eight patients with unique defensive positions that may not be complementary, while creating a milieu that allows patients to feel sufficiently secure to risk relinquishing long-held ways of relating and viewing themselves.

THE THERAPEUTIC ALLIANCE

The *therapeutic alliance* is that part of the therapeutic relationship between patient and therapist that is realistic and free of distortion or transference elements (Greenson, 1978; Kiesler, 1996; Zetzel, 1956). Contemporary clinical writers and researchers have defined the therapeutic alliance as having three components: (a) the collaborative agreement between therapist and patient on goals of therapy, (b) an agreement on tasks of therapy or how the therapy will proceed, and (c) the affective bond between therapist and patient (Greenson, 1978). The therapeutic alliance is the most researched concept of psychotherapy. A recent meta-analysis of 296 studies indicated that the association between the therapeutic alliance and patient outcome was moderately large ($r = .29$) and highly reliable (Flückiger et al., 2018).

Therapeutic orientation, method of assessment of the alliance or outcomes, perspective of assessment (patient, therapist, observer), or time at which the alliance was measured had little impact on the degree of association between alliance and patient outcomes. There is also a growing consensus that a positive therapeutic alliance is a causal factor in determining patient outcomes for some (Zilcha-Mano, 2017).

Kiesler (1996) argued that a therapeutic alliance is established when therapists respond to patients in an interpersonally complementary manner at the outset of treatment, thereby allowing patients to feel that their concept of self is not threatened. Black et al. (2013) found that internalizing defenses, such as interpersonal withdrawal or attacking the self, erode the quality of intimate relationships, including the therapeutic alliance. Many individuals seeking group therapy are likely to possess an insecure attachment style (i.e., they harbor a negative view of self and/or a negative view of others) and so are apt to rely on internalizing defenses as a means of managing anxiety (for case examples, see Lo Coco et al., 2019).

A positive therapeutic alliance requires that at the core of the therapist's person, there exists a reverence for the struggle and vulnerability of the patient. The therapist's aim is to convey such respect in the face of a patient's defenses, distortions, transference reactions, and projections. As suggested earlier, in the context of group therapy, the therapist has the added challenge of creating an environment in which members experience and communicate this sense of reverence for each other and with the group as a whole.

This can be particularly challenging if a group includes several members whose interpersonal style falls within the hostile–dominant quadrant of the interpersonal circumplex (see Figure 1.4). Typically, these individuals possess a dismissing attachment style that tends to evoke a complementary hostile–submissive response from others, including the therapist (Pincus et al., 1999). If allowed to continue unabated, such complementary interactions may contribute to mistrust among group members and reduce their sense of safety and confidence in the therapist, thereby potentially leading to a poor alliance and outcomes (Samstag et al., 2008). The task of the therapist is to foster an alliance with a hostile–dominant patient early in treatment without reinforcing further hostility (Maxwell et al., 2012). Following from Tasca and McMullen's (1992) research, it is important for therapists to avoid hostile interactions to establish and maintain a therapeutic alliance. We suggest that therapists in this situation be selectively complementary with the hostile–dominant patient. That is, the therapist can maintain a friendly stance but complement the patient's dominance with a submissive stance (Maxwell et al., 2012). To foster a therapeutic alliance, a therapist must remain friendly on the affiliation dimension of the interpersonal circle but complement the patient on the status/power dimension (Figure 1.4). Later in treatment, the therapist may wish to be more friendly–dominant as a means of challenging the hostile–dominant patient's maladaptive interpersonal stance (more about that later).

As noted in Chapter 3, the therapeutic alliance can also be compromised through the enactment of microaggressions, particularly those occurring in response to themes of identity and diversity. These can take the form of subtle comments disguised as friendly banter, teasing, or joking. Alternatively, they may involve dismissing, minimizing, or even ignoring expressions of pain or anger arising out of experiences of exclusion, derogation, or injustice. An even more problematic form of microaggression is the passive-aggressive stance of victimhood that can serve to actively deter other patients from challenging or confronting self-limiting aspects of the victim's interpersonal stance. Interventions aimed at addressing microaggressions must be guided by the stage of group development, a topic that is incorporated in our discussion of stages of group development later in the chapter.

As indicated earlier, establishing a therapeutic alliance in part requires that therapists and patients develop a collaborative agreement on goals and tasks of therapy. This is aided by the therapist understanding the patient's case formulation based on the CMIP and the triangles of adaptation and object relations (Figure 1.2). As we described in Chapter 2 on pre-group assessment, the GPIP case formulation allows the therapist to articulate goals of therapy tailored to the individual patient (e.g., self-assertion, increasing behaviors to get attachment needs met, self-acceptance, more adaptive defense mechanisms, a less punitive introject). The tasks of GPIP follow from these goals, with group interactions serving as the primary vehicle of change aimed at (a) helping each patient develop a new understanding of self (i.e., introject), (b) exposing each patient to new interpersonal experiences in the group that challenge one's expectations of others and offer unfamiliar reactions of others to the self, and (c) encouraging each patient to risk engaging in new behaviors within the group that can ultimately generalize to other relationships in their life (acts of self).

THERAPEUTIC ALLIANCE RUPTURES AND REPAIRS IN GROUPS

Emerging evidence suggests that alliance ruptures are common in psychotherapy and that identifying and repairing therapeutic alliance ruptures can improve patients' outcomes (Eubanks et al., 2018). An alliance rupture occurs when there is a disagreement on tasks or goals of therapy or when there is a strain in the relational bond between therapist and patient. Alliance ruptures can take one of two forms. A *withdrawal rupture* occurs when the group member moves away from the group or therapist by being silent, evasive, or acquiescent. A *confrontation rupture* occurs when the group member moves against the group by lashing out or being hostile toward other patients or the therapist. An added complexity of working in group therapy is that alliance ruptures can occur between a member and another member, between a member and the group, or between a member and the therapist (Garceau et al., in press; Lo Coco et al., 2019). To illustrate, we provide the following example of Joe, an African American man in his late 20s, who experienced criticism, diminishment, or perceived mis-attunement from attachment figures in his life. In this early session of Joe's membership in the group, the therapist's response was misattuned to Joe's anxiety, which caused a withdrawal rupture.

JOE: To be honest, I was very reluctant to consider joining this group when Dr. Marks suggested it. I've often been put down by my parents and girlfriends—they seem only to see shortcomings in me. My last girlfriend was always on my case for not standing up to my mother, telling me I should be more of "a man." So, when Dr. Marks said that group therapy would give me an opportunity to get a better sense of how other people see me, I shuddered at the thought of more criticism. I just don't feel that I have the inner strength to deal with that at this point in my life.

THERAPIST: It sounds like one of the challenges for you here will be to let down your guard and try to be less defensive in order to really get the benefit of what the group can offer you.

JOE: Sure, I guess so [*Joe looks down and becomes silent*].

The therapist's response was ill-timed and recapitulated the very dynamic Joe feared. That is, Joe experienced the therapist as being critical and blaming by framing Joe's difficulty as one of defensiveness. This led to Joe becoming silent, and his desire to leave the group grew, thus signaling a withdrawal rupture. An intervention that is more in keeping with building an alliance or repairing the rupture would have been to underscore the courage Joe showed in taking the step of joining the group. Reparation of alliance ruptures might include the therapist clarifying misunderstandings among group members, taking responsibility for a misattuned statement, or helping members see how current interactions are consistent with problematic aspects of a patient's CMIP. However, as we discuss next, interpreting the CMIP is best kept for the middle stage of GPIP when group cohesion is well established. A key therapeutic skill for a GPIP therapist is to use meta-communication of the rupture event (i.e., commenting on how the rupture occurred and its interpersonal impact on the individual or group in the here and now) to increase group members' ability to reflect on the event and their role in precipitating or repairing the rupture. Had the therapist recognized Joe's silence as a withdrawal rupture, the therapist could have attempted to repair the rupture by first acknowledging that the comment was poorly timed, leading to Joe's withdrawal.

THERAPIST: Joe, I noticed that you looked hurt and became quite silent after my challenge. On reflection, I wonder if my comment felt like just another criticism—similar to what you've endured much of your life.

JOE: Yes, it did. This is exactly what I was afraid of and what made me so reluctant to join this group in the first place.

THERAPIST: It's clear that you're carrying a lot of hurt, and my comment added to that just now. I apologize. What strikes me is that despite the hurt you've been carrying, your willingness to be here shows real courage, and I really admire that.

It is key for the group therapist to recognize the individual's CMIPs and defense mechanisms as understandable but self-limiting ways of managing anxiety and perceived threat that have their basis in efforts to adapt to previous difficult life circumstances. As treatment progresses and the therapeutic alliance is strengthened, the therapist and group can work on the patient's CMIP in a gentle, yet therapeutic manner. Group therapists also must attend to member-to-member interactions that have the potential to reinforce distortions in the self-system that can contribute to alliance ruptures.

IDENTIFYING UNIVERSAL THEMES TO FOSTER AN ALLIANCE

Building a therapeutic alliance begins by identifying universal themes, such as feelings of brokenness, alienation, isolation, anxiety, or the various ways in which members have adapted to difficult life circumstances. Yalom and Leszcz (2020) identified *universality* (the shared life experiences of group members and the sense of not being alone in one's difficulties) as a key therapeutic factor in group treatment. The process of identifying universal themes starts at the point of introducing members to the group in which new members articulate the issues that led them to seek group therapy. Kiesler (1996) noted that a patient's introductory comments comprise "rehearsed" stories about one's problems and concerns. The stories are apt to contain both realistic and distorted aspects of the self. To foster the formation of a positive therapeutic alliance at this early juncture, the therapist must listen respectfully to both realistic and distorted parts of patients' narratives while selectively reinforcing the realistic and adaptive components.

Group therapists can further help to establish the therapeutic alliance and universality by connecting the seemingly disparate stories of members so that common themes and struggles emerge. This may be accomplished by attending to the content and detail of members' stories. Typically, these stories contain elements of the defense vertex of the triangle of adaptation (Figure 1.2). Establishing an alliance by focusing on universality also can be accomplished by attending to the affective tone with which the patients' narratives are told and retold. This generally comprises a mix of the attachment needs vertex and the affect pole of the triangle of adaptation (Figure 1.2). By using an interpersonal framework, GPIP therapists pay attention to the paralinguistic or nonverbal elements of communication, particularly when there is an apparent discrepancy between what a patient says and how they say it. Kiesler (1982, 1996) pointed out that an important axiom of interpersonal theory is that one cannot not communicate. Thus, silence, facial expression, vocal tone, rate of speech, and so forth, all convey relational information that can be considered in understanding the patient's and group's responses.

A final means a GPIP therapist has of fostering universality, and thereby solidifying the alliance, includes gentle, nonconfrontational *metacommunication* (i.e., comments about how people communicate and the interpersonal impact on others). Metacommunications are aimed at highlighting aspects of the group members' experience of their emerging relationships in the group, including the relationship with the therapist. Metacommunication may include cognitive, affective, and interpersonal impacts of the patients' narrative and thereby how patients communicate. In the early stage of group formation, therapist metacommunications may include comments about patients' ambivalence regarding the desire to connect and the need to assume certain roles, such as that of rescuer, authority, victim, teacher, or coach. In developing these interventions, GPIP therapists are guided by their knowledge of the patient's CMIP as gleaned in the pre-group assessment and how the CMIP defines two of the vertices of the triangle of object relations: current relationships with self and other and the therapist and group (see Figure 1.2). With regard to the clinical vignette described earlier, an alternative intervention by the therapist in response to Joe's trepidation about starting group would use metacommunication to foster universality:

THERAPIST: It's understandable that you'd feel apprehensive about joining the group, and you should know that others have expressed very similar feelings—so you are not alone. [*The therapist may invite others in the group to share their feelings about joining the group.*] I really admire the strength you've shown in taking this step and letting the group and me know that what you need is to be seen more fully as the man you are, not the person your girlfriend or your parents want you to be.

THERAPIST TASK BOX
THE THERAPEUTIC ALLIANCE

1. Be aware of patients' internalizing defenses and their eroding impact on intimacy and the therapeutic alliance.

2. To foster a therapeutic alliance early in treatment, complement a patient's interpersonal stance on the status dimension of the interpersonal circle but remain friendly on the affiliation dimension.

3. Use the triangle of adaptation and CMIP case formulation of the patient to come to an agreement with the patient on the goals and tasks of therapy.

4. Identify universal themes among group members.

5. Identify and repair therapeutic alliance ruptures if they occur member-to-member, member-to-group, or member-to-therapist.

6. Be attentive and responsive to instances of microaggression.

7. Attend to content, affective tone, and patterns of relating among patients.

8. Highlight emerging relationships within the group and with the therapist, and understand these in the context of each patient's CMIP.

9. At early stages, do not interpret patient behaviors in the context of the past, but stay in the here and now.

In the early stage of GPIP, particularly when conducting open-ended groups, it is prudent that therapists avoid metacommunications that refer to past relationships with others from the triangle of object relations (Figure 1.2). This could undermine the sense of safety necessary to establish an alliance by heightening feelings of vulnerability and contributing to patients feeling exposed. Alternatively, it might be experienced as confrontational rather than supportive by patients, contributing to an adversarial tone or climate in the group. The therapist's objective at this early stage is to reinforce the group norm of working in the present (here-and-now). Furthermore, the likelihood of offering interpretations or feedback that resonate with patients is greatly enhanced if therapists work with what is immediately observable rather than interpretations that require greater extrapolation and a level of self-reflection of which the patient may not yet be capable.

INTERPERSONAL COMPLEMENTARITY IN A GROUP CONTEXT

In the initial stages of group formation, most patients may experience a high degree of uncertainty and anxiety, much like Joe from the clinical vignette described earlier. Under conditions of uncertainty and perceived interpersonal threat, relational patterns and coping mechanisms tend to become more rigid (Kiesler, 1996). Hence, patients may seek a greater sense of security by relying on ways of coping and relating that are most familiar, even if they are maladaptive (e.g., the defense vertex of the triangle of adaptation, Figure 1.2). For example, an individual with histrionic personality traits may present in a more dramatic and exhibitionistic manner at the outset of treatment. An individual with paranoid traits may be more guarded, hypervigilant, critical, and silent. Someone with obsessive–compulsive traits may get lost in the details of their story and a need for control. In the face of the disequilibrium that comes with the anxiety common in early sessions of group therapy, each individual may unwittingly pull the therapist and other group members to respond in a manner that confirms their view of self and the world; that is, they may pull for complementary responses.

This dynamic illustrates the intersection between the triangle of adaptation and the triangle of object relations in the GPIP model. For example, Joe, who wishes to connect to others and to feel a sense of self-pride (attachment needs) but who has a history of receiving rejection or criticism from others, may experience anxiety (affect) as he joins the group.

He may start by minimizing his need for the group, and he may withdraw (defense). This intrapersonal dynamic had its origin in his relationships with his parents (past others), repeats itself in his relationship with his girlfriend (present others), and is evident in how he begins to engage with the group (therapist and group). The anxiety brought on by the new and unfamiliar group setting activates his preferred defenses that are intended to decrease anxiety. However, the dynamic perpetuates relationship patterns that reinforce Joe's original fears of expressing his attachment needs and activating affect. Figure 4.1 illustrates the triangle of adaptation and triangle of object relations and how they represent aspects of Joe's case formulation and experiences in relationships, including with the group.

Interpersonal theory posits two principles that emerge under these conditions. First, the more rigid interpersonal styles will prevail (Kiesler, 1996). In other words, individuals possessing a more intransigent character structure are more likely to "succeed" in moving others into a complementary response. Second, group members having interpersonal styles that are naturally complementary will be more engaged and aligned with one another (Kiesler, 1996). For example, an individual with a competitive interpersonal style (hostile–dominant quadrant of the interpersonal circumplex) will likely engage more with a group member who has an unassured or passive-aggressive interpersonal style (hostile–submissive quadrant).

FIGURE 4.1. Triangles of Adaptation and Object Relations as Part of Joe's Case Formulation

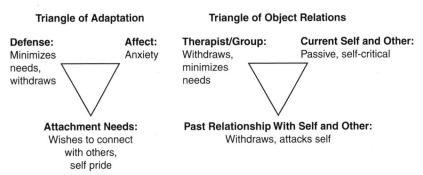

Triangle of Adaptation

Defense: Minimizes needs, withdraws

Affect: Anxiety

Attachment Needs: Wishes to connect with others, self pride

Triangle of Object Relations

Therapist/Group: Withdraws, minimizes needs

Current Self and Other: Passive, self-critical

Past Relationship With Self and Other: Withdraws, attacks self

Note. From "Group Psychodynamic Interpersonal Psychotherapy: Summary of a Treatment Model and Outcomes for Depressive Symptoms," by G. A. Tasca, S. F. Mikail, and P. L. Hewitt, in M. E. Abelian (Ed.), *Focus on Psychotherapy Research* (p. 165), 2005, Nova Science. Copyright 2005 by Nova Science. Adapted with permission.

See, for example, the two-headed arrows in Figure 1.4 that illustrate which behaviors are complementary. Therapists who can attend closely to these early behaviors will gain considerable insight into the personality dynamics of a given patient and their interaction patterns with other patients. This knowledge will help the therapist get a clearer picture of patients' CMIP. In the middle phases of group therapy, these observations form the basis of interventions in which the therapist intentionally links together two or more members whose interpersonal styles are not complementary to create the tension required to shift aspects of patients' relational patterns. We discuss this in further detail later. Next, we turn to the qualities of each stage of the GPIP group and the associated therapist tasks.

STAGES OF GROUP DEVELOPMENT IN GPIP

Group development is a product of the interactions among members of the group and their response to the therapist. Group interactions are defined and categorized by attending to two themes or levels related to the therapeutic alliance: the task level and the emotional level. *Task level* pertains to specific activities geared toward achieving the agreed-on outcome or objective of the group at a particular point in its existence. It reflects the reason the group exists and an agreement on how the group will work (a focus on relationship patterns and the here-and-now interactions within the group) and includes goals of individuals, as well as the group as a whole. The *emotional level* consists of how group members interrelate and their affective experience at a particular juncture in the life of the group. It comprises group norms, the emotional climate of the group, and the depth of relationships among members, including with the therapist.

In their most crude form, models of group development provide benchmarks regarding the progression of the group along these two dimensions or levels. Benchmark stages of development serve as organizing principles guiding the therapist's understanding of group interactions and related therapeutic tasks and objectives specific to the stage. A useful group development model identifies the optimal focus of group work, relevant tasks for therapists and participants, and expected interactions. Adhering to a group developmental model allows the therapist to steer the work of the group and prioritize the type of intervention necessary to achieve the goals specific to each stage. Factors that are considered to be therapeutically potent or curative at one stage of development may be inert or even iatrogenic at other points in the group's life.

Tuckman (1965) presented a model of group development that postulates four stages he termed forming, storming, norming, and performing. In a subsequent article, Tuckman and Jensen (1977) suggested that groups in which members share a defined end point progress through a fifth stage, termed adjourning. As noted previously, each stage is characterized by a combination of task level and emotional level benchmarks. Our research on time-limited versions of GPIP identified three empirically derived stages based on the development of group cohesion (Tasca, Ritchie, et al., 2006) and change in overall defensive functioning across therapy sessions (Hill et al., 2015). In both studies, GPIP resulted in an early increase in cohesion and change in defensive functioning, followed by a plateau in the middle stage, followed by a further increase in cohesion and decrease in defensive functions during the last stage. We suggested that the early stage was associated with therapist and group behaviors geared toward developing therapeutic norms, cohesion, and culture; the middle stage was associated with therapists challenging maladaptive patterns of relating to the self and others; and the late stage was focused on therapists and patients consolidating these changes (Tasca, Balfour, et al., 2006).

Our outcome and process research examining GPIP used 12- and 16-week time-limited groups in which three stages of group development were identified. In our view, GPIP is also a viable treatment modality for open-ended groups that use staggered or rolling admissions. We acknowledge that Tuckman's concept of stages of group development in open-ended GPIP groups has yet to be supported empirically. Nevertheless, Tuckman's stages are a useful heuristic for group therapists to aid in framing group interventions. Next, we elaborate and describe a stage model of GPIP that incorporates Tuckman's (Tuckman & Jensen, 1977) five stages rather than simply presenting the empirically derived three-stage model. We present this version based on Tuckman's conceptualization because it captures some of the nuances within the middle stage that are likely to occur in open-ended groups, but that may not be as apparent in time-limited groups.

THERAPIST TASK BOX
STAGES OF GROUP DEVELOPMENT

1. Use a stage model to conceptualize group development.
2. Adhere to the model to prioritize interventions and manage anxiety.
3. Understand the stages of development to develop optimal interventions.

Stage 1: Forming

The first hours of the group's life are dominated by an effort to define the task of the group. During the pre-group preparation meeting with a patient, therapists will have discussed group rules and how group therapy works, provided each member with an overview of their unique CMIP, and discussed individualized treatment goals based on the GPIP case formulation. Nevertheless, the anxiety inherent in the first few sessions of treatment contributes to an effort by some patients to clarify and possibly refine the rules and primary objectives of the group. For example, some patients may state that their treatment goal is to resolve grief, improve their self-esteem, or learn strategies to manage stress. Although each of these is a legitimate focus for treatment, the overriding assumption of the GPIP group therapist is that patients' difficulties arise from transdiagnostic factors such as problems in their important relationships, including the relationship with the self. Given this assumption, the central focus of a GPIP group is to understand and examine the interpersonal (i.e., components of the CMIP and vertices of the triangle of object relations) and intrapersonal (i.e., vertices of the triangle of adaptation) patterns of group members and how these pattern interface with patients' presenting complaints.

During Stage 1, forming, patients tend to focus on identifying behaviors deemed to be acceptable within the group and to the therapist. Much of the communication that occurs at this stage is therapist focused. In other words, patients typically direct their comments to the therapist and are most concerned with the leader's judgment of them. In their efforts to determine what is acceptable, patients are most responsive to cues from the therapist and much slower to engage directly with peers. As we discuss next, managing this process appropriately is critical to establishing adaptive therapeutic norms that will facilitate growth.

A related dynamic revolves around patients' search for structure. This involves "living" the agreement that was outlined during the pre-group preparation session, as well as becoming familiar with the rules of engagement in the group. Questions that are often on the minds of patients include the following: How long am I allowed to speak? Do we take turns speaking? Is everyone expected to say something during the session? Do we offer solutions and answers to others' questions? An important task in which the group is engaged during this stage is to define the type of information and the manner of interacting that is needed and valued by the therapist.

At the emotional level, group members are faced with a number of challenges. Each patient must accommodate a shift in status from being an individual in relation to the therapist to being a member of a group.

Having to make room for others in one's relationship with the therapist can serve to recapitulate early family dynamics of sibling rivalry for some individuals and awaken emotions that are not fully recognized. For some members with attachment-related issues of competition, fear of judgment, need for approval, or preoccupation with relationship loss, early recapitulation of family dynamics in the group will be reflected in the components of their CMIP. Relatedly, group members must explore the extent to which dependence on the group leader is acceptable and/or tolerable. Members may seek out information regarding expectations, such as the expected level of self-disclosure, amount of historical material to be shared, and how to resolve conflict and competing needs.

For most people, clarity on these issues emerges through hesitant participation. Although it is important for therapists to respect the pace with which each member participates, the therapist must also serve as a catalyst and guide the group through this stage by gently challenging members to go beyond their polite and understandably cautious exchanges. Patients whose developmental history has been marked by enmeshment, sexual abuse, or other forms of blurred interpersonal boundaries can present in quite the opposite manner by being indiscriminately self-disclosing. In these instances, the therapist must be equally active in aiding these patients to maintain a sense of dignity and avoid pseudo intimacy that can contribute to intolerable anxiety, followed by a desire to withdraw.

Invite Group Members to Engage
In Stage 1, forming, the leader has two primary objectives. At the level of the individual, the task is to help each patient increase their capacity for self-observation and judicious self-disclosure. At the level of the group-as-a-whole, the primary objective is to foster cohesion and the formation of a group identity. The therapist begins by inviting group members to introduce themselves. How members approach the introduction reveals important aspects of their CMIP. For example, some members might choose to focus on the nature of their work, others may emphasize their symptoms, and others might speak of previous ineffective treatments in which they engaged. Depending on the tone with which this latter focus is expressed, it may represent a subtle form of microaggression toward the therapist if the patient perceives differences with the therapist's culture or identity. Overt microaggressions are less likely to be enacted during Stage 1, forming. If they do occur, they tend to be directed toward the therapist. At this stage of the group, expressions of microaggressions are most effectively managed by focusing on the triangle of adaptation and empathizing with the patient's unfulfilled attachment needs.

Each introduction offers a glimpse into the interpersonal and inner world of the speaker, how they define themselves, and the defense mechanisms they engage in to manage anxiety. Similarly, each introduction will have a particular interpersonal impact on other members of the group. Therapists can glean a great deal about a patient's relational style and self-concept through these early interactions by considering whether they draw others near, push others away, evoke indifference, or convey a stance of dominance or submission. Therapists can draw on this information to further their understanding of the patient's CMIP—that is, how each individual is likely to relate to others in the group and how others may respond. During the forming stage, therapists should limit their use of this information to refining their conceptualization of the patient's CMIP. That is, we recommend that at this juncture in the life of the group, therapists not yet describe, interpret, or confront a given group member's interpersonal dynamics (CMIP). Rather, emphasis should be placed on identifying aspects of the triangle of adaptation (e.g., attachment needs, anxiety, defenses). In as much as possible, therapists should use empathic reflection to underscore shared emotional experiences and needs among group members.

> During the introductions, Diane, a rather shy and interpersonally submissive White woman in her 50s, stated that she had struggled with her weight and body image for her entire life. She became tearful as she recounted instances in which she believed her weight contributed to the failure of her marriage and interfered with career advancement. A subtle hint of anger became evident in her voice as she described how ugly she feels and what an outcast she has been throughout her life.

Figure 4.2 illustrates how this brief self-description begins to inform the therapist's understanding of Diane's CMIP.

> Another group member, Susan, an Asian American woman in her late 40s who has a pattern of interpersonal enmeshment in relationships and rigid, overbearing nurturance of others, began to reassure Diane that she has "a lovely face, and an even more beautiful heart" and a flawless complexion. Susan stated to Diane, "I'm sure you are very competent at work, and I can't imagine that men wouldn't be attracted to you."

Figure 4.3, indicates possible aspects of Susan's CMIP based on this brief description of her interactions with Diane.

> It was evident that Susan could not tolerate Diane's expression of sadness and despair. Susan assumed an interpersonal stance that was familiar to her—that of caretaker (friendly–dominant on the interpersonal circle). Her response to Diane, a woman she did not know yet, was placating and inauthentic and had the potential to minimize Diane's pain and push her away. At this point, the therapist commented to Susan, "It seems that you are very attuned to

FIGURE 4.2. Illustration of Diane's Cyclical Maladaptive Interpersonal Pattern

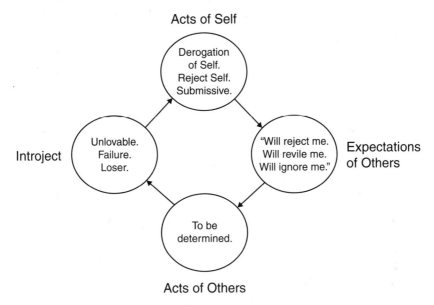

Acts of Self

Derogation of Self. Reject Self. Submissive.

Introject

Unlovable. Failure. Loser.

"Will reject me. Will revile me. Will ignore me."

Expectations of Others

To be determined.

Acts of Others

Note. From *Perfectionism: A Relational Approach to Conceptualization, Assessment, and Treatment* (p. 163), by P. L. Hewitt, G. L. Flett, and S. F. Mikail, 2017, Guilford Press. Copyright 2017 by Guilford Press. Adapted with permission.

FIGURE 4.3. Illustration of Susan's Cyclical Maladaptive Interpersonal Pattern

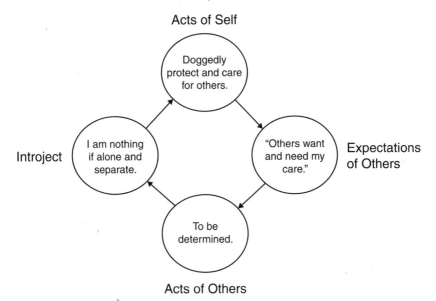

Acts of Self

Doggedly protect and care for others.

Introject

I am nothing if alone and separate.

"Others want and need my care."

Expectations of Others

To be determined.

Acts of Others

Note. From *Perfectionism: A Relational Approach to Conceptualization, Assessment, and Treatment* (p. 163), by P. L. Hewitt, G. L. Flett, and S. F. Mikail, 2017, Guilford Press. Copyright 2017 by Guilford Press. Adapted with permission.

Diane's pain and that you would like to comfort her. The challenge for the group will be to allow Diane and others to be with their pain." The therapist then turned to Diane and commented, "And for you, Diane, your presence in this group will be an opportunity to see yourself through the eyes of others as they see you rather than what you believe they see."

The focus of this intervention was for the therapist to acknowledge Susan's efforts to connect with Diane and to support her in those efforts. At the same time, the therapist intended to establish and model useful group therapeutic norms by encouraging group members to tolerate the discomfort of intense affect and by underscoring the centrality of interpersonal feedback to redefine one's introject. Note that the therapist refrained from commenting on Susan's dynamic of rigid caretaking because it would have been too challenging for Susan at this early point in the group's development.

As indicated earlier, one of the therapist's primary objectives is to create a sense of safety and cohesion in the group. Thus, interpreting CMIPs is ill-advised during the forming stage. Rather, therapists should primarily focus on the adaptive components of members' communication and defenses. In doing so, the leader can draw on Benjamin's (1993) view that defense mechanisms and rigid interpersonal patterns emerge out of an effort to protect the integrity of the self. These coping mechanisms may well have been reasonable ways of surviving an unreasonable set of circumstances in the past. Over time, however, these interaction patterns and defense mechanisms become internalized, habitual, and indiscriminately applied to current situations that present no apparent threat to the self.

Had the interaction occurred at a more advanced stage of group development (e.g., Stage 2: Storming), the therapist's intervention would have been quite different. At that juncture, the principles of GPIP would guide the therapist to use an intervention that disrupts the self-limiting nature of both patients' CMIP. Susan's compulsive caretaking and overbearing nurturance may be a means of feeling relevant and warding off the pain of isolation. Yet, her efforts to connect with others often lead to the very loneliness she fears by pushing others away (Figure 4.3). Diane, however, views herself as undesirable, irrelevant, and having no place in the lives of others, a position that contributes to a painful fear of asserting herself and expressing her emotional needs (Figure 4.2).

Typically, defense mechanisms are triggered by anxiety or fear from a perceived threat or a heightened sense of stress. The early forming stage, particularly the first session, is often a stressful situation for participants.

As Beck et al. (1986) suggested, at this stage, members are focused on assessing each other, each estimating their own ability to cope with the experience and demands of the group. The templates with which these assessments are made reflect core components of the patient's CMIP.

THERAPIST TASK BOX

STAGE 1: FORMING. INVITE GROUP MEMBERS TO ENGAGE

1. Note how patients enact their CMIPs in interactions with other members of the group.

2. Encourage patients to move beyond polite, cautious engagement or indiscriminate self-disclosure in support of adaptive group norms.

3. Task level: (a) Invite group members to introduce themselves, (b) do not interpret CMIP at this stage.

4. Emotional level: Emphasize the adaptive component of members' communications and defenses as a means of establishing a sense of safety.

Create a Sense of Safety

Therapists can foster a sense of safety by emphasizing two components of the triangle of adaptation: attachment needs and affects, both of which may represent shared experiences among group members. In doing so, the therapist can connect group members according to their intrapersonal, as well as interpersonal, dynamics. Thus, therapists can underline patients' common struggles, fears, hurts, wishes, and hopes.

Hostility, such as verbal attacks, pejorative language, or passive-aggressive statements, is corrosive to creating a sense of safety in the group. Parenthetically, we encourage therapists not to equate the expression of anger with hostility. A group member expressing anger in the first person in a way that is acknowledged and owned by the speaker reveals the self in a state of vulnerability and, in turn, has the potential to deepen intimacy among group members.

Binder and Strupp (1997) demonstrated that the emotional tone of the first three sessions of psychotherapy is critical to treatment success. Their research demonstrated that sessions characterized by hostility and the use of pejorative language by the therapist (or other group members) are associated with a negative outcome (see also Tasca & McMullen, 1992). Reversing the effects of hostile within-group interactions can be difficult once they have occurred. This speaks to the importance of therapists focusing on the adaptive aspects of each group member's interpersonal style. This may prove challenging, particularly if the group is composed of a number of members that engage in a hostile and/or disengaging manner. The temptation for the therapist is to shut down or silence these group members in a complementary response to the patient's hostility; however, doing so may be experienced by the group as a form of reciprocal hostility. Often, a patient's hostility can be understood as a defense against the fear of being humiliated or overwhelmed despite their attachment needs. A useful therapist intervention with a patient engaged in hostile interactions might be, "Although a part of you would like to connect to others in here, it seems that most of your energy is going into simply trying to feel safe with us." In this example, the therapist focused her intervention on components of the triangle of adaptation by identifying the attachment need (longing to connect), the affect (fear of rejection or abandonment), and the associated defense (hostile attack or outward rejection of others). Once again, we underscore the importance of therapists not articulating the patient's CMIP at this early stage because that may heighten anxiety and invite either premature termination or further hostility as a means of defending the self.

In contrast to anxious hostility, some group members may assume a stance of rigid friendliness (identified as friendly–dominant on the interpersonal circumplex). This also can be understood as a defensive posture aimed at diluting intense affect and avoiding authentic connection. The defensive nature of intrusive friendliness can erode intimacy or distract the group from deep emotions, as was illustrated in the case of Susan described earlier. In some ways, this friendly–dominant interpersonal style can be more difficult to manage therapeutically. For one thing, being friendly, particularly in the early stages of relationships, is consistent with accepted social norms. The acceptability of such behavior combined with the ease that it evokes in others may obscure the defensive and self-limiting elements of this interpersonal style. Therapists are likely to be drawn to patients that assume this stance, particularly if the therapist is feeling uncertain or anxious. Conversely, therapists who attempt to interpret this relational style too early in the group's development run the risk of alienating group members and evoking more defensiveness. That is, members may begin to feel that every aspect of their behavior is open to interpretation, thereby leading to a lack of safety.

Rigid friendliness can be handled in a similar way as hostility. The emphasis should be placed on the adaptive component of the behavior (i.e., friendliness [defense] to diminish fear related to the possibility of attack and/or rejection [affect] and/or a deep longing to belong [attachment need]). Despite the longing for connection, the defensive behavior results in avoidance of intimacy (acts of self), often driven by a belief that the self is deficient (introject). An individual entering into a close interpersonal relationship while viewing the self as deficient may harbor a fear that their deficiencies will be exposed and a belief that abandonment by others and isolation will surely follow (expectation of others). The therapist can intervene by commenting,

> It seems that you are putting a lot of effort into making others feel at ease in the group, which I think is familiar to you and allows you to find your way in these new relationships. I hope that you will gradually give equal voice to your needs so that we have the opportunity of encountering the richness of who you are.

Comments such as this one may normalize the patient's behavior and permit group members to assess the climate before prematurely exposing their vulnerability.

THERAPIST TASK BOX
STAGE 1: FORMING. CREATE A SENSE OF SAFETY

1. Use the GPIP case formulation to understand each person's early interactions in the group relative to defense mechanisms and acts of self.
2. Refrain from interpreting the CMIP or the triangle of adaptation at this stage.

Task Level

3. Emphasize the adaptive component of behavior and defenses.

Emotional Level

4. Underline common struggles, fears, hopes, and wishes among group members.
5. Identify fears or interpersonal intents beneath any hostility or overly friendly behaviors.

Establish Adaptive Norms

During Stage 1, forming, the therapist is also focused on establishing a set of norms that will facilitate group therapeutic goals. The most central norms include

- being willing to self-disclose and self-reflect;
- verbally expressing affect, fantasy, and impulses, rather than acting out;

- providing interpersonal feedback to group members and the therapist;
- respecting interpersonal boundaries; and
- being willing to remain in the here-and-now.

Although the importance of each of these norms will have been discussed in pre-group preparation sessions, therapists must actively reinforce these behaviors in the first part of the group's life. This may include therapists encouraging patients to speak to each other rather than to the therapist, asking patients to speak in the first person when describing feelings and reactions, redirecting patients to within-group interactions if they focus only on events outside the group, having patients describe their feelings or bodily sensations rather than only their behaviors, asking patients to consider what internal state (attachment needs or affect) led them to behave in a certain manner, and encouraging patients to consider the motivations of others, including those in the group. As we indicated previously, in the early stage, group members look to therapists for what is appropriate behavior, and so therapists focusing on, responding to, and emphasizing desired norms will reinforce and help shape these norms in the group. The reader will find examples of such therapist behaviors to establish adaptive norms in the American Psychological Association video of GPIP (Mikail & Tasca, 2021).

THERAPIST TASK BOX
STAGE 1: FORMING. ESTABLISH ADAPTIVE NORMS

1. Establish adaptive norms of self-disclosure, self-reflection, verbal expression of affect, interpersonal feedback, respect of boundaries, and here-and-now focus.
2. Reinforce these behaviors in the early part of the group.

Encourage Self-Disclosure and Self-Reflection

Self-disclosure, especially if authentic, can be difficult, even when interacting with others who are familiar. And so, self-disclosure can be particularly anxiety provoking within the context of group therapy, especially in the early stages. Patients with self-limiting interpersonal patterns often harbor feelings of shame that extend beyond regret about past actions, decisions, or failures. Often, their shame is about their very being (Saha et al., 2011). As a consequence, statements about the self are likely to be guarded and superficial at first. Repeated interpersonal conflict in patients' lives may contribute to chronic feelings of guilt or anger (affects); a belief that the self is flawed, bad, and undesirable (introject); or that others cannot be trusted or relied on for acceptance and care (expectations of others).

In light of these negative introjects, it is not unusual for affirmation and compliments from others to evoke in the patient unpleasant affects and a state of dissonance. Compliments or expressions of support from others may be experienced by some patients as discordant with their negative introject. And so, the self-pride (attachment needs) that such statements may awaken in the patient could result in anxiety or fear (affect). The latter is often resolved through defensive operations, including the dismissal of positive interpersonal feedback, interpersonal retreat, use of contradiction, or escalation of behaviors that have the effect of pushing others away or shutting them down. This pattern reaffirms a patient's view that the self is flawed and unworthy (introject). Overlearned defensive responses usually operate outside the individual's awareness; that is, they tend to be automatic. Such behaviors can be understood as efforts to protect and maintain the integrity of the individual's self-system (Sullivan, 1953), thereby allowing a state of homeostasis that reduces or manages difficult affect.

Encouraging self-disclosure in a group may require therapists to selectively direct and reinforce such behaviors among group members. Group members may not know how much and to what extent to disclose, and so therapists must make a judgment about what quantity and quality of disclosure are therapeutic. Early in groups, it is key for therapists to evoke self-disclosure that provides enough information about the individual but that does not leave the patient feeling overexposed. If a therapist is concerned about the potential for a patient overdisclosing leading to shame, the therapist can slow down the patient, ask about their level of comfort or anxiety with what they have said so far, or ask other group members to comment or react. Conversely, if a patient is reluctant to disclose, the therapist may decide not to pressure the patient but rather rely on other group members to model the benefits of self-disclosure.

Self-reflection involves patients asking questions to understand themselves and their behaviors as determined by their mental states. It requires a sense of curiosity about the self and a willingness to consider new ways of understanding one's behaviors, feelings, and relational patterns. GPIP therapists can use their case formulation of patients based on the CMIP and the triangles to gently encourage patients to consider why they behaved in a certain way, what they may be feeling, or why they might have responded defensively. The therapist can model self-reflection by asking such questions, judiciously disclosing their hunches and reactions, and engaging others in the group in the process of trying to understand a group member's behaviors, thoughts, and feelings. For example, a therapist may ask the group, "Jane is having trouble identifying her feelings about her argument with her husband. What do you imagine Jane could be feeling about the argument?" or "How would you feel in that situation?"

In this instance, the therapist's intervention invited the group to engage in the process of mentalizing—that is, for patients to access their capacity to consider the mental state of another person and one's own and see these mental states as separate from one's behaviors yet potentially causing behaviors (Bateman & Fonagy, 2006; p. 70).

Foster Genuineness and Authenticity

It is critical for group therapists to note and respond to individuals' defensive behaviors in the early stages of the group's life. Failure to do so allows for the emergence of group norms that reinforce maladaptive patterns of relating to the self and others. Earlier, we emphasized the importance of guarding against the therapist's or other group members' use of pejorative language, pathologizing, or criticizing other members. However, it is equally important to address the criticisms that patients make toward the self. In doing so, the therapist must diffuse the patient's hostility toward the self (introject) without reprimanding or sounding confrontational or hostile. Rather, therapists must remain steadfast in their efforts to

- solidify the therapeutic alliance (agreement on goals and tasks and affective bond),
- establish adaptive norms, and
- create an atmosphere of safety.

The overall goal is for group members to grow toward a state of authenticity in which the hidden and suppressed aspects of the self and attachment needs can be encountered or experienced with less fear and without repulsion. To this end, group therapists can rely on what Rowe and MacIsaac (1991) referred to as *expanding attunement*, a process that requires "continuous empathic immersion in the patient's shifting states of thinking and feeling" (pp. 136–137). Through this process, the therapist distills the meaning of the individual's thoughts, feelings, fantasies, needs, and impulses that are aspects of the attachment needs vertex of the triangle of adaptation and the acts of self component of the patient's CMIP. At times, it may be sufficient for therapists to summarize the unspoken meaning implied by the patient's communication. For example, a group therapist might say,

> It seems that there is a part of you that you would like to destroy [*acts of self in response to a negative introject*]. My impression is that you have borrowed words from another time that others said to you [*internalization of acts of others that reinforce and maintain the negative introject and result in aversive affects*]. I invite you to be gentler with yourself here as you move forward in your work with the group.

The last comment in this statement serves multiple functions: (a) for the patient, it counters their expectations of others and invites alternate acts of self, and (b) for the group, it establishes an adaptive norm and creates a sense of safety in the face of hostility toward the self.

Primarily, the goal is for patients to know their attachment needs and experience less aversive affects without requiring the distortions of maladaptive defenses. This may include therapists helping patients to act in ways that are consistent with the way they are feeling, express attachment needs directly, say what they mean without fear of reprisal or shame, and take in information and feedback from others without the distortion caused by defenses or their expectations of others.

Use Metacommunication

An effective intervention for GPIP therapists involves metacommunication by identifying the interpersonal intent and interpersonal impact of a patient's statement or behavior. Metacommunication can be used when the therapist attempts to keep two or more group members focused on either the affiliative or disengaged or hostile elements of their interactions. A therapist can encourage patients to voice their intentions or motivations that give rise to affirming statements. For example, in responding to a compliment John offered to Rita about how nice she looked on this particular day, the group therapist could say to John, "I can see that you want to get close to her. I wonder whether you'd be willing to tell her that directly just now."

In this instance, the therapist is reinforcing an adaptive group norm that invites group members to express their feelings and desires directly rather than enacting them indirectly. At the same time, the metacommunication encourages John to try out new acts of self that serve to counter the expectation that expressing a desire for connection and closeness will be met with dismissal and rejection (expectations of others).

Similarly, metacommunication by highlighting the self-protective components of hostile behavior can short-circuit the potential for disengagement among patients that can create more distance and a chronic state of threat within the group. The leader can address Rita's retreat from John by giving voice to both sides of her ambivalence:

> Part of you is hungry to hear more of the kind of thing that John is saying to you. At the same time, part of you is terrified and unsure of the risk involved in seeing yourself through John's eyes and what it might mean if you allowed yourself to feel connected to him.

The "public" nature of group therapy leads to a multitude of negative reactions in response to invitations to engage in self-reflection and self-disclosure. These include feelings of anxiety, fear, irritation, or numbness (affects). Most group members are likely to experience internal conflict between their expressed desires for change and the feelings of safety and familiarity afforded by guarding their established ways of relating and defending the self. The resulting tension manifests in the appearance of interpersonal ambivalence and variability in the degree to which patients engage and disengage with others in the group. If allowed to continue without comment by the therapist, such a climate dilutes the individual's commitment and identification with the group. For example, members may silently compare themselves with others, viewing others as "sicker" or more in need of help. Or they may feel that the group cannot meet their therapeutic or relational needs. These reactions distance individuals from the group as a whole and erode efforts by the therapist to forge a sense of group identity and cohesion. Therapists can move the process forward by looking for opportunities to give voice to this inner tension and ambivalence as it becomes apparent for various members of the group. In doing so, the patient's ambivalence is normalized and reframed as an adaptation.

In introducing himself, a group member commented,

> My problems don't seem so bad compared to what everyone else has said. I came here thinking that I was a real loser. But the fact is I have a wife and children that love me; I have a good job and a nice house. So really, there is nothing to complain about. Maybe I just need to stop whining, get back to basics, and get on with life.

The group therapist can respond to this scenario in several ways, including the following:

> It sounds like you have a number of things to be proud of. At the same time, you have a number of needs and struggles that were the reason for your decision to come here. Perhaps, right now, those needs and struggles are overshadowed by the anxiety of walking in this room and assessing whether it will be safe to express those needs openly in here. My impression is that you are not alone in that and that several people are struggling with that very same thing.

Alternatively, the leader may make a comment that strikes at the heart of the ambivalence:

> As each of you [*speaking to the group as a whole*] is trying to find your footing in here, it's understandable that you might feel some trepidation and anxiety in trying to connect and share your struggles openly with people you just met.

Use Group-as-a-Whole Interventions

Patients may experience the latter metacommunication as more challenging and anxiety provoking. It exposes the process of the group as seen through the eyes of the therapist and reiterates a basic expectation of group therapy to patients. The use of such group-as-a-whole interventions in the early stage of group development invites individual members to view themselves as being part of a collective. Therapists injecting a tone of "we-ness" about the group experience may be both welcomed and threatening for group members. Typically, therapists' group-as-a-whole interventions are aimed at connecting members to one another and increasing identification with the entire group. Two forms of group-as-a-whole statements have been described in the literature: deductive and inductive. Ezriel (1973) suggested a *deductive approach* to group-as-a-whole interventions, whereby a therapist identifies a concern that is shared by the group (or most of the members), followed by the therapist exploring how individual patients relate to it. For example, a therapist might say, "The group is angry with me today. I wonder whether it feels safe enough in here for each of you to tell me directly about your anger."

Alternatively, Horwitz (1977) described an *inductive approach* to group-as-a-whole statements in which the group therapist responds to an individual concern, links some aspect of the concern (content, affect, interpersonal impact) to the experience of another member, and gradually moves toward identifying a group-level issue. For example, a therapist might say,

> Cindy, it seems that you have been feeling very angry with your boss for making you feel controlled. That sounds a lot like John's experience with his father last week. . . . [*Wait for both members to share more of their reactions with each other*] I wonder whether the group is angry with the parent figure in this room.

Both deductive and inductive group-as-a-whole interventions draw on the vertices of the triangle of object relations (Figure 1.2), with the therapist's statement emphasizing the here-and-now relationship between patients and group and the therapist. In so doing, the therapist communicates several critical messages: (a) "I can tolerate and even welcome expressions of anger or other feelings that are directed at me," (b) "The group is a safe place to take interpersonal risks," and (c) "Anger, conflict, or other affects are an expected and acceptable part of healthy relationships." If the group's anger was triggered by an empathic failure by the therapist (or some other therapeutic error), the therapist should communicate humility and a willingness to acknowledge her or his humanness, as was illustrated earlier in the chapter when the therapist used an ill-timed confrontation to challenge Joe's ambivalence about group therapy.

The impact of group-as-a-whole interventions is somewhat paradoxical. Such interventions communicate empathic attunement with an individual's subjectively felt personal experience, while underlining the universality of the experience in a manner that builds on the collective identity of the group as a whole. The choice of deductive versus inductive group-as-a-whole interventions depends on the dynamics of the individual members. Brabender and Fallon (1993) suggested that if the majority of members show a greater propensity for isolation and overt fear about group involvement, it is more advisable to use inductive group-as-a-whole intervention in the early stages.

THERAPIST TASK BOX
STAGE 1: FORMING. FOSTER THERAPEUTIC NORMS

1. Gently note and respond to defensive behaviors early in the group to promote self-disclosure and self-reflection.
   - Highlight the self-protective component of hostile or defensive behaviors.
   - Address criticisms group members make toward self and others.
   - Give voice to inner conflict stirring within individuals.
2. Use metacommunication to identify and state the interpersonal intent or impact of a patient's statement or behavior.
3. Use deductive or inductive group-as-a-whole interventions to encourage a view of the individual as part of a collective.

Build Cohesion

Building a sense of "we-ness" and attraction to the group is critical in Stage 1, forming. Research has demonstrated that greater cohesion is related to better patient outcomes in groups (Burlingame et al., 2018). Research in social psychology has demonstrated that people who perceive themselves as having shared experiences or goals tend to feel a greater degree of connection to one another (e.g., Widmeyer & Ducharme, 1997). Developing cohesion tends to be an easier task when conducting groups that are homogenous with respect to presenting concerns. However, regardless of group composition, the therapist can foster cohesion by deliberately drawing the attention of patients to aspects of their shared experience: "It's evident that a number of people in this group have struggled with feelings of isolation and shame and seeing yourself as inherently flawed."

In this intervention, the therapist drew on the universality of distorted introjects that is prevalent among patients referred to group therapy. Similarly, summaries, reflections, and other interventions can be aimed at highlighting shared goals: "The group would like to find ways to join the rest of the world in feeling that it's okay to be fully yourselves in relationships."

Here the therapist focused on the triangle of adaptation by identifying the unfulfilled attachment needs and the longing for healthy connection. Therapists can also build cohesion by connecting smaller groups or pairs of individuals: "John, it sounds like your experience growing up is very similar to what Pat described earlier" or "Both of you seem to want to feel less afraid and more alive in your marriages."

The risk associated with this latter type of intervention is the possibility of creating antitherapeutic subgroups (Yalom & Leszcz, 2020). However, the group therapist can easily include the group-as-a-whole by following such statements with the question "I wonder whether others share the same experience or wish?"

THERAPIST TASK BOX
STAGE 1: FORMING. BUILD COHESION

1. Draw attention to aspects of group members' shared experiences.
2. Highlight shared goals.
3. Connect smaller groups or pairs of individuals based on common themes.

Stage 2: Storming

The storming stage is marked by an increase in interpersonal tension. Members begin to compete with each other and the leader for time, attention, and dominance. For some, this may be an enactment of a CMIP characterized by competition with peers and siblings or anger and resentment toward a parental figure. These dynamics can contribute to increased member-to-member conflict or expressions of disapproval toward the therapist. Individuals may resist the assumed roles and ideas of other members (expectations of others), leading some to become silent and passive while others become increasingly vocal and sometimes hostile (acts of self). From the vantage point of the individual patient, the primary task is one of individuation. For some patients, the need to distinguish themselves from others in the group is a function of anxiety evoked by therapist interventions intended to foster cohesion and identification with the group. This anxiety is common, yet the dynamics giving rise to it are unique to each person. For example, patients whose attachment style is predominantly dismissing will mistrust invitations to identify with the experiences of other patients because the dismissing patient views others as ill-equipped to respond to their needs (attachment needs, expectation of others). Those with a preoccupied attachment style may monopolize a session through the urgent expression of their needs and distress (acts of self) but with little room for mutuality that betrays a view of self as inadequate (introject).

The storming stage is characterized by a reduction in or a plateauing of cohesion (Tasca, Balfour, et al., 2006). Individual objectives and needs take on greater prominence and become framed as unique. During this stage, microaggressions become more prominent. When enacted by a given patient toward the group, they are apt to take the form "I am not like you, nor will I ever be." This can either betray a stance of superiority or self-protection. In contrast, microaggressions that occur at a more dyadic (member-to-member) level typically are overt expressions of rejection or efforts to exclude a specific other, such as "you are not one of us." In both instances, the most effective interventions by therapists are those that address attachment-related anxiety. Here, the clinician must look beyond the surface statements to the underlying emotions that may not be within the patient's conscious awareness.

Some clinicians refer to this as the phase of "terminal uniqueness," during which some patients view their struggles and needs as distinct and perhaps beyond the comprehension of others in the group, including the therapist. Other patients may express unattainable goals, including expecting people in their lives to change their behavior or personality. Patients whose CMIPs are characterized by issues of struggle with authority and power may challenge the therapist by expressing concerns about what they perceive the group and/or the leader is pushing them to do.

These dynamics are generally outside conscious awareness for most patients. They involve enacting one's prototypic pattern of relating, and in so doing, they confirm long-held views about the self and world as expressed by the patients' CMIP. Some patients exhibit increased rigidity and patterns of relating that are polarizing, whereas others may actively resist the subjective experience of "we-ness" or belonging with the group that is key to group cohesion to protect their individuality. Some patients insist that their needs are not being met in the group, whereas others preserve individuality through infighting, defensiveness, or competitiveness. In essence, the group may become engaged in an effort to establish a hierarchy, sometimes giving rise to a climate of disunity, jealousy, and subgrouping.

Beck et al. (1986) called this the stage of personal influence and survival. The hallmark of Stage 2, storming, is a heightened intrapersonal and interpersonal tension. As group therapists work through this period in the life of the group, it is helpful to be mindful that the histories of most individuals entering group therapy are filled with experiences of disappointment and hurt in significant relationships and groups. Thus, the insistence on individuation reflects a relational ambivalence characterized by a simultaneous longing for acceptance (attachment needs) and fear (affects) of connection with both self and others. As individuals are exposed to the narratives of other group members and the unifying statements of the group therapist, they encounter an image of self (introject) that is reflected in the painful disclosures of fellow group members. Such encounters are both comforting and disturbing. On the one hand, the universality of shared disappointments, hurts, fears, and disillusionment diminishes the pain of isolation and rejection. On the other hand, coming face to face with emotions that one has worked hard to contain through repression, avoidance, distraction, or any number of defense mechanisms can be a most unwelcome encounter. It is at this point that patients are most vulnerable to premature termination. Each individual is faced with the task of choosing between relinquishing well-learned, familiar, and comforting defenses, or maintaining their current maladaptive means of being in the world. The degree of anxiety that emerges from this internal conflict may contribute to increased symptoms, which can serve as another precipitant to premature termination.

JACKIE: So, I have some doubts I want to bring to the group. I've been struggling about whether I want to continue. I think my doubt is that I'm not sure that this group has been all that helpful so far. Part of it is that I would prefer a process that has a clearer marker that I'm getting it, but so far, the only marker I have is the number of weeks we've met. I tried to assess the cost in coming, given the traffic and other demands. If I was certain that it would be helpful, I would drive twice the distance.

Instead, I feel frustrated and disappointed that we are half-way through, and it feels like nothing has changed. This is a renowned clinic, so I expected quicker and clearer answers, but I'm afraid that I may get to the end of my time here without anything changing. It's very uncomfortable for me to say all this, but I had to say it.

THERAPIST: It takes a lot of courage to share those feelings so openly. What I'm hearing is that we haven't given you what you feel you need. Can you say more about the discomfort you're feeling in sharing this with us?

JACKIE: Well, I think it's a mix of anger and frustration. Without having some clear way of assessing this process, my doubt just gets bigger. This is supposed to be a cutting-edge clinic that's produced all sorts of research about the kind of issues that I'm struggling with. Yet, that knowledge isn't being shared, and instead, we're told to talk to each other. It feels like the blind leading the blind. How is anyone in here supposed to have answers for me when they're just as confused as I am? I'm used to doing things on my own and taking care of myself.

HELEN: I, too, have been having doubts. I really haven't seen changes in my own behavior, and I don't see any clear path to that.

THERAPIST: (To Helen) So, you share many of the feelings that Jackie just voiced.

HELEN: Yes, I feel the same ambiguity because we haven't been given a clear road map. But I don't feel anger. For me, it's more apathy because I don't know where this is going, so I find myself just checking out. I keep hearing the same phrases from both of you [*referring to the two therapists*], like "How do you feel?" or "Where do you want to start?" Personally, I would appreciate some clarity. Will we even get some explanation at the end of this experience?

THERAPIST: My sense is that both of you feel like we've been withholding something that you need. I wonder if that has raised questions in your mind about the extent to which you can actually trust us and trust that something of value will come from this.

NANCY: The theme of trust resonates for me as well because when I was in individual therapy, the psychologist started by telling me how she approaches treatment. Personally, I'm not thinking of quitting, but I feel apathy. But Jackie, I have to say I would be sad to see you go. As for me, I plan to see this through, and I told myself that when this group ends, I'll know if it worked or not.

MATT: I would be sad to see you go as well, Jackie.

NANCY: For me, it's easy to stay because really there is nothing else that's pulling me away. I feel a separation from both of you [*therapists*]. It's like us versus them.

THERAPIST: There is some healthy anger in here, and it's really helped a number of you connect with your needs and your expectations of us. I'm encouraged to know that you feel safe enough with us to voice your disappointment, apathy, or anger.

In this segment, the therapist remained open and inviting in the face of expressions of disconnection and questions about the value of the group. One can conceptualize these reactions as indicating a defense against the affects related to attachment needs (triangle of adaptation). Jackie described feeling angry and disappointed. Other patients then voiced feeling apathetic or "checking out." These are variations on the same dynamic enacted by Jackie—that is, an effort to defend against the anxiety caused by the implicit demands of group cohesion and by the possibility of intimacy with others in the group (an attachment need). By encouraging these disclosures and resisting the urge to retaliate, respond defensively, or indulge the group's desire for an explanation, the therapist allowed the group members to experience yet another point of connection and sameness. The therapists also disconfirmed the CMIP expectation of others as judgmental or retaliatory. As a consequence, several patients were able to describe their disappointment as well, whereas other patients expressed their feelings of attachment and loss should Jackie leave. In essence, group members were asking for a powerful and more capable parental figure to offer them a secure base in the face of the unknown and unfamiliar. The therapist picked up on this and responded with a statement to the group that their expressions of attachment needs indicated that they felt safe enough to risk challenging the leaders without shame or fear of reprisal (affects).

Therapist Interpersonal Stances

Meaningful therapeutic progress requires the therapist to become both participant and observer in the interpersonal world of group members (Sullivan, 1954). Entry into the patient's interpersonal world is an essential component of empathic attunement that, on occasion, involves the therapist responding to the patient in ways that are all too familiar to the patient. There is no error in being drawn into the patient's interpersonal dynamics (i.e., complementary responding) and patterns of relating (i.e., aspects of the patient's CMIP) for brief periods, as long as the therapist remains friendly or affiliative. In the face of heightened anxiety often experienced in therapy groups, members may rigidly embrace their CMIPs as a means of gaining a sense of security and predictability.

We have observed two distinct patterns of interpersonal tension during Stage 2, storming. First, group members whose defenses are organized around an interpersonal pattern characterized by hostile–dominance on the interpersonal circumplex (Figure 1.4) may react by challenging the therapist's authority. The individual with an interpersonal style that is hostile–dominant may feel threatened by the confidence and interpersonal strength of the therapist and may either ignore or challenge the therapist and other patients who exhibit a capacity for dominance. Challenges can take the form of "yes-butting," pointing out errors in logic, assuming the stance of expert, or simply ignoring the comments of the therapist. At times, therapists may feel incompetent or simply insignificant, as if the group would do well without them. Such countertransference reactions signify that the therapist, having touched the patient's vulnerability, has been drawn into the patient's maladaptive relational pattern (i.e., CMIP). The therapist's task in this context is to avoid retaliating against the hostile–dominant individual, while also working to protect other members of the group without shaming or rejecting the hostile patient. This can be accomplished by normalizing the hostile–dominant individual's anxiety and felt a sense of threat. For example, the therapist might offer one of the following comments:

> People in the group are becoming increasingly anxious, particularly because each of you encounters parts of your pain through the stories of others. There is some healthy anger in the room. Anger is an old companion that a number of you have relied on for protection. The goal here is to find additional ways to feel alive and connected to others and risk giving others a chance to stand with you at times like this when you're feeling most uncertain about how to move forward.

Second, group members whose defenses are organized around an interpersonal pattern of friendly–submissiveness on the interpersonal circle tend to be conflict avoidant and self-effacing. Their relational stance is aimed at dissipating the anger or hostility that is part of all intimate relationships. Thus, for these patients, the increased tension characteristic of Stage 2, storming, is generally more intrapersonal, or internally, felt. Their coping style reflects a pattern of internalization, a process consistent with their tendency to be highly self-referent and self-critical. Often, they will respond in one of two ways: by assuming the role of peacemaker to diffuse criticisms levied toward the therapist or by becoming increasingly withdrawn or sulking due to their harsh internal critic and propensity to personalize the comments of others. The first type of response is best dealt with through deductive group-as-a-whole statements that point to the ongoing process or interaction: "I wonder whether the group is willing to tolerate the messiness of intimacy" or "Perhaps the group is sorting out the extent to which people are willing to be honest and direct with each other" or "The group is showing a great deal of courage in its willingness to challenge the constant need to be polite and careful" or "Joe's willingness to challenge me seems to evoke some anxiety in some of you."

Self-critical responses can be addressed through a variety of individual and inductive group-as-a-whole interventions, each of which targets the self-destructive elements of the individual's behavior and introject. Examples include "Jane, it seems to be a struggle to forgive yourself, much like what Julie described last week" or "I wonder, Sue, whether it is more tolerable to blame and even punish yourself than it is to express disagreement with John?" or "At times, a number of people seem to struggle intensely with a harsh internal critic" or "It appears that the group has just expanded. We've been joined by Stan's critical parents and Sue's schoolyard bullies. I wonder if whether others are struggling with the same thing."

The primary themes of Stage 2, storming, are "Do I count?" and "Am I safe from myself and/or others?" The conflict inherent in this stage is aimed at answering these two questions. In challenging the leader, a group member unconsciously expects to encounter criticism or the coldness of dismissal that may have been all too familiar during childhood and adolescence. Usually, this is the foundation of expectations of others that forms part of the CMIP. In some cases, these critical responses are internally generated, taking shape in an image of self as tainted or deficient (i.e., introject) and echoing throughout a member's internal dialogue that, in turn, is projected onto others (i.e., in the form of the patient's expectations of others). The therapist can counter this self-limiting pattern by assuming a friendly, accepting, yet inquisitive stance that disconfirms the patient's expectation of rejection, retaliation, or criticism. The therapeutic objective is to have group members begin considering the possibility that the self is fundamentally worthwhile and that one's attachment needs are legitimate and adaptive.

THERAPIST TASK BOX
STAGE 2: STORMING

1. Be aware of the "pull" to respond to hostile or cold individuals with counterhostility.

2. Protect group members from hostility by normalizing anxiety and the perceived threat that underlies the hostility.

3. Counter self-limiting self-critical elements (introjects) of friendly-submissive patients.

4. Counter CMIP expectations of dismissal and criticism (expectations of others) by assuming a friendly, accepting, and inquisitive stance toward the patient's introject and attachment needs.

5. Encourage the group to consider their attachment needs as legitimate.

Stage 3: Norming

The norming stage signals the group's entry into a state of growing emotional and interpersonal equanimity. As the turbulence of Stage 2, storming, subsides, members gradually expand their capacity for relating to one another with less fear of losing autonomy, being hurt, or feeling forgotten. Patients become less preoccupied with questions regarding group norms. During this stage, members possess increased clarity regarding their expectations of each other and what the group can offer. As the fear of being engulfed by others or losing one's identity lessens, self-disclosure deepens, with some patients exhibiting a willingness to take interpersonal risks by offering feedback to others and working in the here-and-now. Typically, this involves greater expression of attachment needs with less inhibiting affect, a reduction of maladaptive defenses, and a more genuine expression of the self or introject. Given that these ways of engaging may be unfamiliar to most patients, they are likely to be enacted awkwardly. For example, a supportive comment from one patient to another might be expressed in a curt tone or in the absence of direct eye contact. During this stage, it is critical that the therapist encourages members of the group to make room for clumsiness as the members risk engaging each other in ways in which they may have little experience.

Beck and colleagues (1986) suggested that in the norming stage, there tends to be at least one member of the group who begins to exhibit significant growth and is most poised to take interpersonal risks by relinquishing the more self-limiting patterns of relating that have characterized their CMIP. Beck and colleagues referred to this individual as the *emotional leader* of the group, who is often expressive, extraverted, and well-liked by other patients. The emotional leader does not necessarily dominate the interaction but rather exhibits a willingness to engage in honest self-examination, offer and receive feedback, and express attachment needs and a range of feelings openly. The emotional leader serves as an important source of modeling for other patients and, when these efforts are managed effectively by the therapist, the emotional leader has the potential to facilitate the therapeutic work of others. It is critical for the therapist to remain vigilant to the temptation of becoming overly engaged with the emotional leader to the exclusion of more challenging patients. Doing so can give rise to scapegoating and feelings of resentment among members of the group. Should the therapist become aware of having fallen into this pattern, it is essential to respond by showing humility and acknowledging the error. Such a disclosure allows group members to explore and work through past wounds and themes of sibling rivalry or parental neglect.

One of the therapist's primary tasks in Stage 3, norming, is to bring to conscious awareness the harsh internal critic at the core of patients' self-concept (introject) and to invite patients to have greater self-tolerance.[1] Generally, the emotional leader will be most amenable to such interventions. Greater self-disclosure by the emotional leader becomes a conduit for other patients to share their experiences of shame, fear of rejection, and self-repulsion, a process that contributes to mutual empathy and a deepening of intimacy among group members. An especially important task during this stage is to foster group members' capacity to tolerate the differences and limitations of others, both within and outside the group. The therapist's consistent modeling of nurturance and acceptance, particularly when confronting maladaptive interpersonal patterns, is critical to facilitating this shift as it disconfirms both expectations of others and patients' negative introjects.

Although the norming stage is considerably less turbulent than the storming stage, some members who tend to have a hostile interpersonal

---

[1]Self-tolerance is used here deliberately and should not be confused with self-acceptance. The focus is on aiding the individual to tolerate the self and the incompleteness of the self. For many group members, being with the self is highly intolerable, a state that mirrors the intolerance and lack of interest exhibited by people that were or are significant in the person's life. The lack of self-tolerance also reflects frequent demands placed on the individual by significant others to be someone other than who the person is.

style may remain aloof and argumentative, often by dismissing, minimizing, or ignoring other patients' painful disclosures. This manner of relating can become accentuated during this stage and is best understood as the hostile patient's effort to manage anxiety evoked by others' expressions of vulnerability and the group's growing intimacy and cohesion. Hostile patients often are likely to possess a dismissing attachment style stemming from a history in which they experienced attachment figures as unavailable and/or incapable of meeting their attachment need for security. It is not surprising then that expressions of vulnerability within the group that are met with empathy and acceptance may evoke mistrust and heightened anxiety in patients with a dismissing attachment style. One effective means of intervening with the hostile or dismissing patient is through the therapist's use of here-and-now comments that encourage member-to-member feedback. Inviting other patients to voice their reactions to the hostile patient's aloofness is a fruitful means of drawing on the therapeutic potential of group therapy. These interventions can be powerful, provided the therapist can help group members offer feedback that includes both their immediate response of wanting to withdraw from, as well as their desire to get closer to the hostile individual.

Patients' risk-taking and transparency during the norming stage are often accompanied by more intense emotional expression. One of the central tasks of the therapist during this stage is to access and facilitate the expression of attachment needs and accompanying feelings that have long been concealed or avoided by defenses. However, it is unrealistic to expect group members to relinquish their defenses spontaneously. Doing so requires entering an unchartered relational world that involves a willingness to reclaim parts of the self that have been rejected or denied and accept parts that have been viewed through a lens of shame or fear (affects). If a solid foundation of trust has been established during the forming and storming stages, the group's progress through the difficult tasks of the norming stage is made possible.

It is often necessary for the therapist to normalize the awkwardness of patients' experiences when taking the risk of relating to others or self in an unfamiliar manner. Therapists should encourage group members to make room for clumsiness and missteps in their interactions because doing so is essential to expanding patients' capacity to tolerate differences and limitations of self and others. This serves as a foundation for the ability to recognize the shortcoming of significant figures in their lives and ultimately to grieve the reality that, in some cases, they may never receive all of what they have longed for in those relationships.

Emotional Processing

During Stage 3, norming, the therapist relies on two primary forms of intervention: emotional processing and process commentary or meta-communication. *Emotional processing* involves an invitation to all levels of the group, individuals, dyads, and the group-as-a-whole, to connect more fully with their attachment needs. This stage is marked by the therapist's use of both inductive and deductive group-as-a-whole interventions. Inductive group-as-a-whole interventions typically should be aimed at the emotional leader of the group. As that individual reveals hidden or rejected parts of self, the therapist endeavors to support the individual and connect him or her to others in the group. This latter process sets the stage for other patients to follow suit, much like a series of concentric ripples in a pool of water when a stone is thrown into it.

The leader must anticipate an increase in the use of both individual and group defenses in response to the anxiety that inductive group-as-a-whole interventions may cause. These defenses may include the use of intellectualization, rationalization, symptom escalation, problem solving, and a general focus on cognition. At such junctures, the therapist can encourage members of the group to be curious about and examine the suppressed fears and anxiety (affects) and/or the attachment needs concealed by these defenses.

Examples of such therapist comments that touch on the three aspects of the triangle of adaptation might include "I wonder what that stirs up inside you? And I wonder what that has evoked in others?" or "Can you tell Betty how you feel toward her right now? . . . Betty, as you hear that, what's the biggest risk you could take at this moment in responding to Sue? . . . If others were in Sue's place, what might be the biggest risk for you?" or "There is a profound sense of sadness that seems to have descended on the group. I wonder if some of you would be willing to put words to it" or "A number of you are struggling to let go of familiar ways of relating to others and yourselves."

Each of these interventions is intended to connect members of the group to their inner experience and each other. The emphasis is on attachment needs (triangle of adaptation), although, at times, it may be helpful to explore core beliefs and assumptions (expectations of others or introjects):

THERAPIST: When Jack tells you that he wants to get closer to you, what impact does that have on how you see yourself? [*Followed by,*] I wonder if that can be the start of changing your image of yourself and of how others see you.

Some patients have little difficulty expressing emotions or using emotional language, particularly if they have been in therapy previously. However, it is critical that the therapist distinguishes between a patient's expression of emotion as a defense versus a genuine attempt to reveal one's self to the group. In instances when the expression of emotion is used as a defense against affects or attachment needs, therapists have to go beyond the surface of what was expressed and invite patients to move deeper into their affective experience: "You sound quite hurt. I wonder what you are feeling underneath that hurt?" or "I've noticed that each time someone broaches this topic, you become quite tearful. The group seems to have taken the tears as a signal to be careful rather than taking the risk of getting closer and being honest with you."

Metacommunication

Process commentary involves metacommunication or a statement of what is happening at the level of the relationship, including how participants feel about their relationship. In metacommunication, there is an under-emphasis on the content of a message and a greater emphasis on the inter-personal impact that the message has on the participants (i.e., the process). In considering a metacommunication, it may be helpful for the therapist to imagine placing him- or herself on both sides of a member's comment. In other words, what would it be like to be on the receiving end of the comment, and what would it be like to have made the comment? Kiesler (1985) developed the Impact Message Inventory (IMI) as a means of determining a target person's interpersonal style. The IMI is a self-report interpersonal circumplex–based measure that asks respondents to define their covert responses or "impact messages" when interacting with a target individual. The IMI provides a vocabulary that can be quite useful when making process comments to group members. Some examples include "*It seems that you feel* superior to him"[2] or "*It sounds like you feel* as important to him as others in the group" or "*You sound* frustrated because she won't defend her position."

Process commentary can also focus on elaborating on the impact the message has on the speaker. This can include either interpersonal or intra-personal components. An *interpersonal* focus is similar to the previous examples: "It sounds like you want to stop her from getting any closer to you" or "It seems that you just retaliated in response to what felt like an attack." An *intrapersonal* focus targets the effect the speaker's communication has on his or her sense of self. When such interventions are well-timed, they

---

[2]The phrase in italics is the actual item wording from the IMI.

can serve as a window into the individual's introject: "It seems that there is part of you that believes that you must always remain alone" or "I wonder whether you are afraid that if you let Julie be right in her understanding of you, you will be overwhelmed by her?"

THERAPIST TASK BOX
STAGE 3: NORMING

1. Identify the emotional leader in the group.
2. Heighten awareness of the harsh internal critic (introject) of the emotional leader's self.
3. Model nurturance and acceptance to disconfirm expectations of others.
4. Access and facilitate patients' expression of attachment needs.
5. Emotional processing: Invite the group to enter into affective experiences.
   - Use inductive group-as-a-whole interventions aimed at the emotional leader to support and connect them to others in the group.
   - Anticipate increased defenses in the expression of attachment needs.
6. Metacommunication: Comment on the interpersonal impact of a statement or behavior (i.e., the process).

Stage 4: Performing

The performing stage is a time of deep inner and interpersonal work. The affect that surfaces during this point in treatment involves revisiting experiences of unmet attachment needs that extend beyond recounting details of past events from a less defended position. At this juncture, patients not only experience more intense affect but also have an expanded capacity for a broader range of emotions, in keeping with their efforts to work toward self-acceptance. Change and growth seldom occur in the absence of anxiety, uncertainty, and a transient yet intense wish to put it all back as it once was.

If conflict emerges during the performing stage, it usually involves wrestling with internalized images of self and significant figures in one's life (introject). Beck and colleagues (1986) referred to this aspect of the process as "self-confrontation in the context of interdependence" (p. 619). Individual group members increasingly recognize unwanted parts of the self (introject) and are open to an emerging clarity about aspects of attachment figures that have contributed to unhealed wounds. There is greater awareness of the contrast that exists between relational patterns that defined interactions with past attachment figures (CMIPs) versus those that have been experienced in the group. If interpersonal conflict has been managed skillfully during the storming and norming stages, group members come to the realization that attachment needs are not destructive or shameful. Tolerating and working through conflict is essential to intimacy and reflects an acceptance of the limits inherent in all relationships. During the performing stage, group members no longer see interpersonal confrontation and conflict as a threat to the integrity of the self or the relationship but as an integral component of growth. Through this experience of emotional and interpersonal growth, the individual's assumptions about relationships (i.e., aspects of their CMIP) shift, resulting in a decreased need to impose their particular view of the world onto others. That is, the expectations of others become less rigid. Group members are more able to withdraw their projections while recognizing their contribution to interpersonal difficulties. By this point, the group has achieved a solid sense of trust, characterized by mutuality and respect. Interpersonal feedback is more carefully considered rather than deflected or contradicted. Themes of intimacy, connection, attraction, and sexuality are explored more openly.

This stage may also include a certain amount of *grief work*, in which members begin to relinquish long-held fantasies about wished-for relationships with significant others and attachment figures. That is, the attachment needs vertex of the triangle of adaptation becomes more easily accessible to the individual. As patients soften their defenses, they become increasingly receptive to the affirmation and validation offered by other patients, and a complex mix of feelings emerges. On the one hand, patients may experience elation and excitement in response to feeling accepted and connected to others. But on the other hand, they may also feel anger, bitterness, and deep sadness that such experiences were unavailable to them in some of their most significant relationships. It is through this admixture of emotions that group members are faced with the challenge of redefining their approach to a number of their formative and attachment relationships.

This is yet another period of heightened vulnerability during which patients must remain intentional and persistent in their efforts to resist being drawn into relational dynamics and interpersonal role assignments (i.e., the CMIP) that were well-established. Interpersonal theory posits that if one attempts to alter a particular manner of relating, relational homeostasis is disrupted, and others in the patient's life may intensify efforts to keep things as they have always been. Thus, when a patient enacts new ways of relating in their life (revised CMIPs), they may face pressure from others to fall back into familiar ways of being. At this juncture, it is important that the group serves as a secure base from which the patient explores new ways of relating to their family of origin and current attachment figures.

The performing stage is also marked by patients' growing acceptance of one another's limitations. This parallels the realization that significant others are limited in their ability to respond to the patient's attachment needs. We view this as an instance of reverse generalization. In other words, as patients realize that family members or life partners cannot satisfy all their attachment needs, there is growing recognition that neither can the group meet all these needs. The group and its leader are no longer idealized but are viewed more realistically. Essential to this development is the therapist's ability to allow themselves to appear both human and professional.

Therapist Interpersonal Stances
In the performing stage, the therapist tends to be less active. By this point in the process, most of the interactions involve member-to-member exchanges. Ideally, this is a time when a significant change in individual CMIPs occurs. As patients experience a shift in at least one component of the CMIP, the scene is set for a chain reaction that eventually results in a realignment of the remaining elements of the CMIP. An effective therapeutic strategy is for therapists to facilitate a change in the most malleable element of the client's CMIP by highlighting subtle shifts that are occurring in that domain. These elements might include patients' use of more adaptive defense mechanisms or patients' ability to express attachment needs without accompanying affects of shame or anxiety. This may not be a dramatic process. Sustained change is often subtle and measured, thereby allowing the patient to test the waters while preserving the integrity of the self. In our experience, many individuals are not fully cognizant of the changes they are making until they are noted by the therapist or other patients in the group. For example, the therapist might comment, "I've noticed that you are much more willing to take in the affirmation that others are offering you now" (less defensive) or "Did you notice that you've been talking about yourself in a much gentler manner? It seems that something has shifted within you" (less punitive introject) or "You seem

to be more willing to let us get close to you. From what you've shared, I sense that you are welcoming intimacy more often in your life, both here and outside of group" (openness to attachment needs) or "It seems that you are more confident that your anger won't destroy John or your relationship with him" (less inhibiting affect).

Even though the therapist may be less active during this stage, their interventions remain critical. One of the leader's primary tasks is to model the integration of being both fallible and an authority figure. This is most effectively accomplished through a willingness to accept and acknowledge one's limitations as a helper. Invariably, there will be times when the group or one of its members feels that the leader has made an error in judgment. Typically, this may be in response to administrative decisions, an empathic failure, or a mistimed interpretation. A patient's or group's criticism or expression of disappointment in the therapist may evoke feelings of shame and self-doubt in clinicians who are, by their nature, conscientious and committed to being helpful. However, some therapists have little tolerance for such feelings and may be too quick to interpret the group's reaction as a function of some unresolved "issue" or to ignore or dismiss the criticism. Doing so diminishes what may be a patient's reasonable and adaptive reaction. Concurrently, some group members may become anxious when another patient is critical of the therapist. They may react defensively by protecting the leader, offering explanations and rationalizations, distracting the group, or blaming the patient with the complaint. In these situations, it is critical that the therapist uses metacommunication as a means of bringing group members to a conscious understanding of the unfolding process: "It seems that the women in the group feel compelled to protect me" or "I wonder how Sue's disappointment in me is affecting others" or "What's it like for the group when it's clear that I've made an error?" or "I haven't been able to meet a number of your needs. What's it like to encounter my limitations in this way?"

When leaders invite the group to examine such questions, members must reevaluate their assumptions about the self and their expectations about others' responses to them, particularly those of authority figures. The leader's openness to examine a group member's disappointment or criticism offers the group an unfamiliar yet welcome experience of benevolent authority that may disconfirm certain expectations of others. Such encounters, when repeated over time, serve as an invitation for group members to reconsider their observed reactions of others (i.e., acts of others), their expectations of others, and ultimately, their introject.

THERAPIST TASK BOX
STAGE 4: PERFORMING

1. The therapist allows him- or herself to appear both human and professional.
2. Facilitate change in one or two aspects of patients' CMIP, including the introject.
3. Point out subtle changes that have occurred in the way members relate to the self and/or others.
4. Openly examine group members' disappointment in the therapist, and link to CMIP.

Stage 5: Adjourning

Termination from group therapy may give rise to anxiety related to past experiences of separation and loss that may amplify attachment insecurity for some group members. The actual process of termination differs depending on how the treatment is structured. In time-limited closed groups in which all members begin and end treatment together, group members are likely cognizant of termination-related themes throughout the course of treatment. A unique aspect of this experience is that the time limit is not under any group member's control. The therapist established the meeting time, length of each session, and frequency and number of sessions. This degree of structure will "pull" for the emergence of certain themes. For example, for individuals who had enmeshed relationships with parental figures, such containment and boundary setting may offer a feeling of relief and security. Conversely, for individuals familiar with emotional abandonment by parental figures who were seldom or variably accessible, these limits may evoke mistrust, resentment, anger, hurt, and deep loneliness.

The therapist's work regarding termination from group therapy is to facilitate the overt expression of these feelings so that they can be addressed without distortion and anxiety. The experience of affect during Stage 5, adjourning, often triggers defenses such as minimizing the importance of the group, feeling anger at the therapist, or avoiding the termination. Resolution of these emotions requires that they are voiced, felt, and given legitimacy. It may be important for patients to understand that their defensive reactions to termination are related to the anxiety (affect) caused by sadness or grief at losing the group, which has become a safe haven (attachment need). For many patients, these adaptive feelings that were historically dismissed or ridiculed by attachment figures lead to shame or anxiety. Defensiveness may result in patients diluting the impact of the feelings that begin to emerge at the end of treatment. They may look for ways to extend the life of the group, discuss the possibility of informal get-togethers after the group ends, exchange contact information, or suggest holding "anniversary" meetings. Such suggestions speak to the extent to which members have valued the experience and one another and the extent of their loss. At the same time, these behaviors represent an unconscious effort to avoid the pain of current and past separations from attachment figures.

In the last few sessions, patients may recount previous losses, such as the death of a loved one, divorce or separation, relocation, children leaving home, or the loss of a valued job. Compelling as these stories are, it is critical for the therapist to connect them to the impending termination of the group. In response to a painful story in which a member tearfully recounted details of a divorce that occurred seven years previously, the therapist commented,

> Your ex-husband was an important part of your life, and it's understandable that the pain of your divorce will revisit you periodically, particularly at junctures like this when you are facing yet another loss. I suspect that you are not alone in what you are feeling right now. Perhaps others in the group are silently struggling with the anticipation of our imminent separation.

Another patient tearfully recounted the death of her father some time ago and how she arrived in town just hours after her father died. The therapist refocused the discussion to the imminent loss of the group:

> It seems that there were many things that you wanted to tell your father before he died. One of the things that I am aware of right now is that in 3 weeks, this group will be ending, and I am wondering what you want to say to me and others while there is still an opportunity to do so.

Termination in open-ended groups in which members end treatment at varying points is somewhat different. Generally, these tend to be long-term groups with rolling admissions in which a patient who decides to bring treatment to a close is expected to give several months' notice. Departing patients in this context also can exhibit a variety of defensive behaviors. These behaviors are designed to reduce the anxiety and pain related to the impending loss and termination. Some may begin to pull away and appear disconnected, others may experience regression in symptoms or old relational patterns, and yet others may respond by pulling for a fight as an unconscious means of avoiding the pain of separation. Some patients assume the role of a pseudo therapist by focusing on the needs and emotions of other group members while avoiding their own. It is critical that the leader balances the task of keeping the departing patient fully engaged while also attending to the needs of the group. For patients who are continuing with treatment, the departure of a long-time member may evoke feelings of abandonment, as well as pride and hope. Group members who have a preoccupied attachment style may respond with rigid affirmation and support intended to appease the departing member and secure their approval and blessing while diluting their own sadness. Those with a dismissing attachment style are apt to respond with stoic indifference or polite resignation. Patients who have a fearful or disorganized attachment style may exhibit a stance of emotional paralysis or confusion. For any remaining group member, the departure of a valued copatient may touch on a particular aspect of their CMIP, such as the expectation that others will abandon them.

Therapist Interpersonal Stances

As members begin to say goodbye to each other or a departing patient, there is a strong pull to idealize the relationships. In time-limited closed groups, it is not unusual for groups to engage in a "go-around" in which each member says goodbye by sharing personal experiences of other members, including the therapist. Frequently, these summaries overemphasize the positive elements of each person's experience. It is natural for patients to feel that they want to leave on a good note. It is also natural for therapists to resist stirring up previous conflicts, with the knowledge that there may not be sufficient time to resolve them fully. Authentic and genuine relationships, however, are multilayered and encompass experiences in which one is faced with having to work through certain feelings and struggles on their own if the other is no longer accessible. The challenge for the therapist is to encourage each patient to offer a balanced statement of their experience, in which they can include expressions of regret, disappointment, frustration, sadness, joy, pride, and pain felt in relation to other group members.

The group therapist is also faced with the task of saying goodbye to the group or an individual who is leaving. Typically, this is an opportunity to express gratitude to members of the group or the departing patient for the gift of having invited the leader into the sanctity of their most intimate struggles. The therapist may wish to highlight the courage that was demonstrated by the patient in their efforts to face their pain and fears and risk new ways of relating through modifying their CMIPs. It is also important for leaders to give voice to their disappointments, concerns, and caution to those ending treatment. In working with time-limited groups, some therapists choose to make a brief comment to each member, whereas others elect to address the group as a whole. Some therapists feel it is important to model how one brings closure to an encounter in an immediate and personal way. Other therapists prefer to preserve the sense of collective identity that the group has achieved as a means of aiding members in their efforts to internalize the experience and carry it with them beyond the life of the group.

As we mention throughout this book, personality is the total of one's history of internalized relationships—especially attachment relationships. A successful therapy group is one that is a safe haven for individuals to explore new ways of being and new self-concepts. As such, a therapy group can be an attachment figure that is internalized by the individual and has a lasting impact on their ability to manage emotions and engage in satisfying relationships with limited distortion and adaptive defenses. To this end, a key task of a GPIP therapist is to encourage individuals to internalize the group. This requires that the ending of the group for an individual not be defensively dismissed, devalued, or minimized—but authentically evaluated and embraced. That is, it is important that the introject of the departing patient include an internalization of the group as a secure attachment figure that helped them to accept their self, feelings, and attachment needs with minimum anxiety or shame and without the need for defensive distortions.

JOHN: I'm anxious about leaving but excited as well. I'm grateful for all that I've gained by being part of this group—and really appreciate that you all have shared so much of yourselves with me. I'll miss you.

THERAPIST: I hope you will take the group with you in your mind and that we will be there when you need us.

JOHN: You know it's funny that you say that. The other day when I was dealing with that crisis at work, I thought of the group and what each of you might say to me, and it calmed me a little.

THERAPIST TASK BOX
STAGE 5: ADJOURNING

1. Make thematic links from early on between loss and separation and termination of the group.

2. Encourage members to express positive and negative feelings about the group and termination.

3. In open-ended groups, keep departing members fully engaged and focused on their own work.

4. The therapist can express gratitude, concerns, or cautions to the group.

5. Encourage group members to internalize the group as an attachment figure to better manage feelings and relationships.

CHAPTER 4 REVIEW EXERCISES

Exercise 4.1

Identify four types of interventions that can be used by group therapists to build a positive therapeutic alliance.

1. _____
2. _____
3. _____
4. _____

Exercise 4.2

Identify the five stages of development based on Tuckman's work that is used in the GPIP model in their sequential order.

1. _____
2. _____
3. _____
4. _____
5. _____

Exercise 4.3

Indicate whether the following statement is true or false and explain your answer:

In the forming stage of GPIP, interpretations of patients' CMIP are an effective means of achieving therapeutic gains.

Exercise 4.4

For the following case example, answer the following questions:

Frank fears intimacy [*acts of self*] and creates a sense of safety for himself by assuming a stance of superiority and condescension toward others [*acts of self, defense*] that contributes to others avoiding him [*acts of others*]. His tone is one of certainty, often speaking as if instructing others on matters that he considers to be blatantly obvious. His outlook is best characterized as pessimistic and negative, with a tendency to "rain on others' parades" whenever others appear hopeful or affirming [*acts of self*]. Frank believes that others will reject and abandon him [*expectations of others*] because, having grown up being bullied and called a "nerd" [*acts of others*], he views himself as dull and unattractive [*introject*]. Frank anticipates outward rejection, annoyance, or indifference from others in both personal and professional interactions [*expectations of others*]. He conceals his loneliness and hurt by assuming a posture of impenetrability and emotional unresponsiveness [*acts of self*]. Colleagues and acquaintances often respond with boredom, impatience, or a silence born of confusion [*acts of others*], but Frank interprets this as their indifference or dismissal [*expectations of others*]. Thus, Frank encounters the very rejection that he fears and tries to avoid. The end result is that Frank continues to view himself as unworthy of others' care and affection [*introject*]. He has a harsh internal critic that is often projected outward [*defense*]. In the first group session, Frank either ignored or dismissed most of the therapist's comments [*acts of self*]. Each time the therapist spoke, Frank felt compelled to contradict her, generally presenting a more pessimistic alternative or referring to esoteric psychoanalytic constructs [*acts of self*]. At other times, he simply ignored the therapist's statements and moved on to an unrelated topic [*acts of self*]. Internally, the therapist felt annoyed in response to Frank's behavior [*acts of others*]. Other group members felt anxious and wary of Frank, lest he treat them the way he treated the therapist, and thus they tended to avoid engaging him directly [*acts of others*].

1. Using the concept of *selective complementarity*, what is required by the therapist in her interactions with Frank to work toward creating a positive therapeutic alliance? Explain how selective complementarity works in this case. Use Figure 1.4 to illustrate your answer.

_____

_____

_____

_____

2. Identify potential therapist interventions that would be appropriate for Frank during each of the following stages of GPIP development:

(a) The forming stage.

_____

_____

_____

_____

(b) The storming stage.

_____

_____

_____

_____

(c) The norming stage.

_____

_____

_____

_____

Exercise 4.5

Jude is about to terminate from a GPIP group in which she gained a lot and had a successful therapy. However, the termination is fraught with problems, such as her missing sessions and dismissing the importance of the group to her life.

1. How do you understand Jude's tendency to miss sessions and dismiss the group therapy?
   A. An inhibiting affect
   B. A defense
   C. An attachment need
   D. An introject

2. What is the main task for Jude's therapist to accomplish for Jude to have a successful termination from the group?
   A. Make sure Jude does not say anything negative to the group members about the group or therapist.
   B. Help Jude to access the feelings of loss, grief, or disappointment.
   C. Convince Jude that the group was, in fact, an important event in her life.
   D. Focus only on the rest of the group and their reactions to Jude's departure.

CHAPTER 4 REVIEW ANSWERS

Exercise 4.1

1. Selectively reinforce the adaptive elements of patients' rehearsed stories.
2. Identify universal themes of alienation, brokenness, or isolation.
3. Connect the stories of various patients, one to the other.
4. Use nonconfrontational metacommunication.

Exercise 4.2

1. Forming
2. Storming
3. Norming
4. Performing
5. Adjourning

Exercise 4.3

False. Interpretations of the CMIP in the forming stage can trigger a level of anxiety that may overwhelm patients and potentially contribute to the patient withdrawing or terminating treatment prematurely.

Exercise 4.4

1. Assume a friendly–submissive stance as a means of countering Frank's hostile–dominance. The therapist's submissive position reduces Frank's "felt anxiety" by offering a response that is reciprocal to Frank's dominance, while the friendly stance gently challenges Frank's hostility.

2. (a) The forming stage. Gently highlight the self-protective component of Frank's criticism and dismissing behaviors (acts of self) without interpreting the CMIP. Encourage him to reflect on his behaviors and their impact on others in his life.

   (b) The storming stage. Refrain from taking a hostile complementary stance to Frank's hostility; that is, remain friendly and accepting. If necessary, protect other group members from his criticism by focusing on his reactions to the therapist. Understand his behavior as a response to his anxiety about being criticized.

(c) The norming stage. Consider interpreting Frank's outward behavior as a defense against his anxiety in social situations. Consider explicitly discussing his CMIP in which others withdraw (acts of others) because of his aloofness (acts of self) and that he interprets as further rejection (expectation of others). Explore whether he can access his attachment needs and recognize the self-limiting nature of his ways of defending.

Exercise 4.5

1. B. A defense
2. B. Help Jane to access the feelings of loss, grief, or disappointment.

5

RESEARCH EVIDENCE FOR GROUP PSYCHODYNAMIC-INTERPERSONAL PSYCHOTHERAPY

Many clinicians might stop reading a clinical book at this point with the thought that they had gained all that they could from such a text on group therapy. Why would a clinician want to go on and read a chapter on the research evidence for group psychodynamic-interpersonal psychotherapy (GPIP)? It is a question that lies at the heart of the practice–research divide in psychotherapy. Clinicians often feel that research has little to offer their clinical practice. Conversely, researchers often disregard or even dismiss clinical wisdom when designing studies (Tasca, Sylvestre, et al., 2015). As a result, clinicians and researchers have inadvertently limited what they can learn from each other, and this has diminished the quality of both clinical practice and clinical research. Because we wrote this book primarily for clinicians, we focus on the clinician's side of the divide for a moment.

Although we believe that clinicians and clinical practice should be informed by research, the typical approach of mandating psychotherapists to follow treatment guidelines has not been effective and has not had a great impact on the way clinicians practice (Tobin et al., 2007). For example, surveys have indicated that even if clinicians are aware of innovations

https://doi.org/10.1037/0000213-006
Group Psychodynamic-Interpersonal Psychotherapy, by G. A. Tasca, S. F. Mikail, and P. L. Hewitt

in clinical practice, they do not often take up the innovations (e.g., Ionita & Fitzpatrick, 2014). Part of the problem is that clinicians, like most people, are less likely to change their behavior solely on the basis of social pressure to do so. Rather, clinicians may be more likely to change their practices if they also have control over the implementation process and feel positively toward the clinical interventions they may implement (Tasca et al., 2014). That is, clinicians are more likely to adopt a practice if they feel aligned to it and deliberately choose it and if they expect the practice to improve their patients' outcomes.

Rather than focusing on the obligations of clinicians to practice according to the evidence, we emphasize what clinicians and their patients can gain by knowing the research. Our goal in this chapter is to provide therapists with research findings regarding GPIP that are accessible and relevant to their practices. Research has indicated that a therapist's considered assessment of an approach's efficacy and the belief in its effectiveness has a positive impact on patient outcomes (Wampold & Imel, 2015). These therapists are likely more knowledgeable, confident, enthusiastic, and diligent in their training and application of the method. Clinicians communicate this confidence to their patients, who, in turn, have a greater expectation of a good result from therapy. And patients' hope and positive expectations are associated with better outcomes (Constantino et al., 2018). Clinicians who understand the evidence for GPIP can be appropriately confident in what they are doing, and they can communicate this confidence to patients who can expect to improve. For this reason, we encourage you to keep reading. To make the research more practically meaningful, we provide clinical vignettes to illustrate the concepts we researched and demonstrate how the findings are directly applicable to clinical practice in GPIP.

Consistent with most research on treatment efficacy and effectiveness, the research that we completed on GPIP used symptom reduction as one indicator of the utility of this group treatment approach. As we discussed in Chapter 1, it is important to tackle more than symptoms in our treatment. Hence, the research on GPIP also evaluated improvements in the underlying transdiagnostic factors as an indication of the treatment's effectiveness and efficacy. Thus, in the following sections, we describe the research showing that GPIP not only reduces symptoms associated with a disorder but also reduces the putative factors that maintain or cause the symptoms. In this manner, we illustrate that GPIP is effective well beyond symptom reduction and has a powerful effect on the underlying transdiagnostic factors that impact the quality of patients' lives.

EFFICACY AND EFFECTIVENESS STUDIES[1]

In two randomized controlled trials (RCTs), we demonstrated the efficacy of GPIP for the treatment of binge-eating disorder (BED; Tasca, Balfour, et al., 2006; Tasca et al., 2019). We developed the original treatment manual for GPIP (Tasca et al., 2005) for the first RCT for BED (Tasca, Ritchie, et al., 2006). In that trial, we randomly assigned 135 patients with BED to receive GPIP or group cognitive behavior therapy (GCBT; Wilfley et al., 1993), or we assigned participants to a wait-list control condition. Both GPIP and GCBT performed equally well to reduce symptoms, including binge eating, depressive symptoms, and interpersonal problems up to 12 months posttreatment. Both GPIP and GCBT outperformed the wait-list control condition on all outcomes. This was the first study to indicate that GPIP was an efficacious treatment and as effective as a well-established evidence-based intervention.

A subsequent RCT of GPIP for the treatment of BED tested a stepped care model of treatment, and so the research design was more complicated. In the first step of the study, a different sample of participants ($N = 135$) all received individual unguided self-help based on a cognitive behavior therapy (CBT) model (Fairburn, 2013). In the second step of the study, we randomly assigned participants either to receive GPIP, or we assigned them to a wait-list control condition. The CBT-based intervention provided in the first step significantly reduced binge eating with a large effect. Adding GPIP in the second step of treatment after CBT did not significantly reduce binge eating much further—after all, participants had already achieved significant symptom reduction. However, adding GPIP did result in further improvement over and above the effects of CBT in interpersonal problems and attachment avoidance when compared with the wait-list control. That is,

---

[1]*Efficacy* refers to findings from RCTs in which researchers randomly assign participants to treatments, treatments are time limited, and therapy protocols are manualized. Some consider the RCT to provide the highest quality of evidence because findings from RCTs may be less biased. However, others argue that the requirements of the RCT study design test treatments that are qualitatively different from what occurs in the real world, and so the findings from RCTs cannot easily inform clinical practice (Westen et al., 2004). *Effectiveness* refers to clinical trials in which researchers do not randomly assign participants to treatments, participants are not as rigorously selected, and treatments may not be manualized. Some consider these studies and findings to represent lower quality of evidence compared with RCTs because of the higher potential for bias. However, effectiveness study designs may be more similar to what occurs in real-life clinical practice, and so the findings may be more applicable (Westen et al., 2004).

GPIP had an additive effect on interpersonal issues, which are problems not targeted by CBT but that many consider to be factors that maintain binge eating and other disorders, such as depression (Ivanova, Tasca, Hammond, et al., 2015; Ivanova, Tasca, Proulx, & Bissada, 2015).

A third RCT of a form of GPIP known as the dynamic–relational treatment of perfectionism (DRTP) is currently underway at the University of British Columbia, led by Dr. Paul Hewitt. In that trial, the researchers are randomly assigning participants with elevated components of perfectionism either to receive DRTP or a supportive group therapy. This randomized controlled trial is based on the promising findings of an effectiveness study of DRTP previously published (Hewitt et al., 2015; Hewitt, Qiu, et al., 2019). In that study, 71 participants with perfectionism received GPIP, and 18 of them were nonrandomly assigned to a wait-list control condition. We found clinically significant decreases in all perfectionism components among treated individuals, and posttreatment scores on all variables were significantly lower in the GPIP condition versus the wait-list control condition.

Finally, we conducted a large effectiveness study of GPIP for BED (Tasca et al., 2013). This study deliberately assigned 102 participants with BED to groups homogeneously composed of those with high versus low levels of attachment anxiety or preoccupied attachment. Composing groups to be homogenous on level of attachment anxiety had little effect on outcomes. However, GPIP did result in improvements in binge-eating, depression, and interpersonal problems, with large effects up to 6 months posttreatment.

The outcome research testing GPIP has demonstrated the efficacy and effectiveness of this treatment for a range of symptom-based outcomes, such as binge eating, perfectionism, depression, and interpersonal problems (Hewitt et al., 2015; Hewitt, Qiu, et al., 2019; Tasca, Balfour, et al., 2006; Tasca et al., 2013, 2019). Such findings indicate that the average patient receiving GPIP will likely benefit in terms of target symptom reduction. These results allow therapists and their patients to feel confident that they are engaging in effective treatment. In addition, as we demonstrate next, the effects of GPIP have broader implications for a number of patient factors known to underlie or maintain a wide range of clinical syndromes.

EFFECTS ON FACTORS THAT CAUSE OR MAINTAIN CLINICAL SYNDROMES

We developed GPIP so that the model and group format would have an impact on a broad array of patient factors implicated in the etiology and maintenance of clinical syndromes. The group therapy aspect of the treatment model, with its emphasis on interpersonal learning, interpersonal feedback, a here-and-now orientation, and the development of cohesion and the therapeutic alliance, provides ample opportunity to target interpersonal and attachment issues that affect many clinical problems. For example, as we described in previous chapters, the components of the triangle of adaptation (attachment needs, affects, defense mechanisms, Figure 1.2) likely lead to and maintain clinical presentations such as binge eating, depression, anxiety, and perfectionism, among others. Further, the interpersonal consequences of the triangle of adaptation, as defined by the cyclical maladaptive interpersonal pattern (CMIP), are those maladaptive relational patterns that may lead to distress, a negative self-concept, and specific symptoms. As a treatment model, GPIP is transdiagnostic in targeting etiological and maintenance factors, including attachment insecurity, interpersonal style and problems, affect dysregulation, and defense mechanisms. Hence, our research that examined the effects of GPIP has gone beyond symptom relief and also focused on outcomes related to these maintenance factors.

ATTACHMENT INSECURITY

There is substantial research on the relationship between attachment insecurity and psychopathology, such that higher levels of attachment insecurity are associated with depressive disorders, personality disorder, and posttraumatic stress disorder (Bakermans-Kranenburg & van IJzendoorn, 2009). Research in clinical samples of those with eating disorders, for example, showed that attachment anxiety is related to greater vulnerability to media internalization and body dissatisfaction (Grenon et al., 2016). In two research and clinical reviews, Tasca and Balfour (2014a, 2014b) concluded that attachment insecurity was a vulnerability factor for developing an eating disorder. Tasca and Balfour (2014b) identified attachment insecurity and the accompanying affect dysregulation and difficulties with mentalizing because key aspects of the triangle of adaptation in the context of stressful life events and biological vulnerability lead to eating disorder symptoms.

In a recent report using the Adult Attachment Interview (George et al., 1985), Maxwell and colleagues (2017) found that women with BED had significantly higher rates of preoccupied and unresolved and disorganized attachment states of mind compared with a matched control group of women without BED. Maxwell and colleagues also reported that among those who had an insecure and/or unresolved and disorganized attachment state of mind pre-GPIP, 60% demonstrated changes to secure and non-unresolved and disorganized states of mind by 6 months post-GPIP. In other words, a time-limited version of GPIP resulted in clinically relevant improvements in attachment insecurity and disorganized mental states related to trauma. In a separate study, Maxwell et al. (2018) found that reflective functioning, an index of mentalizing related to attachment security, significantly improved following GPIP. That is, the emphasis on self-reflection and interpersonal feedback in GPIP likely facilitated a greater capacity to understand patients' mental states and the mental states of others. Mentalization plays an important role in maintaining satisfying relationships and regulating affect, both of which are implicated in binge eating, depressive symptoms, and borderline personality disorder, among others (Bateman & Fonagy, 2006; Ivanova, Tasca, Hammond, et al., 2015).

In the following clinical vignette, the patient, Pauline, a White woman in her late 20s, experienced a disorganized mental state when she began talking about her mother's illness and recent death. The disorganization resulted in a loss of the coherence of her narrative and indicated a lapse in mentalizing. The GPIP therapist helped Pauline regain her mentalizing ability and reflect on the immediate impact of her mother's death on Pauline's interactions with the group.

THERAPIST: Can you describe what the tears are about?

PAULINE: What? Oh. She died last fall after a long illness.

JAN: [a group member] Who died last fall?

PAULINE: Oh. My mother. The last days were really awful. . . . (long pause) What was your question?

THERAPIST: (To Pauline) You seemed to lose track there for a moment. What happened?

PAULINE: I don't know. Sometimes I can't keep my thoughts straight when I talk about Mom's death.

THERAPIST: It seemed to take you out of the group for a moment, and you had trouble thinking.

JAN: I found it a little scary.

THERAPIST: (To Jan) Can you tell Pauline about that?

JAN: (To Pauline) I was worried about you. I could see you drifting away. I wanted you to stay with us, let us help you through it, but I didn't know how.

PAULINE: I didn't even notice. I guess it's hard for me to do sometimes.

THERAPIST: (To Pauline) How do you feel about what Jan said to you just now?

PAULINE: I can see that. And I do want to be more present. (To Jan) I appreciate you bringing me back to the present and wanting to help.

INTERPERSONAL PROBLEMS

A number of authors have proposed an interpersonal model of depression (Weissman et al., 2000) and binge eating (Ansell et al., 2012). In a series of empirical studies, Ivanova and colleagues (Ivanova, Tasca, Hammond, et al., 2015; Ivanova, Tasca, Proulx, & Bissada, 2015) found that interpersonal problems led to binge-eating episodes and that negative affect or affect dysregulation mediated this association. In other words, interpersonal problems may lead to emotion dysregulation, which, in turn, results in depressive or binge-eating symptoms. This model and the research findings suggest that problems in interpersonal functioning may be a good target of group therapy because it is a precipitating factor for a wide range of disorders. The clinical trials described previously that tested the efficacy and effectiveness of GPIP (Hewitt et al., 2015; Tasca, Ritchie, et al., 2006; Tasca et al., 2013, 2019) all indicated that GPIP resulted in a sustained improvement in overall interpersonal problems (see also Tasca et al., 2012).

The quality of interpersonal functioning may be a key variable in treatment because it represents specific relational styles of patients to which a therapist and group must adapt. As we illustrated in previous chapters, both the expression of attachment style and the impact of defense mechanisms on interpersonal relationships, in part, define one's CMIP, interpersonal style, and severity of interpersonal problems. In support of the notion that attachment insecurity is intimately related to interpersonal style, Maxwell and colleagues (2014) found that changes in attachment avoidance and attachment anxiety during GPIP was associated with improved interpersonal problems 1 year posttreatment.

There is evidence that specific interpersonal styles are related to types of clinical syndromes independent of symptom severity. For example, in a series of studies, Zilcha-Mano et al. (2015) identified two interpersonal clusters for panic disorder (domineering–intrusive and nonassertive) and two clusters for major depressive disorder (submissive–affiliative and cold;

Dinger et al., 2015). In our research, we found that those with BED had prototypical profiles on the interpersonal circumplex that differentiated them from matched comparison groups (Brugnera et al., 2018; Lo Coco et al., 2016), such that those with BED had predominant interpersonal problems manifested by nonassertiveness and exploitability (Brugnera et al., 2019). These submissive interpersonal problems were associated with higher levels of depressive symptoms in BED. We also found that GPIP resulted in an increase in dominance among those who previously were overly submissive (Brugnera et al., 2019). However, even though GPIP reduced problems with nonassertiveness, this style remained the predominant interpersonal problem for these patients.

The cumulative findings from our research suggest that when treating those with BED, GPIP therapists might focus particularly on interpersonal problems related to nonassertiveness and exploitability. In the group context, therapists may have to help such patients take their rightful place in the group and consider their issues and feedback to others as valuable and relevant. The following exchange illustrates a therapist's interventions to encourage a self-effacing patient to use the group as a means to enhance assertiveness and self-worth.

SUSAN: I really don't want to take up any time; I don't think this issue is really that important. I know Jan has stuff to talk about.

JAN: I think your stuff is just as important as mine.

SUSAN: No, no, I'm too anxious.

THERAPIST: Susan, I wonder if what is happening here right now in the group is part of the problem that you have been describing. You really wished for your family to take you seriously, but you didn't dare to tell them about what was going on inside of you because you were afraid that they would ignore you. Then you were disappointed when they didn't take you seriously. Here, in the group, Jan and others are inviting you to talk about yourself, but you always defer to someone else. I wonder if you feel disappointed when the group moves on to another member.

SUSAN: I do sometimes feel disappointed. At other times, I'm just relieved, though. It's too hard.

JAN: (To Susan) It's time for you to take your place in this group.

SUSAN: I guess so.

DEFENSE MECHANISMS

As discussed on a number of occasions in this book, defense mechanisms play a key role in the GPIP model. Defense mechanisms form a bridge between the triangle of adaptation and the CMIP. Maladaptive defenses, including acting out, passive aggression, and distortions in the view of self or others, reduce people's ability to be empathic, to mentalize, and to manage emotions, thus causing problems in relationships and one's self-concept. Further, the quality of affect regulation is, in part, determined by whether defense mechanisms work and are adaptive. Overreliance on internalizing defenses such as denial, repression, and intellectualization may lead one to minimize internal reactions, to overcontrol responses to stress, and to experience excessive self-criticism. However, overreliance on externalizing defenses, such as acting out, splitting, or reaction formation, may lead to undue conflict in relationships, undercontrolled responses to stress, and unawareness of one's role in relational dynamics.

As indicated in a previous chapter, the Defense Mechanisms Rating Scale (DMRS; Perry, 1990) clusters specific defense mechanisms, such as isolation and intellectualization, as obsessional-level defenses, whereas one can cluster specific defense mechanisms, such as denial and projection, as disavowal-level defenses (see Table 2.2). These specific defenses and clusters may be ranked in a hierarchy from adaptive (humor, suppression, altruism) to maladaptive (acting out, passive aggression, denial) according to the developmental maturity of the defense (Bond, 2004). Researchers have indicated that lower levels of defensive functioning are associated with greater anxiety, depression, interpersonal problems, and impairment in psychological functioning in patients with various disorders (Hilsenroth et al., 2003; Perry & Cooper, 1989). Researchers have also reported that individual psychotherapy reduces one's reliance on maladaptive defenses (Johansen et al., 2011).

Our research group conducted a study in which we video recorded and transcribed five of 12 sessions (Sessions 1, 3, 8, 12, and 16) of GPIP groups for BED (Hill et al., 2015). The transcripts and videos were coded using the DMRS, with independent ratings provided by several trained raters. Patients self-reported binge eating and depressive symptoms at pretreatment, posttreatment, and up to 12 months follow-up. We found that after 16 sessions of GPIP, participants' overall defensive functioning improved significantly. Specifically, GPIP resulted in patients using more high-adaptive defenses (self-observation, altruism) and fewer major image-distorting (projective-identification, splitting) and action-level (passive aggression and acting-out) defenses. An important finding was that improvement in overall defensive functioning during GPIP mediated or explained a decline in binge eating and depressive symptoms at follow-up. In other words, more adaptive defensive functioning (e.g., less acting out and less projective identification) led to an improvement in symptoms and subjective distress. Increases in adaptive defenses and reductions in maladaptive defenses are consistent with the goals of GPIP, which include more self-reflection, improved relationship quality, and reductions in harsh self-criticism. Adaptive defense mechanisms allow one to engage in greater reflective capacity, which is related to symptom reduction (Maxwell et al., 2017, 2018).

The results of this research suggest that the focus of GPIP on improving defensive functioning is a key element in the effectiveness of the treatment. To illustrate, we provide the following clinical vignette. Don, a Latino man in his late 50s, is a patient who persistently used intellectualization, projection, and devaluation of relationships as defense mechanisms. He likely did so because of the anxiety he felt whenever others tried to get close to him. Don feared the prospect of abandonment, and despite his needs for attachment, he kept others at a distance by engaging in abstract conversations and by dismissing the importance of relationships. These defenses were central to Don's acts of self (CMIP) and, in turn, contributed to others keeping their distance, feeling annoyed with him, or leaving him (acts of others in Don's CMIP). Don's introject suggested that, deep down, he felt unlovable. In the following example from a GPIP group, the therapist drew Don's attention back to the here and now of the group and to his feelings, which were contrary to Don's externalizing defenses. The therapist did so to keep Don connected with the group and his attachment needs.

DON: My roommate is such an ass. He uses me. He owes me money, but I don't ask for it back because I'm fed up. I know I should kick him out, but I'm just not like that.

THERAPIST: You seem angry at him. I wonder if you can let the group give you feedback.

DON: Of course, I'm angry at him. He doesn't carry his weight, he doesn't pay rent . . .

THERAPIST: (Interrupting) Don, I'm going to focus you back to your feelings and to what is going on in the group right now. You said you wanted feedback from the group, but before the group could respond, you kept describing your roommate and what he does.

DON: Yah, okay. I get worked up.

THERAPIST: (To the group) What's it like for the group when Don gets worked up?

SHERRY: It's like he's off in his own world and forgets that we're here.

THERAPIST: And what's the impact on you?

SHERRY: I feel like he's shut me out. He's off on his own topic, and he's not interested in what I have to say. I just feel disengaged from him.

THERAPIST: (To Don) I wonder if focusing so much on your roommate keeps you from really engaging with and connecting with people in the group.

PERFECTIONISM

Perfectionism is a core personality-related variable that underlies psychopathology, relationships, achievement, and health-related problems (Hewitt et al., 2017). Hewitt et al.'s (2017) well-researched model describes perfectionism as made up of three independent components. First, perfectionistic traits include the requirement of perfection of the self (self-oriented perfectionism), the requirement of perfection of others (other-oriented perfectionism), and the perception that others require perfection of oneself (socially prescribed perfectionism). Second, perfectionistic self-presentation, the interpersonal expression of one's purported perfection, involves three facets of perfectionistic self-promotion, nondisplay of imperfections, and the nondisclosure of imperfections. Third, the self-relational component reflects the internal dialogue perfectionistic individuals have that is characterized by automatic perfectionistic self-statements and automatic self-recriminatory statements. Researchers found a strong and consistent relationship between these perfectionism components and several kinds of psychopathology (see Hewitt et al., 2017, for a review). Hewitt and colleagues view perfectionism as a complex defensive personality style that functions to quell negative emotions (e.g., anticipation of rejection, abandonment) but, more important, to secure a caring connection with others, find a place to fit in the world, and repair a defective sense of self. However, perfectionistic behavior produces the opposite effect, resulting in distancing from others, alienation and aloneness, and maintenance of the self as defective, flawed, and never good enough (Hewitt et al., 2006, 2017).

In a study evaluating the effects of DRTP on perfectionism, Hewitt et al. (2015) found significant and large decreases in levels of perfectionism components and that these decreases were associated with reductions in measures of distress, including anxiety and depression. The study demonstrated that the treatment, which focuses on the underlying relational mechanisms of perfectionistic behavior, is effective in treating all components of perfectionism, including state-like cognitions, deeply ingrained perfectionism traits, and self-presentational styles. Hewitt and colleagues' (2015) findings suggest that a treatment that focuses specifically on reducing perfectionistic behavior by addressing the relational underpinnings of perfectionism not only produces significant changes in perfectionism but also that these changes lead to an improvement in symptoms such as depression, anxiety, and interpersonal problems.

In a follow-up, Hewitt, Qiu, and colleagues (2019) asked the family members and close loved ones of patients who received DRTP to report on the patient's perfectionism states and traits pretreatment, posttreatment, and at follow-up. It is possible that perfectionistic people who have a stake in how they present or view themselves may not be able to accurately self-report their perfectionistic states or traits. Asking informants (family members, close loved ones) may give a unique perspective on any change due to group therapy. The findings, in many ways, paralleled those described in Hewitt and colleagues' (2015) study in which patients self-reported their levels of perfectionism. Close-other informant ratings of patients' self-oriented, other-oriented, and perfectionistic self-presentation were significantly lower at posttreatment and follow-up. The only exception was that close-other informants did not report improvement in socially prescribed perfectionism. It may be that socially prescribed perfectionism is harder for informants to comment on because it represents the internal experiences of the patient not easily observed by others. Nevertheless, the study showed that not only did patients report improvements in their perfectionistic behaviors but also that loved ones noted these changes as well.

In the following clinical vignette, we illustrate how a therapy group might address perfectionism in DRTP and how this may have wide-ranging implications for the individual. Sherry, an African American patient in the group in her mid-30s, was highly perfectionistic and self-critical, previously had an eating disorder, and continued to experience negative body image. During her childhood, her father was violent when he was intoxicated, and her mother, who was likely depressed, was unable to offer Sherry adequate love and affection due to her distress and fear. Sherry had two failed adult romantic relationships in which she described herself as feeling insecure despite her partners expressing their love for her. She also reported profound self-doubt about her worth. Eventually, her romantic partners left her, perhaps feeling confused and frustrated by Sherry's seeming inability to accept and reciprocate their expressions of affection and affirmation. Her experience of her father contributed to Sherry viewing love as potentially dangerous, whereas her mother's emotional unavailability led Sherry to view herself as undeserving and unworthy.

Sherry developed strong self-oriented perfectionism traits. As can often happen when a child grows up in a home in which a parent is unpredictably explosive or violent, Sherry tried to manage the chaos of her surroundings by striving to be perfect, in the hope that if she did everything perfectly, her father would have less reason to lash out. Sherry sought respite from the turbulence of her home through competitive skating, where she gained self-confidence and was affirmed by her coach for her success in national competitions. Her perfectionism was particularly evident in the achievement domain and gave rise to a fragile self-esteem that depended on external and tangible outcomes. However, now in her early 30s, Sherry no longer figure skated, continued to struggle to maintain closeness in a romantic relationship, and became depressed, anxious, and extremely self-critical at the slightest hint of perceived failure. Paradoxically, Sherry noted experiencing what she felt was perplexing anxiety and restlessness when relationships with either men or women progressed beyond social nicety. The following exchange occurred after an interaction with Don, in which Sherry expressed caring and compassion to him. However, when the therapist identified the positive aspects of Sherry's responses to Don, she withdrew.

THERAPIST: (To Sherry) You've become very quiet in the past few minutes. Earlier, you looked uncomfortable when I said that it was nice to see how empathic you were to Don.

SHERRY: I don't know what to do with what you said to me. I don't know if I should believe it—and if I do, then what?

THERAPIST: (To the group) What do others in the group think about this?

DON: I agree. (To Sherry) I think what you said was very kind. (Others in the group nod.)

THERAPIST: (To Don) How do you feel about Sherry going quiet?

DON: I got the sense that she wanted space—to be left alone. So, I didn't say anything to her.

THERAPIST: (To Sherry) You seemed uncomfortable with the compliment from me, and then you gave the nonverbal message to me and the group to back off. Is it that you don't feel that you deserve the compliment or that I didn't mean it?

SHERRY: Both, but mainly that I don't deserve it. It really makes me anxious.

THERAPIST: It seems that, in that moment, we saw how you struggle to take in anything that is different from how negatively you see yourself. And instead of inviting me or Don in, you gave the signal to back off. And for a moment, we did.

SHERRY: Yes, it works—well, sometimes (smiling).

THERAPIST: What if you try something different in the group so that you allow yourself to accept what the group has to say to you?

SHERRY: I'd like to, but to be honest, something about that feels dangerous. I don't know what. I can't really explain it.

RESEARCH ON THE PROCESS OF CHANGE IN GPIP

One of the key assumptions of GPIP is that change in one or more aspects of the triangle of adaptation will result in changes in maladaptive interpersonal patterns as reflected in the triangle of object relations and target symptoms such as depression, anxiety, or binge eating. Some of the research reviewed earlier tested this assumption. As indicated, change in defensive functioning (Hill et al., 2015) and change in the interpersonal and intrapersonal aspects of perfectionism (Hewitt et al., 2015) each were related to change in target symptoms and subjective distress. Some of our research has suggested that this process might be specific to GPIP. For example, we found that improvement in attachment anxiety was related to reduced depression in patients receiving GPIP but not for those receiving GCBT (Tasca et al., 2007). That is, attachment insecurity is a specific treatment target of GPIP and differentiates GPIP from a CBT-oriented group treatment, and this focus on attachment insecurity may be an important means by which GPIP works.

STAGES OF GROUP DEVELOPMENT

In a pair of studies, we examined GPIP therapists' interpersonal stances to see whether therapists used principles of interpersonal complementarity in their work. Recall that *interpersonal complementarity* refers to interactions that correspond in affiliation (e.g., friendliness followed by friendliness or hostility followed by hostility) and are reciprocal in terms of interdependence or status (e.g., dominance followed by submission, and vice versa; Figure 1.3). Complementarity is an important factor in developing the therapeutic relationship because complementarity reduces anxiety among the interacting individuals, preserves their self-concept, and is highly reinforcing for participants (Kiesler, 1983). Higher levels of positive complementarity early in individual therapy buttresses the therapeutic alliance and is characteristic of successful therapy cases (Henry et al., 1986; Tasca & McMullen, 1992).

In one study, we rated interpersonal interactions from video recordings of 12 GPIP groups and therapists using the structural analysis of social behavior (SASB; Benjamin & Cushing, 2000). The SASB is an observer rating system of the interpersonal circumplex. We found that greater therapist–patient complementarity in early sessions of GPIP was related to decreases in binge eating at posttreatment (Maxwell et al., 2012). In other words, therapists who matched their interpersonal style to the needs of group members in a friendly complementary fashion early in treatment had patients that achieved greater symptom reduction.

In a second related study, we intensively investigated two groups, a GPIP group and a GCBT group, in which the therapists were highly adherent to their respective models of treatment. Early, middle-, and late-stage transcribed video recordings of interactions between therapists and patients in each of these two time-limited group therapies were coded with the SASB. Overall, the GPIP therapist and her group had higher levels of interpersonal complementary interaction than the GCBT therapist and her group. When we looked at complementarity at different stages of treatment, we found that the GPIP therapist and group had high levels of complementary interactions in the early stage, followed by lower complementarity in the middle stage. Findings from these studies were consistent with the GPIP model of group development described in the previous chapter. A highly adherent GPIP therapist worked to develop cohesion and an alliance early in the forming stage (indicated by high levels of complementarity between the therapist and group) and then moved on to challenge the CMIPs in the middle or storming and norming stages of group (indicated by lower levels of complementarity).

We conducted a more direct test of the developmental model of GPIP groups in a study in which we assessed engaged group climate, a proxy for group cohesion, after every session of GPIP and GCBT (Tasca, Ritchie, et al., 2006). Growth curve statistical methods assessed the best fitting curve to represent the data across the 16 sessions of group therapy. The best fit for GCBT was a straight line representing a steady session-by-session increase in engaged group climate. Group engagement among members of the GCBT groups rose steadily over time. However, the best fit for GPIP was a cubic growth curve representing a sharp increase in engagement in the early sessions, a plateau for several sessions in the middle of treatment, and then a sharp increase in engagement again at the end of therapy. We reported similar findings in the cubic growth of adaptive defensive functioning across sessions of GPIP (Hill et al., 2015). That is, there were three distinct phases of growth in group engagement and adaptive defensive functioning that fit with the developmental model of GPIP groups. The early stage (i.e., forming) saw a sharp rise in cohesion and adaptive defenses, followed by a plateau in the middle stage during which therapists challenged patients' CMIPs (i.e., storming and norming), then followed by a precipitous rise in cohesion and adaptive defenses at the end of treatment to coincide with consolidating patient changes (i.e., performing and adjourning).

THE ROLE OF ATTACHMENT

We indicated earlier that attachment insecurity improves after treatment with GPIP. In two separate studies, we also found that improved attachment insecurity was related to (a) changes in target symptoms such as interpersonal problems (Maxwell et al., 2014) and (b) improved depression but only in GPIP and not GCBT (Maxwell et al., 2012). This difference between GPIP and GCBT was also evident in a study in which patients with greater attachment anxiety had better outcomes in GPIP compared with GCBT (Tasca, Balfour, et al., 2006). The findings from these studies suggested that specifically targeting the attachment needs vertex of the triangle of adaptation is an important process by which GPIP works, differentiating it from other forms of group therapy.

In several studies, we drilled a little deeper into the role of attachment and the process of GPIP. We were interested in why patients with greater attachment anxiety (or preoccupied attachment) had better outcomes in GPIP than in GCBT. So, we measured attachment anxiety and avoidance at pretreatment, group cohesion after each GPIP session, and binge eating pre- and posttreatment. In two separate studies using different samples and different measures of group cohesion, we found that increases in group cohesion were related to reduced binge eating and that this relationship was strongest for those higher in attachment anxiety (Gallagher, Tasca,

Ritchie, Balfour, & Bissada, 2014; Tasca, Ritchie, et al., 2006). The findings suggest that GPIP therapists should emphasize an increasing group cohesion across therapy sessions and that this growth in cohesion was especially important for those patients with greater attachment anxiety. Such patients are preoccupied with relationships and sensitive to fluctuations in the quality of these relationships. They may need their therapy group to experience an increasing level of interpersonal connection, empathy, and warmth for them to benefit from treatment.

Preoccupied attachment or attachment anxiety emerged in our research as a key factor in determining how and why GPIP worked. We took the research a little further by evaluating the ongoing and emerging relationships among group members and their perceptions of group cohesion. Gallagher, Tasca, Ritchie, Balfour, Maxwell, and Bissada (2014) asked group participants after every session to rate (a) their cohesion to the group and (b) each of the other group members' cohesion to the group. This gave us an indication of each person's self-rating of cohesion and the mean of the rest of the group's cohesion across sessions of GPIP. First, we found significant convergence over time between self- and other ratings of the group's cohesion. In other words, patients came to agree on their perceptions of the group's emotional atmosphere as they spent more time together. Second, those with greater attachment anxiety had lower self-ratings of cohesion to the group and greater discrepancy of cohesion ratings from the rest of the group. Third, there was a significant positive relationship between convergence in cohesion ratings across sessions and improved self-esteem at posttreatment. Fourth, the convergence of self- with others ratings were associated with an increase in self-esteem among individuals in group therapy. We interpreted the findings to mean that individuals were developing more accurate self-perceptions (measured by converging self- and other ratings of cohesion over time) and that this was achieved through interpersonal feedback from group members. The findings suggested that GPIP therapists should facilitate interpersonal learning in their groups, especially for those with preoccupied or anxious attachments, by noting discrepancies and then encouraging convergence between an individual and the group in their perceptions of group interactions. We see this process of converging perceptions as a form of interpersonal learning from receiving feedback in group therapy.

The following clinical vignette illustrates how a GPIP therapist might encourage feedback from group members to facilitate interpersonal learning in a patient who experiences a high level of preoccupied or anxious attachment. Rather than providing a "definitive" interpretation of what occurred in a previous session, the therapist allowed the group and patient to work out a mutually agreed-on understanding of what happened.

BRUNO:	(To the group) I was upset at the end of the last session and called Dr. T (the therapist) about it. He encouraged me to come to group this week to talk about it.
JIM:	(a group member) What is it that upset you?
BRUNO:	At the end of the session, I thought you guys were laughing at me, and Dr. T. turned to me and said, "See, they're laughing at you!" I expected him (Dr. T) to protect me instead of encouraging you to pick on me.
THERAPIST:	How do other people in the group remember what happened at the end of last week?
SUSAN:	I remember us laughing about something, and you seemed to join in on it (to Bruno). I certainly didn't mean to offend you.
JIM:	I remember Dr. T asking you what you thought about the laughter. I don't think he said that we were laughing AT you. (Other group members nod in agreement.)
THERAPIST:	Bruno, what do you make of what the group is saying?
BRUNO:	I believe them. . . . I guess I misunderstood what they were doing and what you said.
THERAPIST:	How do you understand that?
BRUNO:	(To the group) I know I'm pretty sensitive about people going behind my back, and so, I might have misinterpreted your intentions (To the group). (To Dr. T) I really did want you to protect me, though.

CONCLUSION

There is value in clinicians knowing the evidence that supports the work they are doing. Understanding the research can increase a therapist's confidence that what they are providing is effective, which in turn increases their allegiance to the treatment model from which they are working. This has a cumulative impact on patients who might develop a higher expectation or hope of achieving a positive outcome from the treatment. Psychotherapy research has demonstrated that therapists' confidence and allegiance and patients' expectations are associated with better patient outcomes (Constantino et al., 2018; Wampold & Imel, 2015).

GPIP is an effective treatment for a wide range of patient factors that cause many symptoms and syndromes (Hewitt et al., 2015; Hewitt, Qiu, et al., 2019; Tasca, Balfour, et al., 2006; Tasca et al., 2013, 2019). Our research demonstrated that GPIP can improve those elements identified in the triangle of adaptation that underlie problems in relationships and intrapersonal distress, such as defensive functioning (Hill et al., 2015), attachment insecurity (Maxwell et al., 2017; 2018), negative affect (Tasca, Balfour, et al., 2006; Tasca et al., 2013), interpersonal problems (Tasca et al., 2012, 2019), perfectionism (Hewitt et al., 2015; Hewitt, Qiu, et al., 2019), and low self-esteem (Gallagher, Tasca, Ritchie, Balfour, Maxwell, & Bissada, 2014; Tasca, Balfour, et al., 2006). Also, the evidence suggests that GPIP targets specific interpersonal problems and attachment insecurities evident in the CMIPs of individual patients to improve symptoms and subjective distress (Brugnera et al., 2019; Maxwell et al., 2017, 2018; Tasca et al., 2012). When we looked closer at how and why GPIP works, we found that the course of GPIP followed predictable stages, including developing cohesion early in therapy, challenging CMIPs in mid-treatment, and consolidating changes in the last phase (Hill et al., 2015; Tasca, Ritchie, et al., 2006). In particular, GPIP therapists used interpersonal principles, such as complementarity, differently at different stages of group treatment to facilitate changes in patients (Maxwell et al., 2012; Tasca et al., 2011). The research indicated that GPIP therapists modify their interpersonal stances to fit the patient's needs and depending on the particular requirements of a developmental stage of the group. Finally, we found that through its emphasis on group therapeutic factors such as group cohesion, GPIP can facilitate known group therapeutic factors, such as interpersonal feedback and learning, especially for those with greater attachment insecurity (Gallagher, Tasca, Ritchie, Balfour, & Bissada, 2014; Gallagher, Tasca, Ritchie, Balfour, Maxwell, & Bissada, 2014).

Therapists communicating this knowledge of the evidence for GPIP to patients will increase patients' expectations of a good outcome, which we know has a positive impact on how well therapies work for patients (Constantino et al., 2018). However, just as important is the clinician's capacity to inform administrators, third-party payers, and policy makers about the utility of GPIP as an evidence-based treatment. Knowing the research evidence will help therapists advocate for treatments that can be tailored to individual patients' intrapersonal and interpersonal issues that underlie many problems in living. Understanding the evidence for GPIP's efficacy and its impact on those transdiagnostic factors that maintain symptoms will allow the therapist to feel comfortable with and confident in applying GPIP in their practices.

THERAPIST TASK BOX
GPIP: THE RESEARCH EVIDENCE

1. Know the research evidence for GPIP, and communicate this knowledge to your patients. Use this knowledge to facilitate patients' realistic expectations of a positive outcome.

2. Adjust your interventions and interpersonal stances to the patient's particular interpersonal problem or style. For example, if the patient is too submissive, encourage them to be more assertive in the group.

3. Encourage interpersonal feedback among group members as a means of enhancing their ability to mentalize and self-reflect.

4. Be aware of the requirements of each stage of group development and adjust interventions and interpersonal stances accordingly.

   - Early stage: Engage in more friendly complementary interactions and emphasize similarities and converging experiences of cohesion among patients.

   - Middle stage: Engage in fewer complementary interactions, elicit more interpersonal feedback, and gently challenge CMIPs.

   - Late stage: Engage in more complementary interactions to consolidate changes in behaviors and introjects.

CHAPTER 5 REVIEW EXERCISES

Exercise 5.1

Which of the following statements are true (T) or false (F) about the research evidence for group psychodynamic-interpersonal psychotherapy (GPIP)?

1. GPIP is effective but not as effective as evidence-based treatments. T/F

2. GPIP reduces attachment insecurity but not symptoms of binge eating in patients with binge-eating disorder (BED). T/F

3. GPIP is as effective as group cognitive behavior therapy (GCBT) to reduce binge eating, interpersonal problems, and depression for patients with BED. T/F

4. GPIP is more effective than no treatment and more effective than GCBT for most symptoms. T/F

5. GPIP reduces the effects of patient factors that underlie syndromes, such as defense mechanisms and attachment insecurity. T/F

Exercise 5.2

Match the following group therapist behaviors to the stage of development according to the research evidence on the stages of group development in GPIP:

A. Early (forming)   B. Middle (storming, norming)
C. Late (performing, adjourning)

_____ 1. The therapist shifted her interpersonal stance to be less dominant and so less complementary to Jane's typically passive interpersonal stance.

_____ 2. The therapist maintained a friendly and complementary stance with group members as a means of encouraging group cohesion.

_____ 3. The therapist encouraged the group to challenge Don's hostile-submissiveness in the group by asking group members to describe their feelings about Don's behaviors.

_____ 4. The therapist commented on how Susan's view of herself had changed, and other members in the group also reported similar experiences of Susan.

_____ 5. The therapist noted differences between group members on how they perceived the same event in the therapy group.

_____ 6. The therapist emphasized similarities between group members in terms of their feelings, experiences, or how they were in the group.

Exercise 5.3

Indicate with a yes (Y) or no (N) which of the following is most likely to occur in GPIP regarding changes in patients' defense mechanisms, according to the research.

1. Joanne used to immediately say what was on her mind in group. Now she can be more reflective before talking. _____

2. Jane used to try to explain her behaviors to the group by using somewhat vague constructs ("I used to steal because I was deprived as a child").

More recently, she simply justifies her actions to the group ("I stole it because I wanted it"). _____

3. Don used to get annoyed and say something sarcastic whenever the group challenged him. Now, he makes a joke about it and then considers whether the challenge is valid. _____

4. Previously, Alice used to put a feeling aside in group to focus on another group member, and then she would eventually return to exploring her feeling. Now, Alice will put feeling out of her mind in group and later have no recollection of the feeling. _____

5. Bruno used to attribute negative feelings to others in the group and blame them for how they felt. Now Bruno tries to understand his reactions and the reactions of others according to what he knows about himself and them. _____

Exercise 5.4

Indicate which of the following statements are true (T) or false (F) regarding the research on attachment and GPIP.

1. Patients with greater avoidant or dismissing attachments are more likely to drop out of GPIP. T/F

2. Patients with greater anxious or preoccupied attachments tend to do better in GPIP than in GCBT. T/F

3. Patients with attachment anxiety or preoccupied attachment show initially lower levels of group cohesion in GPIP, but then their group cohesion increases significantly across sessions. T/F

4. Initially, patients with attachment anxiety or preoccupied attachment have diverging experiences of group cohesion compared with other group members, but as they spend more time in GPIP groups, their experiences of group cohesion converge with those of other group members. T/F

5. Patients with attachment insecurity do not benefit as much from GPIP's focus on interpersonal learning and feedback from other group members. T/F

6. The emphasis on self-disclosure and interpersonal feedback in GPIP may be the reason patients' ability to mentalize improves from pre- to posttreatment. T/F

CHAPTER 5 REVIEW ANSWERS

Exercise 5.1

1. False
2. False
3. True
4. False
5. True

Exercise 5.2

1. B. Middle (storming, norming)
2. A. Early (forming)
3. B. Middle (storming, norming)
4. C. Late (performing, adjourning)
5. B. Middle (storming, norming)
6. A. Early (forming)

Exercise 5.3

1. Yes
2. No
3. Yes
4. No
5. Yes

Exercise 5.4

1. True
2. False
3. True
4. True
5. False
6. True

References

Ackerman, S. J., Hilsenroth, M. J., Baity, M. R., & Blagys, M. D. (2000). Interaction of therapeutic process and alliance during psychological assessment. *Journal of Personality Assessment, 75*(1), 82–109. https://doi.org/10.1207/S15327752JPA7501_7

Ainsworth, M. D., Blehar, M., Waters, E., & Wall, S. (1978). *Patterns of attachment: A psychological study of the Strange Situation.* Erlbaum.

American Psychiatric Association. (2013). *Diagnostic and statistical manual of mental disorders* (5th ed.). https://doi.org/10.1176/appi.books.9780890425596

Amianto, F., Northoff, G., Abbate Daga, G., Fassino, S., & Tasca, G. A. (2016). Is anorexia nervosa a disorder of the self? A psychological approach. *Frontiers in Psychology, 7,* 849. https://doi.org/10.3389/fpsyg.2016.00849

Ansell, E. B., Grilo, C. M., & White, M. A. (2012). Examining the interpersonal model of binge eating and loss of control over eating in women. *International Journal of Eating Disorders, 45*(1), 43–50. https://doi.org/10.1002/eat.20897

Baker, H. S., & Baker, M. N. (1987). Heinz Kohut's self psychology: An overview. *The American Journal of Psychiatry, 144*(1), 1–9. https://doi.org/10.1176/ajp.144.1.1

Bakermans-Kranenburg, M. J., & van IJzendoorn, M. H. (2009). The first 10,000 Adult Attachment Interviews: Distributions of adult attachment representations in clinical and non-clinical groups. *Attachment & Human Development, 11*(3), 223–263. https://doi.org/10.1080/14616730902814762

Balfour, L., Kowal, J., Silverman, A., Tasca, G. A., Angel, J. B., Macpherson, P. A., Garber, G., Cooper, C. L., & Cameron, D. W. (2006). A randomized controlled psycho-education intervention trial: Improving psychological readiness for successful HIV medication adherence and reducing depression before initiating HAART. *AIDS Care, 18*(7), 830–838. https://doi.org/10.1080/09540120500466820

Bartholomew, K., & Horowitz, L. M. (1991). Attachment styles among young adults: A test of a four-category model. *Journal of Personality and Social Psychology, 61*(2), 226–244. https://doi.org/10.1037/0022-3514.61.2.226

Bateman, A., & Fonagy, P. (2006). *Mentalization-based treatment for borderline personality disorder: A practical guide.* Oxford University Press. https://doi.org/10.1093/med/9780198570905.001.0001

Beck, A. P., Dugo, J. M., Eng, A. M., & Lewis, C. M. (1986). The search for phases in group development: Designing process analysis measures of group interaction. In L. S. Greenberg & W. M. Pinsof (Eds.), *The psychotherapeutic process: A research handbook* (pp. 615–705). Guilford Press.

Bednar, R. L., & Kaul, T. J. (1994). Experiential group research: Can the canon fire? In A. E. Bergin & S. L. Garfield (Eds.), *Handbook of psychotherapy and behavior change* (pp. 631–663). Wiley.

Benjamin, L. S. (1993). Every psychopathology is a gift of love. *Psychotherapy Research, 3*(1), 1–24. https://doi.org/10.1080/10503309312331333629

Benjamin, L. S. (1996). *Interpersonal diagnosis and treatment of personality disorders* (2nd ed.). Guilford Press.

Benjamin, L. S., & Cushing, G. (2000). *Manual for coding social interactions in terms of structural analysis of social behavior.* University of Utah.

Bernard, H., Burlingame, G., Flores, P., Greene, L., Joyce, A., Kobos, J. C., Leszcz, M., MacNair-Semands, R. R., Piper, W. E., McEneaney, A. M., Feirman, D., & the Science to Service Task Force, American Group Psychotherapy Association. (2008). Clinical practice guidelines for group psychotherapy. *International Journal of Group Psychotherapy, 58*(4), 455–542. https://doi.org/10.1521/ijgp.2008.58.4.455

Beutler, L. E., Kimpara, S., Edwards, C. J., & Miller, K. D. (2018). Fitting psychotherapy to patient coping style: A meta-analysis. *Journal of Clinical Psychology, 74*(11), 1980–1995. https://doi.org/10.1002/jclp.22684

Binder, J. L., & Strupp, H. H. (1997). "Negative process": A recurrently discovered and underestimated facet of therapeutic process and outcome in the individual psychotherapy of adults. *Clinical Psychology: Science and Practice, 4*(2), 121–139. https://doi.org/10.1111/j.1468-2850.1997.tb00105.x

Black, R. S. A., Curran, D., & Dyer, K. F. W. (2013). The impact of shame on the therapeutic alliance and intimate relationships. *Journal of Clinical Psychology, 69*(6), 646–654. https://doi.org/10.1002/jclp.21959

Blatt, S. J. (2004). *Experiences of depression: Theoretical, clinical, and research perspectives.* American Psychological Association. https://doi.org/10.1037/10749-000

Blatt, S. J., Auerbach, J. S., Zuroff, D. C., & Shahar, G. (2006). Evaluating efficacy, effectiveness, and mutative factors in psychodynamic psychotherapies. In PDM Task Force (Eds.), *Psychodynamic diagnostic manual* (pp. 537–572). Alliance of Psychoanalytic Organizations.

Blatt, S. J., & Zuroff, D. C. (2005). Empirical evaluation of the assumptions in identifying evidence based treatments in mental health. *Clinical Psychology Review, 25*(4), 459–486. https://doi.org/10.1016/j.cpr.2005.03.001

Bond, M. (2004). Empirical studies of defense style: Relationships with psychopathology and change. *Harvard Review of Psychiatry, 12*(5), 263–278. https://doi.org/10.1080/10673220490886167

Bowlby, J. (1980). *Attachment and loss.* Basic Books.

Bowlby, J. (1988). *A secure base.* Basic Books.

Brabender, V., & Fallon, A. (1993). *Models of inpatient group psychotherapy.* American Psychological Association.

Bratton, M. (2010). Expanding the script for survivor therapy: Personifying the cognitive distortions associated with childhood abuse. *Annals of the American Psychotherapy Association, 13*(1), 62–64.

Brennan, K. A., Clark, C. L., & Shaver, P. R. (1998). Self-report measurement of adult attachment: An integrative overview. In J. A. Simpson & W. S. Rholes (Eds.), *Attachment theory and close relationships* (pp. 46–76). Guilford Press.

Bretherton, I., & Munholland, K. A. (1999). Internal working models in attachment relationships: A construct revisited. In J. Cassidy & P. R. Shaver (Eds.), *Handbook of attachment: Theory, research, and clinical applications* (pp. 89–114). Guilford Press.

Brugnera, A., Carlucci, S., Compare, A., Tasca, G. A. (2019). Persistence of friendly and submissive interpersonal styles among those with binge-eating disorder: Comparisons with matched controls and outcomes after group therapy. *Clinical Psychology & Psychotherapy, 26*(5), 603–615. https://doi.org/10.1002/cpp.2385

Brugnera, A., Lo Coco, G., Salerno, L., Sutton, R., Gullo, S., Compare, A., & Tasca, G. A. (2018). Patients with binge eating disorder and obesity have qualitatively different interpersonal characteristics: Results from an Interpersonal Circumplex study. *Comprehensive Psychiatry, 85,* 36–41. https://doi.org/10.1016/j.comppsych.2018.06.008

Budman, S. H., Demby, A., Feldstein, M., & Gold, M. (1984). The effects of time-limited group psychotherapy: A controlled study. *International Journal of Group Psychotherapy, 34*(4), 587–603. https://doi.org/10.1080/00207284.1984.11732562

Burlingame, G. M., & Jensen, J. (2017). Small group process and outcome research highlights: A 25-year perspective. *International Journal of Group Psychotherapy, 67*(Suppl 1), S194–S218. https://doi.org/10.1080/00207284.2016.1218287

Burlingame, G. M., McClendon, D. T., & Yang, C. (2018). Cohesion in group therapy: A meta-analysis. *Psychotherapy, 55*(4), 384–398. https://doi.org/10.1037/pst0000173

Burlingame, G. M., Seebeck, J. D., Janis, R. A., Whitcomb, K. E., Barkowski, S., Rosendahl, J., & Strauss, B. (2016). Outcome differences between individual and group formats when identical and nonidentical treatments, patients, and doses are compared: A 25-year meta-analytic perspective. *Psychotherapy, 53*(4), 446–461. https://doi.org/10.1037/pst0000090

Burlingame, G. M., Strauss, B., Joyce, A., MacNair-Semands, R., MacKenzie, K., Ogrodniczuk, J., & Taylor, S. (2006). *American Group Psychotherapy Association CORE Battery-Revised*. American Group Psychotherapy Association.

Carson, R. C. (1969). Interpretive manual to the MMPI. In J. N. Butcher (Ed.), *MMPI: Research developments and clinical applications* (pp. 279–296). McGraw-Hill.

Caspi, A., Houts, R. M., Belsky, D. W., Goldman-Mellor, S. J., Harrington, H., Israel, S., Meier, M. H., Ramrakha, S., Shalev, I., Poulton, R., & Moffitt, T. E. (2014). The p factor: One general psychopathology factor in the structure of psychiatric disorders? *Clinical Psychological Science, 2*(2), 119–137. https://doi.org/10.1177/2167702613497473

Cassidy, J., & Marvin, R. S. with the MacArthur Working Group. (1992). *Attachment organization in preschool children: Procedures and coding manual* [Unpublished manuscript]. Department of Psychology, University of Virginia.

Chambless, D. L., & Hollon, S. D. (1998). Defining empirically supported therapies. *Journal of Consulting and Clinical Psychology, 66*(1), 7–18. https://doi.org/10.1037/0022-006X.66.1.7

Chen, E. C., Kakkad, D., & Balzano, J. (2008). Multicultural competence and evidence-based practice in group therapy. *Journal of Clinical Psychology, 64*(11), 1261–1278. https://doi.org/10.1002/jclp.20533

Clarkin, J. F., Yeomans, F. E., & Kernberg, O. F. (1999). *Psychotherapy for borderline personality disorder: Focusing on object relations*. American Psychiatric Press.

Cone-Uemura, K., & Suzuki Bentley, E. (2018). Multicultural/diversity issues in groups. In M. Ribeiro, J. M. Gross, & M. M. Turner (Eds.), *The college counsellor's guide to group psychotherapy* (pp. 21–35). Routledge.

Constantino, M. J., Vîslă, A., Coyne, A. E., & Boswell, J. F. (2018). A meta-analysis of the association between patients' early treatment outcome expectation and their posttreatment outcomes. *Psychotherapy, 55*(4), 473–485. https://doi.org/10.1037/pst0000169

Cooley, C. H. (1908). A study of the early use of the self-words by a child. *Psychological Review, 15*(6), 339–357. https://doi.org/10.1037/h0071960

Cornoiu, A., Beischer, A. D., Donnan, L., Graves, S., & de Steiger, R. (2011). Multimedia patient education to assist the informed consent process for knee arthroscopy. *ANZ Journal of Surgery, 81*(3), 176–180. https://doi.org/10.1111/j.1445-2197.2010.05487.x

Crittenden, P. M. (1992). Quality of attachment in the preschool years. *Development and Psychopathology, 4*(2), 209–241. http://dx.doi.org/10.1017/S0954579400000110

Crittenden, P. M. (1995). Attachment and risk for psychopathology: The early years. *Journal of Developmental and Behavioral Pediatrics, 16*(3 Suppl), S12–S16. https://doi.org/10.1097/00004703-199506001-00004

Crittenden, P. M. (2006). A dynamic-maturational model of attachment. *Australian and New Zealand Journal of Family Therapy, 27*(2), 105–115. https://doi.org/10.1002/j.1467-8438.2006.tb00704.x

DeKlyen, M., & Greenberg, M. T. (2008). Attachment and psychopathology in childhood. In J. Cassidy & P. R. Shaver (Eds.), *Handbook of attachment: Theory, research, and clinical applications* (2nd ed., pp. 637–665). Guilford Press.

Dinger, U., Barrett, M. S., Zimmermann, J., Schauenburg, H., Wright, A. G. C., Renner, F., Zilcha-Mano, S., & Barber, J. P. (2015). Interpersonal problems, dependency, and self-criticism in major depressive disorder. *Journal of Clinical Psychology, 71*(1), 93–104. https://doi.org/10.1002/jclp.22120

Duncan, B. L., & Reese, R. J. (2015). The Partners for Change Outcome Management System (PCOMS) revisiting the client's frame of reference. *Psychotherapy, 52*(4), 391–401. https://doi.org/10.1037/pst0000026

Eubanks, C. F., Muran, J. C., & Safran, J. D. (2018). Alliance rupture repair: A meta-analysis. *Psychotherapy, 55*(4), 508–519. https://doi.org/10.1037/pst0000185

Ezriel, H. (1973). Psychoanalytic group therapy. In L. R. Wolberg & E. K. Schwartz (Eds.), *Group therapy: 1973, an overview* (pp. 183–210). Intercontinental Medical Book Corporation.

Fairburn, C. G. (2013). *Overcoming binge eating: The proven program to learn why you binge and how you can stop.* Guilford Press.

Flückiger, C., Del Re, A. C., Wampold, B. E., & Horvath, A. O. (2018). The alliance in adult psychotherapy: A meta-analytic synthesis. *Psychotherapy, 55*(4), 316–340. https://doi.org/10.1037/pst0000172

Fonagy, P. (2001). *Attachment theory and psychoanalysis.* Other Press.

Fonagy, P., Gergely, G., Jurist, E. L., & Target, M. (2002). *Affect regulation, mentalization and the development of the self.* Other Press.

France, D. G., & Dugo, J. M. (1985). Pretherapy orientation as preparation for open psychotherapy groups. *Psychotherapy: Theory, Research, & Practice, 22*(2), 256–261. https://doi.org/10.1037/h0085503

Fuendeling, J. M. (1998). Affect regulation as a stylistic process within adult attachment. *Journal of Social and Personal Relationships, 15*(3), 291–322. https://doi.org/10.1177/0265407598153001

Gabbard, G. O. (2004). *Long-term psychodynamic psychotherapy: A basic text.* American Psychiatric Association.

Gallagher, M. E., Tasca, G. A., Ritchie, K., Balfour, L., & Bissada, H. (2014). Attachment anxiety moderates the relationship between growth in group cohesion and treatment outcomes in Group Psychodynamic Interpersonal Psychotherapy for women with binge eating disorder. *Group Dynamics, 18*(1), 38–52. https://doi.org/10.1037/a0034760

Gallagher, M. E., Tasca, G. A., Ritchie, K., Balfour, L., Maxwell, H., & Bissada, H. (2014). Interpersonal learning is associated with improved self-esteem in group psychotherapy for women with binge eating disorder. *Psychotherapy*, *51*(1), 66–77. https://doi.org/10.1037/a0031098

Garceau, C., Chyurlia, L., Baldwin, D., Boritz, T., Hewitt, P. L., Kealy, D., Sochting, I., Mikail, S., & Tasca, G. A. (in press). Applying the Rupture Resolution Rating System (3RS) to group therapy: An evidence-based case study. *Group Dynamics*.

George, C., Kaplan, N., & Main, M. (1985). *The Adult Attachment Interview* [Unpublished manuscript]. Department of Psychology, University of California at Berkeley.

Greenson, R. R. (1978). *Explorations in psychoanalysis*. International University Press.

Grenon, R., Tasca, G. A., Maxwell, H., Balfour, L., Proulx, G., & Bissada, H. (2016). Parental bonds and body dissatisfaction in a clinical sample: The mediating roles of attachment anxiety and media internalization. *Body Image, 19*, 49–56. https://doi.org/10.1016/j.bodyim.2016.08.005

Harwood, T. M., Beutler, L. E., & Groth-Marnat, G. (2011). *Integrative assessment of adult personality* (3rd ed.). Guilford Press.

Hays, P. A. (2009). Integrating evidence-based practice, cognitive–behavior therapy, and multicultural therapy: Ten steps for culturally competent practice. *Professional Psychology, Research and Practice, 40*(4), 354–360. https://doi.org/10.1037/a0016250

Henry, W. P., Schacht, T. E., & Strupp, H. H. (1986). Structural analysis of social behavior: Application to a study of interpersonal process in differential psychotherapeutic outcome. *Journal of Consulting and Clinical Psychology, 54*(1), 27–31. https://doi.org/10.1037/0022-006X.54.1.27

Hewitt, P. L., Flett, G. L., & Mikail, S. F. (2017). *Perfectionism: A relational approach to conceptualization, assessment, and treatment*. Guilford Press.

Hewitt, P. L., Flett, G. L., Sherry, S. B., & Caelian, C. (2006). Trait perfectionism dimensions and suicidal behavior. In T. E. Ellis (Ed.), *Cognition and suicide: Theory, research, and therapy* (pp. 215–235). American Psychological Association. https://doi.org/10.1037/11377-010

Hewitt, P. L., Habke, A. M., Lee-Baggley, D. L., Sherry, S. B., & Flett, G. L. (2008). The impact of perfectionistic self-presentation on the cognitive, affective, and physiological experience of a clinical interview. *Psychiatry, 71*, 93–122. https://doi.org/10.1521/psyc.2008.71.2.93

Hewitt, P. L., Mikail, S. F., Flett, G. L., & Dang, S. S. (2018). Specific formulation feedback in dynamic-relational group psychotherapy of perfectionism. *Psychotherapy, 55*(2), 179–185. https://doi.org/10.1037/pst0000137

Hewitt, P. L., Mikail, S. F., Flett, G. L., Tasca, G. A., Flynn, C. A., Deng, X., Kaldas, J., & Chen, C. (2015). Psychodynamic/interpersonal group psychotherapy for perfectionism: Evaluating the effectiveness of a short-term treatment. *Psychotherapy, 52*(2), 205–217. https://doi.org/10.1037/pst0000016

Hewitt, P. L., Qiu, T., Flynn, C. A., Flett, G. L., Wiebe, S. A., Tasca, G. A., & Mikail, S. F. (2019). Dynamic-relational group treatment for perfectionism: Informant ratings of patient change. *Psychotherapy*. Advance online publication. https://doi.org/10.1037/pst0000229

Hewitt, P. L., Smith, M., Molnar, D., Flett, G. L., & Ko, A. (2019). *The critical relationship with self: A measure of automatic self-recrimination* [Manuscript in preparation]. Department of Psychology, University of British Columbia.

Hill, R., Tasca, G. A., Presniak, M., Francis, K., Palardy, M., Grenon, R., Mcquaid, N., Hayden, G., Gick, M., & Bissada, H. (2015). Changes in defense mechanism functioning during group therapy for binge-eating disorder. *Psychiatry*, *78*(1), 75–88. https://doi.org/10.1080/00332747.2015.1015897

Hilsenroth, M. J., Callahan, K. L., & Eudell, E. M. (2003). Further reliability, convergent and discriminant validity of overall defensive functioning. *Journal of Nervous and Mental Disease*, *191*(11), 730–737. https://doi.org/10.1097/01.nmd.0000095125.92493.e8

Høglend, P., & Perry, J. C. (1998). Defensive functioning predicts improvement in major depressive episodes. *Journal of Nervous and Mental Disease*, *186*(4), 238–243. https://doi.org/10.1097/00005053-199804000-00006

Horowitz, L. M., Alden, L. E., Wiggins, J. S., & Pincus, A. L. (2000). *Inventory of Interpersonal Problems (IIP-32/IIP-64)*. Psychological Corporation.

Horowitz, L. M., Rosenberg, S. E., & Bartholomew, K. (1993). Interpersonal problems, attachment styles, and outcome in brief dynamic psychotherapy. *Journal of Consulting and Clinical Psychology*, *61*(4), 549–560. https://doi.org/10.1037/0022-006X.61.4.549

Horwitz, L. (1977). A group-centered approach to group psychotherapy. *International Journal of Group Psychotherapy*, *27*(4), 423–439. https://doi.org/10.1080/00207284.1977.11491325

Ionita, G., & Fitzpatrick, M. (2014). Bringing science to clinical practice: A Canadian survey of psychological practice and usage of progress monitoring measures. *Canadian Psychology*, *55*(3), 187–196. https://doi.org/10.1037/a0037355

Ivanova, I. V., Tasca, G. A., Hammond, N., Balfour, L., Ritchie, K., Koszycki, D., & Bissada, H. (2015). Negative affect mediates the relationship between interpersonal problems and binge-eating disorder symptoms and psychopathology in a clinical sample: A test of the interpersonal model. *European Eating Disorders Review*, *23*(2), 133–138. https://doi.org/10.1002/erv.2344

Ivanova, I. V., Tasca, G. A., Proulx, G., & Bissada, H. (2015). Does the interpersonal model apply across eating disorder diagnostic groups? A structural equation modeling approach. *Comprehensive Psychiatry*, *63*, 80–87. https://doi.org/10.1016/j.comppsych.2015.08.009

Johansen, P. Ø., Krebs, T. S., Svartberg, M., Stiles, T. C., & Holen, A. (2011). Change in defense mechanisms during short-term dynamic and cognitive therapy in patients with cluster C personality disorders. *Journal of Nervous* and Mental Disease, *199*(9), 712–715. https://doi.org/10.1097/NMD. 0b013e318229d6a7

Kagan, J. (1994). *Galen's prophecy: Temperament in human nature*. Basic Books.

Kagan, J. (2003). Biology, context, and developmental inquiry. *Annual Review of Psychology*, *54*, 1–23. https://doi.org/10.1146/annurev.psych. 54.101601.145240

Kiesler, D. J. (1982). Interpersonal theory for personality and psychotherapy. In J. C. Anchin & D. J. Kiesler (Eds.), *Handbook of interpersonal psychotherapy* (pp. 3–24). Pergamon.

Kiesler, D. J. (1983). The 1982 Interpersonal Circle: A taxonomy for complementarity in human trans-actions. *Psychological Review*, *90*(3), 185–214. https://doi.org/10.1037/0033-295X.90.3.185

Kiesler, D. J. (1985). *Manual for the Impact Message Inventory: Research edition*. Consulting Psychologists Press.

Kiesler, D. J. (1996). *Contemporary interpersonal theory and research: Personality, psychopathology, and psychotherapy*. Wiley.

Kohut, H. (1971). *The analysis of the self: A systematic approach to the psychoanalytic treatment of narcissistic personality disorders*. International Universities Press.

Kohut, H., & Wolf, E. (1978). The disorders of the self and their treatment: An outline. *The International Journal of Psychoanalysis*, *59*(4), 413–425.

Lafontaine, M. F., Brassard, A., Lussier, Y., Valois, P., Shaver, P. R., & Johnson, S. M. (2015). Selecting the best items for a short-form of the Experiences in Close Relationships questionnaire. *European Journal of Psychological Assessment*. Advance online publication. http://dx.doi.org/10.1027/1015-5759/ a000243

Leary, T. (1957). *Interpersonal diagnosis of personality: A functional theory and methodology for personality evaluation*. Ronald Press.

Levenson, H. (2017). *Brief dynamic therapy* (2nd ed.). American Psychological Association. https://doi.org/10.1037/0000043-000

Lichtenberg, J. D. (2013). *Psychoanalysis and motivation* (Vol. 10). Routledge. https://doi.org/10.4324/9780203767191

Lingiardi, V., & McWilliams, N. (Eds.). (2017). *Psychodynamic diagnostic manual: PDM-2*. Guilford Press.

Lo Coco, G., Sutton, R., Tasca, G. A., Salerno, L., Oieni, V., & Compare, A. (2016). Does the interpersonal model generalize to obesity without binge eating? *European Eating Disorders Review*, *24*, 391–398. https://doi.org/10.1002/ erv.2459

Lo Coco, G., Tasca, G. A., Hewitt, P. L., Mikail, S. F., & Kivlighan, D. M., Jr. (2019). Ruptures and repairs of group therapy alliance: An untold story in psychotherapy research. *Research in Psychotherapy*, *22*(1), 58–70. https:// doi.org/10.4081/ripppo.2019.352

Luborsky, L. (1984). *Principles of psychoanalytic psychotherapy: A manual for supportive-expressive (SE) treatment*. Basic Books.

Main, M., Goldwyn, R., & Hesse, E. (2003). *Adult attachment classification system version 7.2* [Unpublished manuscript]. Department of Psychology, University of California, Berkeley.

Main, M., & Hesse, E. (1990). Parents' unresolved traumatic experiences are related to infant disorganized attachment status. In M. T. Greenberg, D. Cicchetti, & E. M. Cummings (Eds.), *Attachment in the preschool years* (pp. 161–181). University of Chicago Press.

Main, M., & Hesse, E. (1992). Disorganized/disoriented infant behavior in the strange situation, lapses in the monitoring of reasoning and discourse during the parent's Adult Attachment Interview, and dissociative states. In M. Ammaniti & D. Stern (Eds.), *Attachment and psychoanalysis* (pp. 86–140). Guilford Press.

Main, M., & Solomon, J. (1990). Procedures for identifying infants as disorganized/disoriented during the Ainsworth Strange Situation. In M. T. Greenberg, D. Cicchetti, & E. M. Cummings (Eds.), *Attachment in the preschool years: Theory, research, and intervention* (pp. 121–160). University of Chicago Press.

Malan, D. H. (1979). *Individual psychotherapy and the science of psychodynamics.* Butterworth-Heinemann. https://doi.org/10.1016/C2013-0-06209-3

Mansell, W., Harvey, A., Watkins, E. R., & Shafran, R. (2008). Cognitive behavioral processes across psychological disorders: A review of the utility and validity of the transdiagnostic approach. *International Journal of Cognitive Therapy, 1*(3), 181–191. https://doi.org/10.1521/ijct.2008.1.3.181

Marmarosh, C. L., Markin, R. D., & Spiegel, E. B. (2013). *Attachment in group psychotherapy.* American Psychological Association Press. https://doi.org/10.1037/14186-000

Maung, H. H. (2016). To what do psychiatric diagnoses refer? A two-dimensional semantic analysis of diagnostic terms. *Studies in History and Philosophy of Science Part C: Studies in History and Philosophy of Biological and Biomedical Sciences, 55*, 1–10. https://doi.org/10.1016/j.shpsc.2015.10.001

Maxwell, H., Tasca, G. A., Gick, M., Ritchie, K., Balfour, L. Y., & Bissada, H. (2012). The impact of attachment anxiety on interpersonal complementarity in early group therapy interactions among women with binge eating disorder. *Group Dynamics, 16*(4), 255–271. https://doi.org/10.1037/a0029464

Maxwell, H., Tasca, G. A., Grenon, R., Faye, M., Ritchie, K., Bissada, H., & Balfour, L. (2018). Change in attachment dimensions in women with binge-eating disorder following group psychodynamic interpersonal psychotherapy. *Psychotherapy Research, 28*(6), 887–901. https://doi.org/10.1080/10503307.2017.1278804

Maxwell, H., Tasca, G. A., Grenon, R., Ritchie, K., Bissada, H., & Balfour, L. (2017). Change in attachment states of mind of women with binge-eating disorder. *Clinical Psychology & Psychotherapy, 24*(6), 1292–1303. https://doi.org/10.1002/cpp.2095

Maxwell, H., Tasca, G. A., Ritchie, K., Balfour, L., & Bissada, H. (2014). Change in attachment insecurity is related to improved outcomes 1-year post group therapy in women with binge eating disorder. *Psychotherapy, 51*(1), 57–65. https://doi.org/10.1037/a0031100

McCullough, L., Kuhn, N., Andrews, S., Kaplan, A., Wolf, J., & Hurley, C. L. (2003). *Treating affect phobia: A manual for short-term dynamic psychotherapy.* Guilford Press.

McCullough Vaillant, L. (1997). *Changing character: Short-term anxiety-regulating psychotherapy for restructuring defenses, affects, and attachment.* Basic Books.

Mikail, S. F., & Tasca, G. A. (2021). *Group psychodynamic-interpersonal psychotherapy in practice* [Film; educational DVD]. American Psychological Association.

Mikulincer, M., & Florian, V. (1995). Appraisal and coping with a real-life stressful situation: The contribution of attachment styles. *Personality and Social Psychology Bulletin, 21*(4), 406–416. https://doi.org/10.1177/0146167295214011

Mikulincer, M., & Shaver, P. R. (2007). *Attachment in adulthood: Structure, dynamics, and change.* Guilford Press.

Mills, J. (2005). *Treating attachment pathology.* Rowman & Littlefield.

Muller, E. J., & Scott, T. B. (1984). A comparison of film and written presentations used for pregroup training experiences. *Journal for Specialists in Group Work, 9*(3), 122–126. https://doi.org/10.1080/01933928408412517

Norcross, J., & Wampold, B. E. (2019). *Psychotherapy relationships that work* (3rd ed.). Oxford University Press.

Norcross, J. C., & Lambert, M. J. (2018). Psychotherapy relationships that work III. *Psychotherapy, 55*(4), 303–315. https://doi.org/10.1037/pst0000193

O'Farrell, T. J., Cutter, H. S., & Floyd, F. J. (1985). Evaluating behavioral marital therapy for male alcoholics: Effects on marital adjustment and communication from before to after treatment. *Behavior Therapy, 16*(2), 147–167. https://doi.org/10.1016/S0005-7894(85)80042-3

Ogrodniczuk, J. S., Joyce, A. S., & Piper, W. E. (2005). Strategies for reducing patient-initiated premature termination of psychotherapy. *Harvard Review of Psychiatry, 13*(2), 57–70. https://doi.org/10.1080/10673220590956429

Ornstein, A., & Ornstein, P. (1990). The process of psychoanalytic psychotherapy: A self psychological perspective. In A. Tasman, S. M. Goldfinger, & C. A. Kaufman (Eds.), *Review of psychiatry* (Vol. 9, pp. 323–340). American Psychiatric Press.

Owen, J., Tao, K. W., Imel, Z. E., Wampold, B. E., & Rodolfa, E. (2014). Addressing racial and ethnic microaggressions in therapy. *Professional Psychology, Research and Practice, 45*(4), 283–290. https://doi.org/10.1037/a0037420

Paquin, J. D., Kivlighan, D. M., Jr., & Drogosz, L. M. (2013). Person–group fit, group climate, and outcomes in a sample of incarcerated women participating in trauma recovery groups. *Group Dynamics, 17*(2), 95–109. https://doi.org/10.1037/a0032702

Perry, J. C. (1990). *The Defense Mechanism Rating Scales* (5th ed.). Cambridge Hospital.

Perry, J. C., & Cooper, S. H. (1989). An empirical study of defense mechanisms. I. Clinical interview and life vignette ratings. *Archives of General Psychiatry, 46,* 444–452. https://doi.org/10.1001/archpsyc.1989.01810050058010

Perry, J. C., & Henry, M. (2004). Studying defense mechanisms in psychotherapy using the Defense Mechanism Rating Scales. In U. Hentschel, G. Smith, J. G. Draguns, & W. Ehlers (Eds.), *Defense mechanisms: Theoretical, research and clinical perspectives* (pp. 165–192). Elsevier. https://doi.org/10.1016/S0166-4115(04)80034-7

Perry, J. C., Hoglend, P., Shear, K., Vaillant, G. E., Horowitz, M., Kardos, M. E., Bille, H., & Kagan, D. (1998). Field trial of a diagnostic axis for defense mechanisms for DSM-IV. *Journal of Personality Disorders, 12*(1), 56–68. https://doi.org/10.1521/pedi.1998.12.1.56

Persons, J. B. (1991). Psychotherapy outcome studies do not accurately represent current models of psychotherapy. A proposed remedy. *American Psychologist, 46*(2), 99–106. https://doi.org/10.1037/0003-066X.46.2.99

Pilling, S., Anderson, I., Goldberg, D., Meader, N., Taylor, C., & the Two Guideline Development Groups. (2009). Depression in adults, including those with a chronic physical health problem: Summary of NICE guidance. *BMJ, 339,* b4108. https://doi.org/10.1136/bmj.b4108

Pincus, A. L., Dickinson, K. A., Schut, A. J., Castonguay, L. G., & Bedics, J. (1999). Integrating interpersonal assessment and adult attaching using SASB. *European Journal of Psychological Assessment, 15*(3), 206–220. https://doi.org/10.1027//1015-5759.15.3.206

Pinquart, M., Feussner, C., & Ahnert, L. (2013). Meta-analytic evidence for stability in attachments from infancy to early adulthood. *Attachment & Human Development, 15*(2), 189–218. https://doi.org/10.1080/14616734.2013.746257

Piper, W. E., Debbane, E. G., Bienvenu, J. P., & Garant, J. (1982). A study of group pretraining for group psychotherapy. *International Journal of Group Psychotherapy, 32,* 309–325. https://doi.org/10.1080/00207284.1982.11492055

Repetti, R. L., Taylor, S. E., & Seeman, T. E. (2002). Risky families: Family social environments and the mental and physical health of offspring. *Psychological Bulletin, 128*(2), 330–366. https://doi.org/10.1037/0033-2909.128.2.330

Rothbart, M. K. (2011). *Becoming who we are: temperament and personality development.* Guilford Press.

Rowe, C. E., & MacIsaac, D. S. (1991). *Empathic attunement: the "technique" of psychoanalytic self psychology.* Jason Aronson.

Sadock, B. J., & Sadock, V. A. (2008). *Kaplan & Sadock's concise textbook of clinical psychiatry.* Lippincott Williams & Wilkins.

Saha, S., Chung, M. C., & Thorne, L. (2011). A narrative exploration of the sense of self of women recovering from childhood sexual abuse. *Counselling*

Psychology Quarterly, 24(2), 101–113. https://doi.org/10.1080/09515070. 2011.586414

Samstag, L. W., Muran, J. C., Wachtel, P. L., Slade, A., Safran, J. D., & Winston, A. (2008). Evaluating negative process: A comparison of working alliance, interpersonal behavior, and narrative coherency among three psychotherapy outcome conditions. *American Journal of Psychotherapy, 62*(2), 165–194. https://doi.org/10.1176/appi.psychotherapy.2008.62.2.165

Schofield, P., Jefford, M., Carey, M., Thomson, K., Evans, M., Baravelli, C., & Aranda, S. (2008). Preparing patients for threatening medical treatments: Effects of a chemotherapy educational DVD on anxiety, unmet needs, and self-efficacy. *Supportive Care in Cancer, 16,* 37–45. https://doi.org/10.1007/s00520-007-0273-4

Segalla, R. (2012). The therapeutic work of the group: Finding the self through finding the other. In I. Harwood, W. Stone, & M. Pines (Eds.), *Self experiences in group, revisited: Affective attachments, intersubjective regulations, and human understanding* (pp. 134–150). Routledge, Taylor and Francis Group.

Silberschatz, G. (2017). Improving the yield of psychotherapy research. *Psychotherapy Research, 27*(1), 1–13. https://doi.org/10.1080/10503307. 2015.1076202

Sroufe, L. A. (1996). *Emotional development: The organization of emotional life in the early years.* Cambridge University Press. https://doi.org/10.1017/CBO9780511527661

Steuer, J. L., Mintz, J., Hammen, C. L., Hill, M. A., Jarvik, L. F., McCarley, T., Motoike, P., & Rosen, R. (1984). Cognitive-behavioral and psychodynamic group psychotherapy in treatment of geriatric depression. *Journal of Consulting and Clinical Psychology, 52*(2), 180–189. https://doi.org/10.1037/0022-006X.52.2.180

Stolorow, R. D., Atwood, G. E., & Orange, D. M. (1999). Kohut and contextualism: Toward a post-Cartesian psychoanalytic theory. *Psychoanalytic Psychology, 16*(3), 380–388. https://doi.org/10.1037/0736-9735.16.3.380

Strupp, H. H., & Binder, J. L. (1984). *Psychotherapy in a new key: A guide to time-limited dynamic psychotherapy.* Basic Books.

Sullivan, H. S. (1953). *The interpersonal theory of psychiatry.* Norton.

Sullivan, H. S. (1954). *The psychiatric interview.* Norton.

Swift, J. K., & Callahan, J. L. (2011). Decreasing treatment dropout by addressing expectations for treatment length. *Psychotherapy Research, 21*(2), 193–200. https://doi.org/10.1080/10503307.2010.541294

Talley, P. F., Strupp, H. H., & Morey, L. C. (1990). Matchmaking in psychotherapy: Patient–therapist dimensions and their impact on outcome. *Journal of Consulting and Clinical Psychology, 58*(2), 182–188. https://doi.org/10.1037/0022-006X.58.2.182

Tasca, G., Balfour, L., Ritchie, K., & Bissada, H. (2007). Change in attachment anxiety is associated with improved depression among women with binge eating disorder. *Psychotherapy, 44*(4), 423–433. https://doi.org/10.1037/0033-3204.44.4.423

Tasca, G. A., & Balfour, L. (2014a). Attachment and eating disorders: A review of current research. *International Journal of Eating Disorders, 47*(7), 710–717. https://doi.org/10.1002/eat.22302

Tasca, G. A., & Balfour, L. (2014b). Eating disorders and attachment: A contemporary psychodynamic perspective. *Psychodynamic Psychiatry, 42*(2), 257–276. https://doi.org/10.1521/pdps.2014.42.2.257

Tasca, G. A., Balfour, L., Presniak, M. D., & Bissada, H. (2012). Outcomes of specific interpersonal problems for binge eating disorder: Comparing group psychodynamic interpersonal psychotherapy and group cognitive behavioral therapy. *International Journal of Group Psychotherapy, 62*(2), 197–218. https://doi.org/10.1521/ijgp.2012.62.2.197

Tasca, G. A., Balfour, L., Ritchie, K., & Bissada, H. (2006). Developmental changes in group climate in two types of group therapy for binge-eating disorder: A growth curve analysis. *Psychotherapy Research, 16*(4), 499–514. https://doi.org/10.1080/10503300600593359

Tasca, G. A., Foot, M., Leite, C., Maxwell, H., Balfour, L., & Bissada, H. (2011). Interpersonal processes in psychodynamic-interpersonal and cognitive behavioral group therapy: A systematic case study of two groups. *Psychotherapy: Theory, Research, & Practice, 48*(3), 260–273. https://doi.org/10.1037/a0023928

Tasca, G. A., Grenon, R., Fortin-Langelier, B., & Chyurlia, L. (2014). Addressing challenges and barriers to translating psychotherapy research into clinical practice: The development of a psychotherapy practice research network in Canada. *Canadian Psychology, 55*(3), 197–203. https://doi.org/10.1037/a0037277

Tasca, G. A., Koszycki, D., Brugnera, A., Chyurlia, L., Hammond, N., Francis, K., Ritchie, K., Ivanova, I., Proulx, G., Wilson, B., Beaulac, J., Bissada, H., Beasley, E., Mcquaid, N., Grenon, R., Fortin-Langelier, B., Compare, A., & Balfour, L. (2019). Testing a stepped care model for binge-eating disorder: A two-step randomized controlled trial. *Psychological Medicine, 49*(4), 598–606. https://doi.org/10.1017/S0033291718001277

Tasca, G. A., & McMullen, L. (1992). Interpersonal complementarity and antitheses within a stage model of psychotherapy. *Psychotherapy: Theory, Research, & Practice, 29*(4), 515–523. https://doi.org/10.1037/0033-3204.29.4.515

Tasca, G. A., Mikail, S. F., & Hewitt, P. L. (2005). Group psychodynamic interpersonal psychotherapy: Summary of a treatment model and outcomes for depressive symptoms. In M. E. Abelian (Ed.), *Focus on psychotherapy research* (pp. 159–188). Nova Science.

Tasca, G. A., Ritchie, K., Conrad, G., Balfour, L., Gayton, J., Lybanon, V., & Bissada, H. (2006). Attachment scales predict outcome in a randomized controlled trial of two group therapies for binge eating disorder: An aptitude by treatment interaction. *Psychotherapy Research, 16*(1), 106–121. https://doi.org/10.1080/10503300500090928

Tasca, G. A., Ritchie, K., Demidenko, N., Balfour, L., Krysanski, V., Weekes, K., Barber, A., Keating, L., & Bissada, H. (2013). Matching women with binge eating disorder to group treatment based on attachment anxiety: Outcomes and moderating effects. *Psychotherapy Research, 23*(3), 301–314. https://doi.org/10.1080/10503307.2012.717309

Tasca, G. A., Sylvestre, J., Balfour, L., Chyurlia, L., Evans, J., Fortin-Langelier, B., Francis, K., Gandhi, J., Huehn, L., Hunsley, J., Joyce, A. S., Kinley, J., Koszycki, D., Leszcz, M., Lybanon-Daigle, V., Mercer, D., Ogrodniczuk, J. S., Presniak, M., Ravitz, P., . . . Wilson, B. (2015). What clinicians want: Findings from a psychotherapy practice research network survey. *Psychotherapy: Theory, Research, & Practice, 52*(1), 1–11. https://doi.org/10.1037/a0038252

Teicher, M. H., & Samson, J. A. (2013). Childhood maltreatment and psychopathology: A case for ecophenotypic variants as clinically and neurobiologically distinct subtypes. *The American Journal of Psychiatry, 170*(10), 1114–1133. https://doi.org/10.1176/appi.ajp.2013.12070957

Tobin, D. L., Banker, J. D., Weisberg, L., & Bowers, W. (2007). I know what you did last summer (and it was not CBT): A factor analytic model of international psychotherapeutic practice in the eating disorders. *International Journal of Eating Disorders, 40*(8), 754–757. https://doi.org/10.1002/eat.20426

Tuckman, B. W. (1965). Developmental sequence in small groups. *Psychological Bulletin, 63*(6), 384–399. https://doi.org/10.1037/h0022100

Tuckman, B. W., & Jensen, M. A. C. (1977). Stages of small-group development revisited. *Group & Organization Studies, 2*(4), 419–427. https://doi.org/10.1177/105960117700200404

van IJzendoorn, M. H. (1995). Adult attachment representations, parental responsiveness, and infant attachment: A meta-analysis on the predictive validity of the Adult Attachment Interview. *Psychological Bulletin, 117*(3), 387–403. https://doi.org/10.1037/0033-2909.117.3.387

Wagner, C. C., Kiesler, D. J., & Schmidt, J. A. (1995). Assessing the interpersonal transaction cycle: Convergence of action and reaction interpersonal circumplex measures. *Journal of Personality and Social Psychology, 69*(5), 938–949. https://doi.org/10.1037/0022-3514.69.5.938

Wallin, D. (2007). *Attachment in psychotherapy*. Guilford Press.

Wampold, B. E., & Imel, Z. (2015). *The great psychotherapy debate* (2nd ed.). Routledge. https://doi.org/10.4324/9780203582015

Weissman, M. M., Markowitz, J. C., & Klerman, G. L. (2000). *Comprehensive guide to interpersonal psychotherapy*. Basic Books.

Westen, D., & Nakash, O. (2005). *Attachment prototype questionnaire manual* [Unpublished manuscript]. Department of Psychology, Emory University.

Westen, D., Novotny, C. M., & Thompson-Brenner, H. (2004). The empirical status of empirically supported psychotherapies: Assumptions, findings, and reporting in controlled clinical trials. *Psychological Bulletin, 130*(4), 631–663. https://doi.org/10.1037/0033-2909.130.4.631

Whittingham, M. (2018). Innovations in group assessment: How focused brief group therapy integrates formal measures to enhance treatment preparation, process, and outcomes. *Psychotherapy, 55*(2), 186–190. https://doi.org/10.1037/pst0000153

Widmeyer, W. N., & Ducharme, K. (1997). Team building through team goal setting. *Journal of Applied Sport Psychology, 9*(1), 97–113. https://doi.org/10.1080/10413209708415386

Wilfley, D. E., Agras, W. S., Telch, C. F., Rossiter, E. M., Schneider, J. A., Cole, A. G., Sifford, L. A., & Raeburn, S. D. (1993). Group cognitive-behavioral therapy and group interpersonal psychotherapy for the nonpurging bulimic individual: A controlled comparison. *Journal of Consulting and Clinical Psychology, 61*(2), 296–305. https://doi.org/10.1037/0022-006X.61.2.296

Yalom, I. V., & Leszcz, M. (2020). *The theory and practice of group psychotherapy* (6th ed.). Basic Books.

Young, D. M., & Beier, E. G. (1982). Being asocial in social places: Giving the client a new experience. In J. C. Achin & D. J. Kiesler (Eds.), *Handbook of interpersonal psychotherapy* (pp. 262–273). Pergamon.

Zetzel, E. R. (1956). An approach to the relation between concept and content in psychoanalytic theory: With special reference to the work of Melanie Klein and her followers. *The Psychoanalytic Study of the Child, 11*(1), 99–121. https://doi.org/10.1080/00797308.1956.11822784

Zilberstein, K. (2014). The use and limitations of attachment theory in child psychotherapy. *Psychotherapy, 51*(1), 93–103. https://doi.org/10.1037/a0030930

Zilcha-Mano, S. (2017). Is the alliance really therapeutic? Revisiting this question in light of recent methodological advances. *American Psychologist, 72*(4), 311–325. https://doi.org/10.1037/a0040435

Zilcha-Mano, S., McCarthy, K. S., Dinger, U., Chambless, D. L., Milrod, B. L., Kunik, L., & Barber, J. P. (2015). Are there subtypes of panic disorder? An interpersonal perspective. *Journal of Consulting and Clinical Psychology, 83*(5), 938–950. https://doi.org/10.1037/a0039373

Zuckerman, M. (1999). *Vulnerability to psychopathology: A biosocial model.* American Psychological Association.

Index

About the Authors

Giorgio A. Tasca, PhD, is a professor in the School of Psychology at the University of Ottawa, and he is a registered psychologist with the College of Psychologists of Ontario. Before going into academia in 2016, he worked in a hospital setting for over 28 years, providing group therapy and psychological consultations. He has published extensively on group therapy, individual therapy, and eating disorders. He is the editor of the journal *Group Dynamics*, a past president of the Society of Group Psychology and Group Psychotherapy, a fellow of the American Psychological Association (Divisions 29 and 49), and a recipient of the Canadian Psychological Association Award for Distinguished Contributions to Psychology as a Profession. Dr. Tasca is also the director of the Psychotherapy Practice Research Networks (https://socialsciences.uottawa.ca/pprnet/), a multidisciplinary collaboration of clinicians and researchers to advance practice-based research and knowledge translation in psychotherapy.

Samuel F. Mikail, PhD, has been in clinical practice for 30 years. He is a member of the College of Psychologists of Ontario and is board certified in clinical psychology with the American Board of Professional Psychology. Dr. Mikail has served on the board of directors of several professional associations, including as chair of practice on the board of directors of the Canadian Psychological Association (CPA) and president of CPA (2018–2019). He is a fellow of CPA and the Clinical Section of CPA. For 12 years, he held the position of clinical director of the Southdown Institute, where he conducted psychodynamic-interpersonal group therapy daily. Dr. Mikail is currently director, Mental Health Solutions with Sun Life Financial, and is a clinical adjunct faculty member in the Department of Psychology at the University of Waterloo. He also maintains a private practice in Newmarket, Ontario.

Paul L. Hewitt, PhD, is a professor in the Department of Psychology and an associate member, Psychotherapy Program, in the Faculty of Medicine at the University of British Columbia, as well as a registered psychologist in British Columbia. He is a fellow of the Canadian Psychological Association (CPA) and the Section on Clinical Psychology of CPA and recent winner of the Donald O. Hebb Award for Distinguished Contributions to Psychology as a Science from the CPA. He received his PhD from the University of Saskatchewan in 1988 and completed his clinical residency in the Department of Psychiatry and Behavioral Sciences, Faculty of Medicine at the University of Washington in Seattle. Recently named in the top 10 Canadian clinical psychology professors for research productivity, Dr. Hewitt's writing and research have focused on perfectionism, psychopathology, and psychotherapy, with over 225 research papers, books, and chapters. His most recent book, coauthored with Gordon Flett and Samuel Mikail, *Perfectionism: A Relational Approach to Conceptualization, Assessment, and Treatment*, synthesizes his research and clinical work on perfectionism and includes detailed information on the dynamic-relational individual and group psychotherapy that he and Dr. Mikail developed over the past 30 years. Dr. Hewitt has had a private practice since 1988 that focuses on individuals experiencing difficulties from perfectionistic behavior, early trauma, depression, anxiety, and interpersonal problems.